Eight Children in Narnia

Other Books by Jared Lobdell

Seeking the Lord (2015, printing limited to 100 numbered copies)

The Rise of Tolkienian Fantasy (2005)

The World of the Rings: Language, Religion, and Adventure in Tolkien (2004)

The Scientifiction Novels of C.S. Lewis: Space and Time in the Ransom Stories (2004)

This Strange Illness: Alcoholism and Bill W. (2004)

A Tolkien Compass (2003, 1975)

The Detective Fiction Reviews of Charles Williams, 1930–1935 (2003)

The Four Corners of the Tapestry: A Casebook of Palmer Hopkins (1999)

Action at the Galudoghson, December 14, 1742 (1994)

Further Materials on Lewis Wetzel and the Upper Ohio Frontier (1993)

Recollections of Lewis Bonnett, Jr. (1778–1850) and the Bonnett and Wetzel Families (1991)

Indian Warfare in Western Pennsylvania and North West Virginia at the Time of the American Revolution (1992)

Sylvia Dubois: A Biography of the Slav Who Whipt Her Mistres and Gand Her Freedom (1988)

England and Always: Tolkien's World of the Kings (1981)

Eight Children in Narnia

The Making of a Children's Story

JARED LOBDELL

OPEN COURT
Chicago

To find out more about Open Court books, call toll-free 1-800-815-2280, or visit our website at www.opencourtbooks.com.

Open Court Publishing Company is a division of Carus Publishing Company, dba Cricket Media.

Eight Children in Narnia: The Making of a Children's Story

ISBN: 978-0-8126-9901-2

This book is also available as an e-book.

Library of Congress Control Number: 2016949427

For C.S.L.

And underneath is written,

In letters all of gold,

How valiantly he kept the bridge

In the brave days of old.

and for my wife

Jane Starke Lobdell

Contents

Introduction

The seven years beginning with 1950 and ending with 1956 saw the publication of seven children's books by the Ulster Irish (but Oxford, then Cambridge) scholar, essayist, literary historian, Christian apologist, versifier and occasional poet, novelist, science-fiction and fantasy writer, philosopher (though old-fashioned), satirist and controversialist, Clive Staples Lewis, known to his early friends and relations as Jacks, and later to many as Jack, and to the world at large as C.S. Lewis.

I counted him as a friend by correspondence, in the last five years of his life, as I now count his younger stepson Douglas Gresham, and have counted his friends Ronald Tolkien, Lord David Cecil, Kenneth Hamilton Jenkin, Nevill Coghill, and two whom I have known also in person, Owen Barfield and Christopher Tolkien. I first read his seven children's books, now known as the *Chronicles of Narnia*, as they came out—not because I was reading children's books in general at that time, but because they were by C.S. Lewis—the same reason I read an old letter by him on *The Kingis Quair* published in the *Times Literary Supplement* in 1929, or the spoof law case he wrote up with Owen Barfield, *Mark v. Tristram*, later on. (I wish I still had the copy Owen gave me.) I read them for the mind of the maker (or, as Professor Tolkien might say, the sub-creator). I read them to be with C.S. Lewis.

He might tell us that is not the best—or even a very good—reason to be reading children's books (after all, he wrote a book—or half a book—*The Personal Heresy*, partly against mixing what is in a book with what is or was in the author, or at least in the author's life). But then, on the other hand, I can recall his lament that there was no weather—no atmosphere, almost no real flavor—in *The Three Musketeers*, and along that line, I think of the flavor of Narnia as coming from his mind and I think of that flavor, in a way, as a major part of Narnia's success. I am not reading—and I have not ever read—the Narnia books as a guide to the mind of C.S. Lewis (though perhaps as a connection), but I am looking at the mind and thought (and experience) of C.S. Lewis, as I understand them (and therefore to some extent my own mind and thought and experience), as something of a guide to his Narnia. And here I should mention there is one book on Narnia (some of it in fact from Lewis) that has contributed greatly to my thought—Walter Hooper's *Past Watchful Dragons* (Collier Books paperback 1979, reprinted from *Imagination and the Spirit*, ed. Charles Huttar, Grand Rapids, 1971).

In connection with my reason for reading the Narnia books (and in my defense), here is one thing Lewis said on the matter of writing for children. He told us, in effect, that if one is going to write a children's story, it ought not to be written with a designed moral, because the only moral of any value comes not by specific design, but from the "whole cast of the author's mind" ("On Three Ways of Writing for Children" given 1952, in *On Stories*, 1982, pp. 41–42), going on to say the story must come from what the author shares with the children in his (or her) audience, and its matter must be "part of the habitual furniture" of the author's mind. And Lewis remarks that an author, to the child, is outside the difficult relations between child and parent or child and teacher, not even an uncle but "a freeman and an equal, like the postman, and the butcher, and the dog next door" (p. 43).

And not only to the child but to any who reads as a child—and of such is the Kingdom—to anyone reading or trying to read as a child. One thing I should make clear. A couple of years ago (or is it a decade ago?) I published a book on C.S. Lewis's "Scientifiction" novels, and was (perhaps predictably) criticized for not spending time summarizing what other writers had to say about those novels—particularly what had been said by David Downing, who teaches a few blocks down the street from where I live, at Elizabethtown College. And it is likely some reviewer of this book will comment that I should have put more in from David Downing's book on Narnia (or from others of the half dozen books on Narnia out in the last few years, or from biographers of C.S. Lewis). But this book is what I have to say on Narnia and C.S. Lewis, from my coign of vantage (with Walter Hooper's help back in 1971 and Lewis's before), and that's based on my experience and my reading and understanding of C.S. Lewis, and my appreciation for the sources and analogues of his Narnia—not anyone else's experience or appreciation or reading or understanding (except Walter's additional information from Lewis)—and unless, of course, their expression of their understanding convinces me that I have been wrong on points where we disagree: the one exception, the work of Michael Ward, will be noted much later on, though not at any great length.

For me, the first knowledge that C.S. Lewis was writing what turned out to be the Narnia series came in Chad Walsh's little 1949 book, *C.S. Lewis: Apostle to the Skeptics*, in which he mentions that Lewis was writing a children's book "after the manner of E. Nesbit." By the time I got around to checking out E. Nesbit (which was actually quite a while later), *The Lion, the Witch, and the Wardrobe* had already appeared, and I had been given a copy—and it was a long time before I made the acquaintance either of E. Nesbit's (Edith Nesbit Bland's) Bastables or of her Five Children (as in *The Five Children and It*). Yet that phrase "after the manner of E. Nesbit" echoes in my ears, made clearer a few years later when I read in *A Preface to Paradise Lost* the words Lewis used to describe Milton's question in making his decision to write *Paradise Lost*: "to which of the great pre-existing forms of literary creation, so different in the expectations they excite and fulfill, so diverse in their powers," is this designed to contribute?

Perhaps a children's book "after the manner of E. Nesbit," is not an ideal qualifier as one of the great pre-existing forms of literary creation, but it was a pre-existing form back in 1948–49, and it remains true that "the first qualification for judging any piece of workmanship, from a corkscrew to a cathedral, to know what it is" (C.S. Lewis, *A Preface to Paradise Lost*, Oxford 1942, pp. 1–2). After all, Lewis had made a conscious decision to write a children's story of a particular kind, with a particular genealogy—that was the first important thing I knew about *The Lion, the Witch, and the Wardrobe*, even before the name of the book, even before the name of the world or the country, and it remains important. And by the way, on the matter of names, we should note that—in common parlance—the name of the world is Narnia and the name of the country is Narnia. (We get to the "origins" of Narnia, the name, later on in this Introduction, and in Chapter 3.) Archenland on the borders of Narnia (the country) is part of the world of Narnia, but not the country. If I were to be given permission to write Narnian books as a kind of sequel to Lewis's, they would be the Chronicles of Archenland—but that is unlikely to happen. (And it would have to be Archenland largely apart from Lewis's "Outline of Narnian History" in *Past Watchful Dragons*.)

In Chapter 1, we will look at Lewis's conscious decision to write a children's story, beginning with what "a children's story" meant to him, looking first at his childhood and childhood reading, and why he thought such a story might say best what was to be said! We will examine the children's story (and at "boys' books") from 1898 to (say) 1950, and then we'll look at another point, at Lewis's boyishness. (In the early part of the period, we'll look especially at G.A. Henty, Kenneth Grahame, E. Nesbit, Rudyard Kipling.) On this other point—Professor Claude Rawson has spoken of Lewis as the "schoolboy [Dr.] Johnson" and we will ask, in line with that, whether he wasn't still in some sense that schoolboy even at the age of fifty when he began the Narnia books, trying (he said) to write "corking good yarns" (to use the slang of his youth) and all that. (And given his statement that the author of children's books writes from what he shares with the child, Lewis's schoolboy attitudes may be a kind of strength in his children's books.)

But on this matter of a collection of books like the seven beginning with *The Lion, the Witch, and the Wardrobe* "saying best what's to be said," we might look briefly here (more in Chapter 1) at what Lewis said about the reason(s) he wrote the Narnia books (in the *New York Times Book Review* in 1956, collected in *On Stories*, 1982, pp. 45–47): He is speaking of Tasso's distinction between the poet as poet and the poet as citizen, and remarks that there are the Author's reason for writing an imaginative work and the Man's reason. The story material bubbles up in the Author's mind—in Lewis's case invariably beginning with pictures in his mind. But this gets one nowhere "unless it is accompanied by the longing for a Form" that completes the Author's impulse. The Man must then ask "how the gratification of this impulse will fit in with all the other things he wants and ought to do or be." He applies this then to his own "fairy tales," where (a famous passage) he remarks: "Everything began with images; a faun carrying an umbrella, a queen on a sledge, a magnificent lion. At first there wasn't even anything Christian about them; that . . . pushed itself in of its own accord . . . part of the bubbling."

Then it becomes apparent that the Form will be that of the "fairy-tale" (though it is scarcely a traditional fairy tale), and then the Man becomes aware that this form will enable the Author to "cast all these things [the basic Christian truths presumably being among these things] into an imaginary world, stripping them of their stained-glass and Sunday school associations, one could make them for the first time appear in their real potency. Could one not thus steal past those watchful dragons? I thought one could. That was the Man's motive. But of course he could have done nothing if the Author had not been on the boil first." It looks as though he was trying to do more than simply write corking good yarns, and that is where we go in Chapter 2, looking at his creation of Narnia (the country or world—less the name), and what went into it. And what went into it begins with his (and his brother Warnie's) created world of Boxen (Animal-Land and India), and the Ulster world they were growing up in, in the very early years of the twentieth century.

India, in the Boxonian combined world, was the creature of Grandfather Hamilton's sojourn there (his diary out, in the days before the Sepoy business, is in Volume I of the *Lewis Papers*, along with other diaries, including the Crimea) and perhaps still more of the Henty books whose mise-en-scène is India or thereabouts: *With Clive in India, The Tiger of Mysore, At the Point of the Bayonet, On the Irrawaddy, To Herat and Cabul, Through the Sikh War, Rujub the Juggler, In Times of Peril, For Name and Fame, Through Three Campaigns.* Animal-Land has perhaps more complicated origins: the timing is not certain, but there seems to have been a shift from contemporary (1906) to medieval (or "knights-in-armor") Animal-Land about the time Conan Doyle's *Sir Nigel* was appearing in instalments in *The Strand*. India, of course (Warnie's realm), might have very different knights and very different armor—but, like contemporary Animal-Land, it is fundamentally a political entity. If anyone doubts that Animal-Land is a creation out of *Punch*, by way of Edward Lear (or perhaps the other way around), then through Victorian illustration generally, let him (or her) look at the young C.S. Lewis's illustrations of the early Boxonian play "The King's Ring" (*Boxen*, p. 29) and of the later "Boxen, or Scenes from Boxonian City Life" (*Boxen*, esp. pp. 64–65, 69, 86).

These are, in short, pretty much the dressed animals of *Punch* or the Nonsense Writers like Lear and Carroll (and C.S. Lewis's father was something like a character out of *Punch*), and even the human beings are comic creations (General Quicksteppe, for example). The dialogue has music-hall (comedy-routine) overtones—in fact, in "Boxen, or Scenes from Boxonian City Life," Viscount Puddiphat is serenaded with "Oh Mister Puddiphat / Where did you get that ha-at?" followed by "Now down D street we will go / That's the place for us, you know / Whoop! [Whoop! Whoopee!]" The only way in which this can be seen as a forerunner or antecessor (certainly not greatly an ancestor) of Narnia is in its illustrating the early furniture of Lewis's mind. And particularly, it is interesting that at the age of nine he is systematizing the history of Animal-Land from 55 B.C. (sic!) to 1212—a more interesting date than 1215 to an eight-year-old, I suppose, the year 1215 being England's Magna Carta to go with England's Julius Caesar in 55 B.C.—and then 1377 (the latest date in the sketch), the death date of England's Edward III. The only well-known English date missing (before the fifteenth century at least) is 1066.

My point is that these stories seem to be constructed from the materials available to the pre-schoolboy C.S. Lewis at his parents' house and in his parents' lives at Little Lea, reflecting the interests of the house and those lives, and while the stories are illustrated, their sources seem to be literary rather than visionary. But then, perhaps the connection is closer than we might think, for if Narnia "all began with a picture," we can reasonably ask, from what book or story did the picture come? And we will. We will also look then at the Ulster world the Lewis brothers grew up in. Here is where the music-hall sketches and the ships that are so important in Boxen come in: the Lewis brothers are living in the Belfast of Harland & Wolff and the *Olympic* and the *Titanic*. They are living in the politically charged atmosphere of Ireland in the years before the Curragh mutiny of 1914 and the Easter Rebellion of 1916. And they are living in the house of their father, a well-known solicitor, literary figure, and political speaker (on the Conservative and Unionist side). And their literary tastes (or at least their mental furniture) might be expected to reflect that of well-to-do political (Unionist) Belfast in the *Titanic* age. We know, for example, that Albert Lewis loved music-hall "variety" shows, and Gilbert and Sullivan, and the verses (sometimes poetry) of Henry Newbolt ("Captain, art tha' sleepin' there below?")—and we know that someone in Lewis's youth in Belfast, perhaps his father, read James Stephens, *The Crock of Gold*. On Gilbert and Sullivan, we know that Lewis's 1945 verses "Awake! My Lute" pick up from the Lord Chancellor's song in *Iolanthe*—"When you're lying awake with a dismal headache / And repose is taboo'd by anxiety." But the question here is, to what degree does all this have a place in the creation of Narnia?

It is likely not very much more than coincidental that in the Boxen stories, the province originally named Frog-land became Piscia, the first Roman place name in Lewis's fiction, as Narnia is pretty much the last. Piscia is, I believe, a small town near Portovecchio on the south coast of Corsica—which has nothing much to do with Narnia (Nequinum) in Umbria. But its appearance in Boxen does suggest that at some time in the first decade of the twentieth century, Lewis was reading something with Latin (Roman) names—and if it was a text rather than simply a map, I believe it is very likely to have been *The Lays of Ancient Rome*, perhaps an edition (like the Harper 1894) with notes. That being said, I doubt if it is coincidental that a good bit of the sentiment of the *Lays* is in the Narnian stories—along with a love of ships and seafaring (though medievalized rather than contemporary, as happened in 1906 with Lewis's childhood creation of Animal-Land). In what way does Tirian at the Stable differ from Horatius at the Bridge—"To every man upon this earth / Death cometh soon or late / And how can man die better / Than facing fearful odds / For the ashes of his fathers / And the temples of his gods?'"?

I do not base any argument on the claim that the return of the Four Children in the Year of Narnia 2303 is akin to the coming of the Great Twin Brethren at *The Battle of Lake Regillus*—though it is akin. But Lake Regillus is simply Macaulay's version of a story told of many divine returns by many hands ("'The gods who live forever / Have fought for Rome to-day / These be the Great Twin Brethren / To whom the Dorians pray"), and Lewis's turn on the story in Prince Caspian is like his turn in "Yellow-Hair" or "After Ten Years"—as we shall see. That is, in this case, he looks at the event from the generally unregarded point of view of the "divine" entities who are being summoned (or of the soldiers inside the Trojan Horse, to take another example).

In any case, whatever were the first stirrings of Narnia, part of what went into that world or country after it stirred was the books Lewis read in those long-gone days, written by E. Nesbit, or Andrew Lang, or even perhaps Thackeray, Kipling, Kenneth Grahame (and in Warnie's case certainly, G.A. Henty). Then—as he said in 1956—he thought that new books after the manner of E. Nesbit (or Andrew Lang)—his own newly written books—could be used to "get past the watchful dragons" guarding modern children from the heritage of the past. Of course, we need to ask, in fact, "Were there watchful dragons?" And what, indeed, were they watching? The implication of Lewis's remark in the *New York Times Book Review* is that they were watching for tell-tale signs of Christian belief. We shall see. In the meantime, the phrase gave Walter Hooper a title for his little book on Narnia, *Past Watchful Dragons*, based in part on that argument, which introduces some very interesting matter, as we shall also see.

Chapter 3 of this present book is entitled "The House in the Country and the First Larger Life," referring both to the house in the country— Professor Kirke's house—where Narnia lies (sometimes) behind the coats in the wardrobe in the spare room and to the house in the country (in the far north of Scotland) where Lewis's mentor George MacDonald may be said to have begun his writing career and which appears in his novel *Phantastes* (and in at least six others of his novels). Here's what Mr. Cupples in Alec Forbes says of the library and the house (quoted from M.R. Phillips, *George MacDonald*, Minneapolis: Bethany 1987, p. 117): "'Efter I had ta'en my degree . . . I heard o' a grit leebrary i' the north . . . Dinna imaigin' it was a public library. Na, na. It belonged to a grit an' gran' hoose —the Lord hae respec' till't!" ["After I had taken my degree, I heard of a great library in the north. Don't imagine it was a public library. No, it belonged to a great and grand house, the Lord have respect to it!"] Greville MacDonald—George MacDonald's son—suggested that the great and grand house with the great library where his father spent 1842–43 was the Castle of Thurso in the far north of Scotland, in Caithness. But whether there or at Dunbeath (also in the far north of Scotland, in Caithness), the important thing was the great and grand house and its great library and the "jump start" its books gave MacDonald in the realm of imagination—books by authors like Novalis, one of the founders of German Romanticism. Professor Kirke's house in *The Lion, the Witch, and the Wardrobe* is as much the great house in the north that led MacDonald to the realms of Faerie as it is anything like Little Lea. A great and grand house in the north would have empty rooms and long corridors (and tourists), much more than the book-crowded Little Lea.

For the life of Faerie, or the life of the imagination, is the First Larger Life, and it is into this life that Lucy first steps through the wardrobe. And indeed, I see in Professor Kirke (and think of the ramifications of that name in Lewis's mind, and the figure of Mother Kirk in *The Pilgrim's Regress*!) a teacher not unlike George MacDonald, as he was in Lewis's mind. For Professor Kirke is a Platonist and a rational man and a Romantic—and more than that, he is opening the children's minds to that first larger life, as *Phantastes*, in 1914 or 1915, opened the mind of C.S. Lewis. And then, eventually, to the second larger life. The Wardrobe in the great and grand house of Digory Kirke (Father Kirk?) is a gate to the first larger life and eventually to both.

This chapter looks also at "the pictures it all began with" (in reference to Lewis's *Times Book Review* essay "It All Began with a Picture"), then at the name of Narnia (which we first look at in this Introduction), then at *The Lion, the Witch, and the Wardrobe*, with its beavers, fauns, Father Christmas, Sons of Adam, Daughters of Eve, witches, [Old Uncle Tom Cobbleigh] and all. The key point here, I think, is that the pictures it all began with are literary pictures. Lewis had never seen in his quotidian life the Queen on the Sledge, or the Great Lion. Jadis, the White Witch, sometime Queen of Charn, the Queen on the Sledge, is out of E. Nesbit. The Great Lion bears the name Aslan (but shouldn't it be Arslan?), and He is essentially a lion rampant (as he is indeed on Peter's shield), an heraldic lion, a medieval lion, as Alp Arslan was a medieval warrior-king (though not on the Christian side). Now why did these particular pictures produce Narnia—the country and the world by whatever name we call it—we're not asking about the name itself. The question, *why the name Narnia?*—that will be considered later in this Introduction and in Chapter 3.

But how did the world come out of the pictures? Certainly the pictures that started *The Lion, the Witch, and the Wardrobe* must include the Lion and the Witch (as Lewis said they did), though not perhaps the Wardrobe, which was part of the furniture of Lewis's mind and perhaps of his past when he began to write the Narnian books. There has been considerable argument as to which wardrobe was (or is) The Wardrobe? one at Wheaton College? one out in California? Let me recall here a remark made by Edmund Burke, back in the eighteenth century, and quoted by the twentieth-century scholar Russell Kirk: "in Burke's rhetoric, the civilized being is distinguished from the savage by his possession of the moral imagination—by our 'superadded ideas, furnished from the wardrobe of a moral imagination, which the heart owns, and the understanding ratifies, as necessary to cover the defects of our naked shivering nature, and to raise it to dignity in our estimation.'" I'm not suggesting that the wardrobe in Professor Kirk's house is solely from Burke—we know there were wardrobes in the house at Little Lea, and presumably in the earlier house at Dundela Villas—but I believe nonetheless that it is the "wardrobe of moral imagination" from which the children take the coats that "cover ... their shivering nature" as they enter Narnia (and the coats are left there in Narnia when they return).

Other pictures? Tolkien complained that Narnia was an untidy jumble, with Talking Beavers, Fauns, Father Christmas, Sons of Adam, Daughters of Eve, Witches and all—"*L'Après-midi d'un faune*, indeed!," we can hear him remarking (and a very good remark it would be, I think, though the humor might be more Lewis's than Tolkien's). The "faun carrying the umbrella and parcels in a snowy wood" was, we know, one of the original pictures ("It All Began with a Picture" in *The Radio Times* 1960, reprinted in *On Stories* 1982, p. 53), "This picture had been in my mind since I was about sixteen [why?]. Then one day, when I was about forty, I said to myself: 'Let's try to make a story about it!'" This would give the beginning of the Narnian stories a date around 1938—which would tie in with Lewis's remark to Chad Walsh in 1948 that, in effect, he was taking this book "After the manner of E. Nesbit" off the shelf. But it leaves unanswered the interesting question, where did this picture come from? When he was sixteen, C.S. Lewis was studying under his father's tutor W.T. Kirkpatrick at Great Bookham in Surrey, and any teacher less likely to encourage or produce visions of fauns in the snow with an umbrella and parcels, can only be imagined with extreme difficulty—but perhaps it came from reading George MacDonald on the train.

Or perhaps it came from something as quotidian as a description of a man in a fawn-colored overcoat carrying an umbrella and parcels on the streets of London or Belfast or wherever. Or perhaps—I think I incline to this explanation, as agreeing with Lewis's sense of humor)—young Lewis heard the music of *L'Après-midi d'un Faune* (Débussy's tone-poem of 1894) and the picture came from that. After all, the humorist who described a Portuguese gourmet trying haggis as a "Vascular da Gama" certainly had a ready and witty way with words and their connections.

We go on from there to Chapter 4, on writing the Chronicles of Narnia and "realizing" the world of dragons—and specifically we look at "Cair Paravel and the Past in the Present" in *Prince Caspian*, at the character of Eustace Clarence Scrubb in *The Voyage of the Dawn Treader*, at the question proposed in *The Silver Chair*, "What exactly is the real world?" and then at the cry "For Narnia and the North" and all it means and suggests in *The Horse and His Boy*. By "realizing" we mean here "making real"—which is what the authors of works of fiction generally do with their imagined worlds. The difficulty comes, in particular, when there are what we generally think of as unreal components in the imagined world—as, for example, dragons. Or castles like Cair Paravel (or should that be Caer Perlesvaus or something of that sort?).

On Cair Paravel and the past in the present, we can say this experience of the past in the present that is a hallmark of Edwardian (and late Victorian, and early Georgian) fiction—say from the mid-1880s to 1914—might reasonably be expected in the work of a children's author who was a child at that time. What are the earmarks of this "Edwardian adventure story"? First, the story is framed in familiarity. In this, it is like a fairy-tale, but unlike the fairy-tale, its action is time-specific. Second, the characters are types, though they may rise to the dignity of archetypes (my example from Lewis's youth would be Sherlock Holmes). Third, and connected with the second characteristic, it is the character of Nature (even a Nature containing dragons), not the characters of the actors, being "realized" (in the French sense of the word). Fourth, the adventurers are not solitary, but they are frequently (in fact, almost universally) a happy few. Fifth, the adventures are narrated (frequently in the first person), by the most ordinary of the happy few. Sixth, there is a recurring *motif* (perhaps the recurring *motif*) of the past alive in the present. And seventh, the world of the adventurers is essentially an aristocratic world.

It might also be argued that there are fewer shades of grey in the actions of the characters than we are accustomed to seeing in our present-day world (on all this, see Jared Lobdell, *The Rise of Tolkienian Fantasy*, 2005, p. 167). While there are two time-schemes in the books, they are time-specific, and if the English world is not aristocratic, the Narnian world certainly is. The stories have an omniscient (or almost-omniscient) narrator, which is characteristic of the fairy-tale mode rather than the Edwardian-adventure mode, but they are Edwardian for all that.

Coming to the fifth of our children in Narnia, Eustace, in *The Voyage of the "Dawn Treader,"* it is noteworthy that Eustace Clarence Scrubb is a humorous name, like Otho or Lotho Sackville-Baggins—or (but this was a real man, in our world and the world of Lewis's childhood), Archibald Willingham de Graffenreid Clarendon Butt. In fact, it combines, like the full name of Major Butt (who went down on the *Titanic*), or like Otho or Lotho, Medieval or Norman names with an absurdly English last name. The humor is not far removed from the humor of juxtaposition in the old music-hall song, "I'm 'Enery the Eighth, I Am!"

Eustace and Clarence are noble names from Medieval England and Scrubb is the resounding anti-climax. But Eustace's coadjutor in *The Silver Chair*, Jill Pole, should be recognized as having a royal name. When the Welsh claimant to the Lancastrian line, Henry Tudor (nephew of the half-blood to Henry VI Plantagenet), took England by conquest in 1485, there remained (besides his wife, Elizabeth of York), several other Yorkist claimants to the late rights of Edmund Mortimer from Lionel Plantagenet, Duke of Clarence. One of these was Margaret Plantagenet, Countess of Salisbury, daughter of the Duke of Clarence, who married Sir Richard Pole. She was put to death by Henry VIII, possibly because her claim was better than his, certainly because her children's claims would be better than his children's. I doubt if Lewis was unaware that Pole was a royal name. (Jill is, I suppose, from the child evacuee Jill Flewett, who became a friend for the rest of Lewis's life.) I suspect the "Eustace Clarence Scrubb" name lay dormant in Lewis's mind a very long time—we shall say more about the name itself in Chapter 4.

But what is real? Not a child named Eustace Clarence Scrubb, to be sure, though possibly a child named Jill Pole. Not a marsh-wiggle named Puddleglum—though certainly Fred Paxford, Lewis's gardener, who was a model for some of Puddleglum's characteristics. Of course, the real philosophical question in *The Silver Chair* is whether the "Overworld" is real—but then, we already know it is, even though Rilian, in captivity, has been brought by the Green Witch to believe the

"Underworld" is all. But this is Lewis seeking to get past the watchful dragons, not to realize ("make real") the world of the dragons, the world of imagination. This is Lewis the apologist, the controversialist, not so much the artist. The artist made Puddleglum on Paxford's model—that is a work of imagination, with overtones from *Punch*. The gnomes of Bism (if not the name of Bism) are a work of imagination (even if their origins lie in part in *Punch* caricatures of workers in Lewis's youth). We will look a bit more at the philosophical point later on, in Chapter 4: here we are merely noting some other matters along the way.

Here, for starters on the matter of Narnia and the North (and what the North meant to Lewis), is Lewis's description of the three great imaginative experiences of his earlier youth: "The third glimpse [of 'enormous bliss'] came through poetry. I had become fond of Longfellow's *Saga of King Olaf*; fond of it in a casual shallow way for its story and its vigorous rhythms. But then, and quite different from such pleasures, and like a voice from far more distant regions, there came a moment when I idly turned the pages of the book and found the unrhymed translation of *Tegner's Drapa* and read 'I heard a voice that cried / Balder the beautiful / Is dead, is dead.' I knew nothing about Balder; but instantly I was uplifted into huge regions of northern sky, I desired with almost sickening intensity something never to be described (except that it is cold, spacious, severe, pale, and remote), and then, as in the other examples, found myself already falling out of that desire and wishing I were back in it" (C.S. Lewis, *Surprised by Joy*, New York, 1954, paperback ed., p. 17). Remember, we are not looking here at the North in the Narnian world, but at what "The North" meant to Lewis, in this world, in his world.

And then, some few years after the experience with Balder, but still in his youth (pp. 72–73), there came another such experience. "A moment later, as the poet says, 'The sky had turned round.' What I had read was the words Siegfried and the Twilight of the Gods. What I had seen was one of Arthur Rackham's illustrations to that volume. I had never heard of Wagner, nor of Siegfried. I thought the Twilight of the Gods meant the twilight in which the gods lived. How did I know, at once and beyond question, that this was no Celtic, or silvan, or terrestrial twilight? But so it was. Pure 'Northernness' engulfed me: a vision of huge clear spaces hanging above the Atlantic in the endless twilight of Northern summer, remoteness, severity . . . and almost at the same moment I knew that I had met this before, long long ago (it hardly seems longer now) in *Tegner's Drapa*, that Siegfried (whatever it might be) belonged to the same world as Balder and the sunward-sailing cranes.

And with that plunge back into my own past there arose at once, almost like heartbreak, the memory of Joy itself."

In Chapter 5, "First Things, Last Things: The Second Larger Life," we conclude our separate looks at the separate volumes of the Chronicles of Narnia, beginning with the way in which the first and last volumes (by Narnian chronology) show the consciousness that "In my ending is my beginning." Here we consider Digory and Polly in *The Magician's Nephew* as they might have been friends of Jacks (they were certainly his older contemporaries)—that is, beginning the whole story in the familiar times of his youth before going off to adventures not really within his timeline at all, inside the stable (but what stable? and where?) in *The Last Battle*, before going "Higher up and further in" in the Delectable Mountains, in a time-line that includes Christ and Christian, but not the quotidian days of Clive Staples Lewis. This is the beginning of the Second Larger Life. (For those of my readers unfamiliar with the prayer on the anniversary of one departed in the Episcopal *Book of Common Prayer* it reads this way: "Almighty God, we remember this day before thee thy faithful servant [N.], and we pray thee that, having opened to him the gates of larger life, thou wilt receive him more and more into thy joyful service; that he may win, with thee and thy servants everywhere, the eternal victory; through Jesus Christ our Lord. Amen.)

But that, as John Donne might say, rather leaves us hanging. After we have looked at "chronicles" one by one, ending with the first and last (the book-end "chronicles" we might say), we will, in Chapter 6, ("Child! I Tell No-One Any Story but His Own"), consider some questions of style and content—including the style of the content and the content of the style. When Aslan tells Lucy that she really does not need to know the stories of others (and tells Shasta and Aravis)—and that she will not be told what would have been (ever!)—no stories of *If!*—he is asserting, for the author's purposes in this creation, that the content of what is being told is universal, which is probably why it is told in the narrator's voice of C.S. Lewis.

This sixth chapter looks at certain questions and connections—1. real children and unreal estates? 2. avuncular stories or parental stories? 3. Narnia and the "Greatest Story Ever Told"—and then 4. a discussion of what has come after. This bears the title, "Pevensies, Peregrinations, and Potter." The Pevensies, of course, are Peter, Susan, Edmund, and Lucy. (I connect their name with the Sussex location that plays so great a role in Kipling's children's books.) I do not think of them as real children in unreal estates, as I do of E. Nesbit's five children, or Kipling's

Dan and Una. Eustace and Jill are neither more nor less real than the Pevensies, to my mind—but Digory and Polly seem to come out of C.S. Lewis's childhood, when he said determinedly to his parents, "I'se Jacks!" Jadis comes out of a book (by E. Nesbit, as it happens)—whether Digory and Polly come from one too (or several) we cannot say, but they are (to me) a little more flesh and blood than the others. The wonderful illustrations of Pauline Baynes have almost guaranteed that the four Pevensies would need the medium of film to take full form.

Peregrinations (a word connected with "pilgrimages") refers—in this context—both to Peregrine (Pippin) Took (Tûk), the Hobbit of that ilk, in *The Lord of the Rings* and to the Narnian stories as pilgrimages. Potter is, of course, Harry Potter in the J.K. Rowling heptology of that name. No doubt the Narnia books had some influence on Rowling, but what we will be looking at in Chapter 6 is the children's milieu (for want of a better word) in both sets of books, and their place in the Arcady of childhood. Here we may briefly suggest the relation of some of the classic children's books to the idea of Arcady.

First, G.A. Henty (1832–1902) is Arcadian—though his is a slightly different vision of Arcady from Grahame and Kipling—his novels are certainly not part of the same stream as *The Wind in the Willows*. Nor are they part of quite the same stream as Kipling's, though they are much closer to being school stories (they are essentially about schoolboys), as indeed are the Narnian stories. The schoolboy excursions in defiance of authority in Kipling's *Stalky & Co* (1899) are Arcadian, and I believe they suggest that the book is pastoral, that there is an amorality to pastoral (to which the English, at least, have found it necessary to add some kind of moral judgment), and that this exemplifies the natural linking of youth and pastoral—and thus Arcady (or Arcady and thus pastoral). And then there is the matter of the houses—the great grand houses—in the country.

There are dwelling-places in Arcady in Henty's boys' books (and his occasional girls' book), and, for that matter, with Bevis. Inns are dwelling-places in the Arcady of the open road. For, after all, there are wolves in the pastoral (else why do we need the pastor?) just as there are dangers in the Wild Wood, dangers from which, in *The Wind in the Willows,* Ratty and Moley are rescued by Badger's House. This too is surely a dwelling-place in Arcady. But it is also in the Wild Wood, and beyond that is the Wide World, of which it is forbidden to speak. Now for Lewis, as it is for Lewis's friend Tolkien, it may be that recapturing the past (even the Arcadian past) is a kind of advance. Come to think of it, that is a theme in Kipling's *Puck of Pook's Hill* and *Rewards and*

Fairies, as it is in E. Nesbit's *The House of Arden*. And in all these, irony aside, Kenneth Grahame's vision of children as Arcadians among the Olympian adults holds true.

Whatever the age of the children, Arcadia is beset with perils, so an agreeable dwelling-place is all to the good—but note, there is a link between child and countryside, as well as between schooldays and golden days: the link is the link of Arcady. There is also a strong sense of the past somehow immanent in the present, not always a golden past but at least a past streaked with gold. And also we remember, that in the ninth chapter of *The Wind in the Willows*, "Wayfarers All," the Rat is entranced by the call of the Sea Rat, and is only kept from leaving all his world behind, by the forcible action of the Mole. He is not to be a wayfarer: home is sweet, *dulce domum*, and the call of the Wide World is a siren call.

There's a pattern beginning to take shape. Even if we go wide in this world, wonders to hear, we will come back—the pattern is "there and back again." (Yes, I know, that's the pattern of *The Hobbit*—and *The Lord of the Rings*—but so it is of the first six Narnia books.) And this leads us to Chapter 7, on what has come after—not only the competition (so to speak) in the form of Harry Potter at Hogwarts and elsewhere, but the glorification of the Narnia books over the past half-century as being (at least almost) C.S. Lewis's greatest achievement.

Several of them have been made into movies, and doubtless the others will follow (or are already following)—and while I would have said once that no one is likely to make any films of Lewis's other books, barring *Screwtape* and *The Great Divorce*, I think it possible that the Ransom stories will be made into films, with the (true but exaggerated) claim that Elwin Ransom is really based on Professor Tolkien. Nevertheless, it has been Narnia that has led that way, Narnia whose achievement has continued C.S. Lewis's name as a house-hold word for more than half a century. No matter that his finest sustained work is *English Literature in the Sixteenth Century, Excluding Drama*. You can't make a movie out of that, and Oxford even changed the book's name some years after Lewis's death.

My approach in this book, as I have suggested, is individual and personal, and reflective—some critics may even say it is idiosyncratic. For example, to anticipate some of what I write in Chapter 3, the name Narnia, in combination with Lucy, suggested to me at my first reading, the name of the Blessed Lucia da Narni—presumably because I had seen that name very recently in a book assigned as summer reading for my class at the Episcopal boarding school I was then attending. It was, I think, Samuel Shellabarger's *Prince of Foxes* [1947]).

I do not suppose many others first reading *The Lion, the Witch, and the Wardrobe* around 1952–53 would have had that reaction, though of course I cannot be sure—but there was certainly a reference to "Saint" Lucia of Narni abroad in a popular book of that time, and it may have had an influence on Lewis, already writing a book "for" his godchild Lucy Barfield. (The whole matter of the ancient Umbrian Narnia and the present Narni is now well-known, of course, and I believe that the town of Narni has a website with references to C.S. Lewis, but I am speaking of what happened with me more than sixty years ago.)

Though "Narnia" appears in Macaulay's *Lays of Ancient Rome* (a book very much part of Lewis's mental furniture), it is in fact under the name "Nequinum" in that passage in Horatius at the Bridge that I once memorized (and I daresay the Lewis brothers, or at least their father, did too): "Aunus from green Tifernum / Lord of the Hill of Vines / And Seius whose eight hundred slaves / Sicken in Ilva's mines / And Picus, long to Clusium / Vassal in peace and war, / Who led to fight his Umbrian powers / From that grey crag where girt with towers / The fortress of Nequinum lowers / O'er the pale waves of Nar." The identity of Nequinum with Narnia is found (for example) in the notes to the Harper English Classics (W.J. Rolfe and J.C. Rolfe) 1894 edition of the *Lays*, p. 138, "Nequinum. The name applied before the Roman conquest [454 A.U.C.] to Narnia, one of the most important cities of Umbria, situated on the Nar, eight miles above its junction with the Tiber"—thus fifty-six miles from Rome.

Lucia (Brocadelli) da Narni (1476–1544), a Third-Order Dominican and recipient of seven divine visions, was a young lady of Umbria who married in 1494, was absolved from her vows, entered a convent at the age of twenty in 1496, under the protection of Ercole d'Este, Duke of Ferrara, at which time (or shortly thereafter, by 1500) she received the stigmata. She remained there at the Convent until her death, eventually as Prioress. I know of no similarity between the visions of Santa Lucia da Narni and the experiences of Lucy of Narnia (nor even if Lewis read her *Visione*), but I do not believe the similarity of names is accidental. (Walter Hooper, by the way, recalls a map Lewis once owned with the name of Narnia underlined.) The only part of the Umbrian Narnia (other than the name) that seems to have made its way into Lewis's creation is the castle girt with towers (which in fact is Macaulay and not Umbrian) and perhaps the almost subterranean (certainly Arcadian rather than Olympian) classical world of fauns and satyrs and strange powers.

We know very little of the Umbrian Narnians, except that the Umbrian leader, Lar or Lars Porsena, under whom Picus of Nequinum

(Narnia) fought, did in fact conquer Rome, the efforts of Horatius and Spurius Lartius and Herminius notwithstanding. But if we remember how Morgan le Fay set all Britain on fire with ladies that were enchantresses, we can see how the mysterious pre-Roman history of Rome—or possibly (but less likely) the intrigues of the Borgias with the countervailing piety of Lucia da Narni—could have helped set Lewis's imagination on fire. He was, after all (as Ronald Tolkien once told me), a "voracious and retentive" reader prone to "echoic borrowing"—and the furniture of whose mind, by my understanding, was stored in many mansions.

In a way, this matter of the name of Narnia can serve as an introduction to the story I want to tell here of my experience of C.S. Lewis. When I was studying for my confirmation into the Episcopal Church my parents urged me to read some of his little books we had on the library table, *The Case for Christianity*, *Beyond Personality*, *Christian Behavior*, *The Problem of Pain*, *Miracles*. Besides these works of what I learned were called apologetics, there were also *The Screwtape Letters* ("You would enjoy that!"), *The Great Divorce*, *Out of the Silent Planet*, *Perelandra*, *That Hideous Strength*, *The Abolition of Man*, *The Weight of Glory*, the reprint of *Pilgrim's Regress*.

Being twelve years old when I was confirmed, I read none of them, but the next year, being thirteen, curiosity got the best of me—though I turned almost automatically to the books my parents had not specifically recommended, beginning with *Out of the Silent Planet, Perelandra, That Hideous Strength*, and then *The Great Divorce*—and only then the apologetics and *The Screwtape Letters*.

And once I began reading C.S. Lewis, I read him voraciously and retentively. And if he even so much as mentioned a book in one of his, I sought to read it. That was why, a few years later on, I asked my parents for the three volumes of *The Lord of the Rings* as a Christmas present— and why I read George MacDonald's Curdie books, and Layamon, and Malory, and Brother Lawrence and Julien Benda and—once I came across his volume on *English Literature in the Sixteenth Century* in the Oxford History of English Literature ("OHEL")—why I read the "Scottish Chaucerians" and indeed the Bannatyne Manuscript (four volumes from the Scottish Text Society), even translating "The Reed in the Loch Says" in my collegiate days for the Yale Literary Magazine. "Though raging storms make us to shake / And winds make waters overflow / We yield to them but do not break / And in the calm bent up we grow / So banished men, though princes rage, / And prisoners, be not despaired / Abide the calm while it assuage / For time such causes has repaired."

And along the way, I read Chad Walsh's *C.S. Lewis: Apostle to the Skeptics*, and then my parents began to give me the "children's books" as birthday and Christmas presents, along with anything else Lewis published in those years. I had been raised on some of Lewis's favorite books, *The Wind in the Willows* among them, and Andrew Lang's *Prince Prigio*, besides the Henty books Warnie (W.H.) Lewis read, but not his brother. And, by the way, as soon as they began to come out, I bought or my parents bought me the W.H. Lewis books on seventeenth- and eighteenth-century France, and one of these days I'll publish in that field also—I began some of the essays and studies long ago ("Letters from the Huguenot War of 1627–28" or "Charles de Batz-Castelmore")—and I had his encouragement through Owen Barfield. Maybe I will finally get back to them when this is finished. It's only been nearly fifty years. And since I own the letters, no one has gotten to them before me.

I enjoyed the Narnia books, but they couldn't be part of the furniture of my mind as the Ransom books were (*Out of the Silent Planet, Perelandra, That Hideous Strength*), and I did not enjoy them the same way I had enjoyed *The Wind in the Willows* or *Prince Prigio*, which, of course, I had read at the appropriate age. To me *The Lion, the Witch, and the Wardrobe* was a kind of helter-skelter grab-bag of a book, not unlike *That Hideous Strength* in that respect, though far less recondite—and I valued it for the aspects of *roman* (or *fairy-tale*) *à clef* and for the references as much as for the story. One thing: I certainly did not read the books as character studies. Perhaps because of my age, perhaps because I was reading the books as a kind of literary exercise, or simply to be in touch with the mind of the author, rather than simply as story-books, I did not think of the four Pevensies as real children.

On the rare occasions earlier in grade school when my friends got me to read the Hardy Boys books, I couldn't think of the Hardy boys as real "teenagers" or "big kids" either. Every once in a while there was a real "kid" moment in Narnia—Edmund saying (in *Prince Caspian*, p. 99) that he should challenge Trumpkin because "it will be more of a sucks for him if I win!"—but they were few and far between. Certainly it was the stories and not the characters that were of interest, perhaps in line with Lewis's saying that those who have strange adventures should not themselves be strange. In any case, these are children's books and not "young adult" books, and I believe they are in many ways "improving" books like the Sunday School tracts of the nineteenth century—but with far greater imagination, accepting imagination and literary tradition as legitimate parts of the endeavor. At least, that is how I saw them, and still see them.

Before I finished the Narnia books—indeed before they were all published—I read *Surprised by Joy* and Lewis's own favorite, *Till We Have Faces*, and one of mine, his inaugural address at Cambridge, *De Descriptione Temporum*, with its great peroration. And then I went to Yale, where I searched down index references to Lewis in the *Times Literary Supplement*, in *Time & Tide*, in the *Review of English Studies*, and so on, then read the pieces. I had already read (almost memorized) my favorite Lewis verses ("Awake! My Lute"), quoted in full in *C.S. Lewis: Apostle to the Skeptics*, the verses that begin "I stood in the gloom of a spacious room / Where I listened for hours on and off / To a terrible bore with a beard like a snore / And a heavy rectangular cough." (Verses reminiscent of "When you're lying awake / With a dismal headache / And repose is taboo'd by anxiety . . . ") By the time *The Last Battle* came out, I was far more familiar with Lewis's whole work than I had been when I first read *The Lion, the Witch, and the Wardrobe*. But I cannot say my view of Lewis had changed, and my view of Narnia remained that of a literary critic or historian, more than that of a child reading a set of children's books.

In November 1958, when I was home on leave from college, my mother told me she had written to C.S. Lewis, telling him how much our family enjoyed his books, and that her son's (my) twenty-first birthday was his sixtieth (November 29th, 1958), and "Happy Birthday!" She received a very gracious letter in reply, inviting me to visit him if ever I came to England, and from that began our correspondence. My last letter from him was dated October 22nd 1963, having as its principal topic the origins of the bubble-trees in *Perelandra* (from a childish mispronunciation of laboratory as bubble-tree, "and the delightful word seemed to suggest the thing").

All my letters from Lewis (and some of those from Ronald and Christopher Tolkien, and my Lewis books, including *Mark v. Tristram*, and my first American edition of *The Lord of the Rings*) were stolen in a break-in when I was in Massachusetts in 1976–77. Three of the books, which had my name in them (*Till We Have Faces*, *Studies in Words*, *Christian Reflections*), were purchased by or given to Wheaton College and returned by them to me in 1985, when I was there for a Conference. Another, the Hooper-Green life of C.S. Lewis, found its way back to me through Taylor University in 2003, when I was there for a Conference. So I no longer have the letters, or my first American editions of all the Narnia books, or much else of the actual copies of the Lewis books I grew up on.

And perhaps in part for that reason, I have something more than I might otherwise have of the voice that speaks through his books. I think

Lewis had something to do with my wanting to be a teacher; I know he had something to do with my being a Christian (but then, my being a Christian, and of his denomination, had something to do with my being—you might say—a "Lewisite"). What I tried (in my better times) to learn from C.S. Lewis, and hope I have learned from him, was what I recognized as a habit of thought, engaged but judicious, convinced but reasoning, knowing the value of tradition and the past but carrying out today's daily tasks, with the strengths of a life of the mind such that (in Scipio's sense) I would never be less alone than when alone, with other minds—like Lewis's—and "all the company of Heaven" to be with me. (And, indeed, the *Somnium Scipionis* was another book I read because Lewis mentioned it.)

I finished writing a first draft of this book eight or nine years ago, but time went on—as it has a way of doing—until it was evident it would be necessary to bring the book up to date if it were to be published at all. So I began extensive revisions, finished some of them, cut some of them short, and finally assembled the book we have here. Along the way, the title changed, and some of the chapters and their titles changed, but the cast of my mind has not, nor has my understanding of the cast of Lewis's—rebellious, ironic, witty—versifier, editorialist, and satirist. And *makar* (as we will shortly see).

But this book is not the one I finished first-draft back in 2006. One cannot think—even off and on—about a project for eight years without that project changing shape in one's mind. Particularly I have thought more about Lewis and History—as part of thinking more about Lewis, Williams, and Tolkien (and Barfield), and the Figure of Arthur. Some of the results of that additional thought may be seen, especially, in Chapter 7.

[1]

The Conscious Decision
to Write a Children's Story

So let us take up this matter of the "conscious decision to write a children's story" in somewhat greater detail. We'll begin with Lewis's childhood and his childhood reading, and here he has carved part of the way for us, in his memoir, *Surprised by Joy*. What is a little curious about that memoir is his relative indefiniteness as to the books that greatly influenced his childhood. It's true that he records how the idea of Autumn came to him (*Surprised by Joy*, p. 16) from Beatrix Potter's *Squirrel Nutkin* (1903), which he could easily have read at the "appropriate" age, and which may have come into his life at the same time as the toy garden he mentions in *Surprised by Joy* (p. 7). That was the toy garden which gave him the first idea of the beauty of nature. But there is little or no trace of Beatrix Potter in his dressed animals in Boxen. As he records, the mood of the systematizer was already strong in him—not the mood of the Romantic. That was the eighteenth-century mood of Swift or Defoe, the Medieval mood of Lydgate or Aquinas (or earlier Isidore of Seville)—not the Romantic mood of the century into which he was born.

He read Conan Doyle's *Sir Nigel* (he doesn't mention *The White Company*) and Mark Twain's *A Connecticut Yankee in King Arthur's Court* for its Arthurian story, not for its "vulgar ridicule"—but better was E. Nesbit's trilogy, *Five Children and It* (1902), *The Phoenix and the Carpet* (1904), *The Story of the Amulet* (1906). "The last did the most for me. It first opened my eyes to antiquity, 'the dark backward and abysm of time'" (*Surprised by Joy*, p. 14—though he doesn't have all the original titles quite right in the book—*The Phoenix and the Wishing Carpet*, for example). And then "Gulliver in an unexpurgated and lavishly illustrated edition was one of my favorites, and I pored endlessly over an almost complete set of old Punches which stood in my father's study. Tenniel gratified my passion for dressed animals . . . Then came the Beatrix Potter books, and then at last beauty" (pp. 14–15).

After that came *Tegner's Drapa* in the Longfellow version, and that is where his story of his childhood reading ends, at least in *Surprised by Joy*. One might say, "But that is quite a lot about his reading as a child— you said there was very little." But there is no mention of Lewis Carroll or Edward Lear, no mention of popular books at the time (barring *Sir Nigel*, in parts in *The Strand*). Nothing else mentioned of Conan Doyle's, though much more was available to him in *The Strand*. The Longfellow was his father's (and there was Tennyson also), I believe, but of his father's favorites, Trollope (for example), he says little—possibly he didn't read them until later. He apparently did not have *The Boy's King Arthur*, or Dasent's *East of the Sun and West of the Moon*, or *Heroes of Asgard* (though one writer, Ruth James Cording, says he did have that one). And he did not read George Alfred Henty's books for boys (or not with pleasure), though his brother "Warnie" (W.H. Lewis) did.

From his account (and from reading Boxen), one is left with the conclusion that the great neglected pieces of C.S. Lewis's mental furniture from his childhood (neglected by the critics and historians) were *Gulliver's Travels* and the back files of *Punch*. The importance of *Punch* we mentioned in the last chapter; the importance of *Gulliver* (as I have pointed out in my book on *The Scientifiction Novels of C.S. Lewis*) may be greater for the Ransom stories (especially *Out of the Silent Planet*) than for Narnia—but it is still there for Narnia. And also, because of his negative comments on Macaulay's *Lays of Ancient Rome*, the importance of the *Lays* has been underrated. What all these portend, when we put them all together, we will see in our final chapter, which I have called (for the pun) "A Good Swift Kick toward Success."

The curious thing about his childhood reading, as he recounts it, is how little of it was books that other children of his time seem to have read—but against this we may set his choice (for the "Book Club" as noted in a letter home 22nd November 1908) of *The Strand* (with Warnie getting *Pearson's* and "Field *The Captain*"). We know he read *Sir Nigel* in *The Strand*, though we have no evidence he read Sherlock Holmes. A study of *The Strand* from, say, 1905 (perhaps earlier) to 1910 or 1911 or even 1912 might well be of considerable value here (*Pearson's* and *The Captain* less). In *The Strand*, E. Nesbit, H.G. Wells ("The First Men in the Moon" in 1901), W.W. Jacobs, Morley Roberts ("The Fog" in 1908), Arthur Conan Doyle, Somerville and Ross (*The Further Adventures of an Irish R.M.*), even (in 1901) Lewis Carroll, all come to mind.

In fact, it may be suggested that much of Lewis's childhood reading, apart from the books—including bound volumes of *Punch*—at Little Lea, was determined by what was in *The Strand*. And yet, he certainly exercised choice—*Sir Nigel*, but not, apparently Sherlock Holmes, or at least not with anything like the same interest. (Though certainly he was aware of Sherlock Holmes, as *The Magician's Nephew* shows, and his father enjoyed detective stories.) We know Lewis read Somerville and Ross (from his description of meeting Somerville's nephew Nevill Coghill), though we don't know whether he read their books when he was young (but *Further Adventures of an Irish R.M.* were in *The Strand* in 1906.). Many of the classic children's stories that were among Lewis's favorites in later life—*The Wind in the Willows*, for example—do not seem to have been an important part of his own childhood. Certainly George MacDonald only came into his ken when he was sixteen, and then not with the Curdie books or *At the Back of the Northwind*, not with the children's books. So in a way, Lewis's experience with children's books—apart from the *Strand* experience—was like mine with his children's books, with the Narnia books. We were reading not as children but as adults, in a way, though not the same way, reading critically. (Lewis may have read *The Wind in the Willows* early on, but it was clearly not so important to him as E. Nesbit.) But what could children's books say best? (Because it was "children's books" for all he said "fairy-tales.")

Actually, his remark indeed was that a fairy-tale "may say best what is to be said!" He pointed out in that connection that he was using the phrase "fairy tale" and not the phrase "children's stories" though it might seem children's stories were, in fact, what he was talking about. But he was (he said) bowing to his friend Tolkien's demonstration that the connection between children and fairy-tales was not as close as was generally thought—so his Narnia books were fairy-tales, and were "'for children' only in the sense that I excluded what I thought they would not like or understand" (*On Stories*, p. 47). He goes on:

> As these images [faun with umbrella in the snow, queen on a sledge, magnificent lion] sorted themselves into events (i.e., became a story) they seemed to demand no love interest and no close psychology. But the Form which excludes these things is the fairy tale. And the moment I thought of that I fell in love with the Form itself [my emphasis]: its brevity, its severe restraints on description, its flexible traditionalism, its inflexible hostility to all analysis, digression, reflections, and 'gas.' I was now enamored of it. Its very limitations of vocabulary became an attraction; as the hardness of the stone pleases the sculptor or the difficulty of the sonnet delights the sonneteer. (pp. 46–47)

I have emphasized Lewis's statement that he fell in love with the form when he came to begin writing the Narnia books, because it suggests that he was not previously enamored of the form, which may be important for us. I have not emphasized the severe constraints on description or the difficulty of using the form delighting the user, the first because I'm not sure of its relevance, the second because I am not sure the experience is universal.

Not all fairy-tales—not even all of Grimm's fairy-tales—eschew description, and it is certain neither E. Nesbit nor the Narnia books show the fairy-tale restraint. But let us look briefly at that restraint in two of Grimm's lesser-known tales, both of which begin with a descriptive passage, "Master Pfriem" and "The Little Folks' Presents"—the first begins "Master Pfriem was a short, thin, but lively man, who never rested a moment. His face, of which his turned-up nose was the only prominent feature, was marked by small-pox and pale as death; his hair was grey and shaggy, his eyes small, but they glanced perpetually about on all sides" (*Grimm's Complete Fairy Tales*, Doubleday, n.d., p. 395). "The Little Folks' Presents" (p. 155) begins:

> A tailor and a goldsmith were traveling together, and one evening when the sun had sunk behind the mountains, they heard the sound of distant music, which became more and more distinct. It sounded strange, but so pleasant that they forgot all their weariness and stepped quickly onwards. The moon had already arisen when they reached a hill on which they saw a crowd of little men and women, who had taken each other's hands, and were whirling round in the dance with the greatest pleasure and delight.

One is reminded of the example I have read of how economy in description can be a great strength—"They came out of the castle by a gate toward the sea, and the moon shown clear." The point is that we, the readers (or listeners), bring our experiences, or images, or vision, to give descriptive substance to the simple words, and by our co-operation, our being part of the process, what is described becomes more real to us. But while this is certainly true of the fairy-tales in Grimm (though in differing degrees as they are from different sources), it may be less true of Narnia, as it is less true of E. Nesbit.

Here is a description of the Dance of Plenty from *Prince Caspian* (p. 205):

> Then Bacchus and Silenus and the Maenads began a dance, far wilder than the dance of the trees; not merely a dance for fun and beauty (though it was that too) but a magic dance of plenty, and where their hands touched, and where their feet fell, the feast came into existence—sides of roasted meat

that filled the grove with delicious smell, and wheaten cakes and oaten cakes, honey and many-colored sugars and cream as thick as porridge and a smooth as still water, peaches, nectarines, pomegranates, pears, grapes, strawberries, raspberries—pyramids and cataracts of fruit. Then, in great wooden cups and bowls and mazers, wreathed with ivy, came the wines; dark, thick ones like syrups of mulberry juice, and clear red ones like red jellies liquefied, and yellow wines and green wines and yellowy-green and greenish-yellow.

In one sense, of course, there is economy in this description—much of it is by nouns and there are a couple of simple similes. But it is scarcely the restricted description under severe restraint of the fairy-tale (though of course what it is describing isn't restrained either). And here, for comparison, is a passage from one of E. Nesbit's books:

"I see" said the Queen, "a sort of play-thing. Well, I wish that all these slaves may have in their hands this moment their fill of their favorite meat and drink." Instantly, all the people in the Mile End Road, and in all the other streets where poor people live, found their hands full of things to eat and drink. From the cab window could be seen persons carrying every kind of food, and bottles and cans as well. Roast meat, fowls, red lobsters, great yellowy crabs, fried fish, boiled pork, beef-steak puddings, baked onions, mutton pies . . . (E. Nesbit, *The Story of the Amulet* [1906], in Octopus ed., 1979, pp. 515–16)

The Queen here is the model for the Empress Jadis in *The Magician's Nephew*, but the point here is that severe economy of description in the fairy-tale mode is no more a characteristic of E. Nesbit and the Five Children (Robert, Anthea, Jane, Cyril and "The Lamb") than it is of C.S. Lewis and the Four Pevensies—even though there is a kind of restraint imposed by restrictions on vocabulary for the proximate audience. And what of the other point Lewis made in his "Fairy Tales May Say Best What's to Be Said" is the pleasure in conforming the artist's creation to a strict form, his example (besides the fairy tale) being the sonnet?

I think I see what he is getting at, though I am not sure it is the way I would put it (but I may not have his point quite right). Certainly there is a pleasure in playing the creation against the form, as Lewis does with the novel in *Perelandra*—or as I have done in writing sonnets (not very expert ones)—but a difficulty in exact conformity seems to me something apart from the creative process. I recall that when A.E. Housman spoke of difficulty in the creative process (in his lecture on "The Name and Nature of Poetry"), he carefully concealed which lines in the poem in question had come easily and which with difficulty. I suggest that Lewis's excitement with the form was part and parcel of his love for epigram, for "short-form" fiction (short story or story in instalments), and for certainty —as in (for example—it is G.K. Chesterton's example) *The Song of Roland,* where "Païens ont tort et Chrestiens ont droit!"

"Short-form" fiction and certainty are part of the "children's story" or the "fairy-tale" mode. One other point here—a person writing a sonnet can feel part of the great tradition gathered about that form, as indeed can anyone using an established form: that is part of what Lewis was talking about when he was talking about John Milton's decision to write a secondary epic. And that can serve as inspiration. I believe Lewis was inspired to further creation by his writing in the manner and tradition of E. Nesbit, rather as Andrew Lang had been inspired in *Prince Prigio* by writing in the manner and tradition of Thackeray's *The Rose and the Ring.* One other thing might be mentioned here (we'll take it up in a subsequent chapter in talking about the watchful dragons) a matter frequently overlooked, I think, in the discussion of such fairy-tale collections as the Grimms'—which is, just how Christian (in many ways) many of them are.

We will not look here at the whole history of children's books from Lewis's birth (or before, since there were older books in the house) to his final creation of Narnia, but a few glances over the field should be useful, remembering that while Lewis read children's books after his childhood years, the books he read were mostly ones that were like those of his childhood years, or even books from those years (or close to them). He did not read *The Wind in the Willows* (or E. Nesbit's Bastable stories) until he was in his late twenties (*On Stories,* p. 33), but we may reasonably include in our look both *The Wind in the Willows* (1908) and the Bastable stories—and even John Buchan's boy's book *Prester John* (1910), which left its mark on *Perelandra* and possibly on *The Silver Chair.* Whether he read *Puck of Pook's Hill* (1906) or *Rewards and Fairies* (1910) is open to doubt—though we know he read Kipling "on and off all my life," as he said (in "Kipling's World" in *They Asked for a Paper,* London 1962). Instead of looking at the history of the children's story from, say, 1898 to 1950, let us concentrate on two of Lewis's immediate antecessors, two we know he read (Andrew Lang and E. Nesbit in her "Psammead" stories), and then on Kenneth Grahame, with a few words on John Buchan.

We turn first to Andrew Lang, with *Prince Prigio* (1889) and *Ricardo of Pantouflia* (1893), where W.M. Thackeray's earlier mixture of satire and high spirits in *The Rose and the Ring* has given way to Lang's sophistication and inward smile. Or almost so—for the fact is, Lang is in some ways better than he tries to be. On this matter of satire and high spirits in *The Rose and the Ring*, one of Thackeray's Christmas books— there are five of these, published as a collection in *The Christmas Books of Mr M.A. Titmarsh*, in 1887 and 1891 and 1897 in Thackeray's Works. I know *Our Street* (the second in the collection) was first published in 1848 and *The Rose and the Ring* (the last) in 1854. They are written for children, in the manner of children's books of the time, we would say, except that (barring John Ruskin's *The King of Golden River*) we have no children's books of the time much beyond Sunday School tracts—and none of these really provide Thackeray with the model either for *The Kickleburys on the Rhine* (1851) or *The Rose and the Ring*, or *The History of Prince Giglio and Prince Bulbo* (1854).

We will look briefly here at *The Rose and the Ring*. In the midst of wars and rumors of wars, at Christmas-time in 1854, Thackeray (under the name M.A. Titmarsh) gave to the world, as his Christmas book for that year, *The Rose and The Ring*, in which—it will be recalled—the first chapter "Shows How the Royal Family Sate Down to Breakfast" and opens with the words "This is Valoroso the XXIV, King of Paflagonia, seated with his Queen and only child at their royal breakfast-table, and receiving a letter which announces to his Majesty a proposed visit from Prince Bulbo, heir of Padella, reigning King of Crim Tartary" (p. 1). Of course, a letter from Crim Tartary would appropriately arrive at an over-groaning board (notice the number of egg-cups in front of the Queen), and we should keep in mind, as we tread warily through the Italianate names of Thackeray's fable, that King Bomba of the Two Sicilies (Ferdinand II, 1810–1859) had been headline and breakfast-table news in England for a dozen years in 1854, and would be for nearly half a dozen more.

So had been the Russians and the Poles, and the Russians were fight-ing the British in the Crimea (home of the Crimean or Crim Tartars)— though it is uncertain whether it is this, or a recollection of Marshal Kutusov in the Napoleonic Wars forty years before, that has given us Count Kutasoff Hedzoff (pp. 27ff). The point is that Thackeray's Christmas-book is in part a topical satire. All these foreigners are faintly ridiculous—and some, like Bomba, are quite ridiculous and also cruel and evil and illiberal (it is a very English view)—so if we are to write about ridiculous people who are also cruel, we will write about foreign-ers. But note that the edge of the edged weapon, and the recognition of the satire, comes from a knowledge of what was going on in 1854: it does not inhere in the book itself. What does inhere in the book is a cer-tain magic, a classical fairy-tale pattern (the lost princess), the character of the Fairy Blackstick, and the tearing high spirits of the whole performance. "'Well, hang the prince.' 'I don't understand you,' says Hedzoff, who was not a very clever man. 'You Gaby! He didn't say which Prince,' says Gruffanuff.

It is far from accidental that *The Rose and The Ring* was published as a Christmas Book, and indeed the Victorian—and particularly the early Victorian—institution of Christmas is one of the few examples of Victorian carnival. And even later, there were the great English Christmas parties given (among others) by Friedrich Engels in the last decade of his life. In his story of Scrooge, as certainly in his earliest work, Dickens enters that realm of carnival, of bouleversement, of suspension of normal rules: the very name of Scrooge has the sound of carnival, and while the story is comedic (in Northrop Frye's sense), it is told very much in the comic vein. Of course, it too is a Christmas book. These Christmas books existed before Victoria's reign, but they are essentially an early Victorian phenomenon. We may briefly look at some of Thackeray's (or Titmarsh's) own remarks on the phenomenon of Christmas books. After all, these Christmas books are one part of the creation of children's literature. The quotations given here are from his "About a Christmas Book" from *Fraser's* in December 1845 (Vol. 32, pp. 744–48), and from his "A Grumble about Christmas Books" in *Fraser's* in January 1847 (Vol. 35, pp. 111–126).

From the first comes the following, in the persona of M.A. Titmarsh to Oliver Yorke, Esquire: "Do you not remember, my dear fellow, our own joy when the 12th came and we plunged out of school, not to see the face of Muzzle for six weeks?" (p. 744). And again, of the Christmas-book illustrators, "Messrs. Cope, Redgrave, Townsend, Horsley, &c., who go back to the masters before Raphael" (p. 745). And again, "Mr. Tenniel's 'Prince and Outlaw' represent a prince and outlaw of Astley's . . . the ballads to which the pictures are appended are of the theatrical sort, and quite devoid of genuineness and simplicity" (p. 748).

And from the second come these, also in a letter from M.A. Titmarsh to Oliver Yorke, Esquire:

I have read Christmas books until I have reached the state of mind most deplorable. "Curses on all fairies!" I gasp out; "I will never swallow another one as long as I live! Perdition seize all Benevolence! Be hanged to the Good and the True! Fling me every drop of the milk of human kindness out of the window! —Horrible curdling slops, away with them! Kick old Father Christmas out of doors, the abominable old impostor! Next year I'll go to the Turks, the Scotch, and other Heathens who don't keep Christmas. Is all the street to come for a Christmas box? Are the waits to be invading us by millions, and yelling all night? By my soul, if anybody offers me plum-pudding again this season, I'll fling it in his face! (p. 111)

Now while all this is pleasurable to quote (and Scrooge did no better than the second—Bah! Humbug! Indeed!), it is quoted here not for the pleasure of it, but because it shows Thackeray's conviction of the nature of Christmas, as of the Christmas book. There is a serious point to all this. We may add one more line, from the "Grumble" (p. 125): "Love is the humorists' best characteristic, and gives that charming ring to their laughter in which all the good-natured world joins in chorus." So the Christmas book should be genuine and loving, humorous in the best sense, simple (perhaps even "homely" in the British meaning of the word), calling back the days of one's own childhood, or boyhood, or girlhood.

And so, presumably, Mr. Titmarsh's own Christmas book was intended to be and do, though there seems to be some alloy—even of sarcasm—in the laughter. But surely this is a very mild form of carnival, almost (so to speak) an ordered form, that Thackeray is writing about. Quite so—yet when he wrote his own Christmas books, just as when he wrote these passages, his high spirits are themselves the spirits of carnival, of excess, of turning things topsy-turvy. That's true, but for our purposes here, there's more. We talk about Lewis's conscious decision to write a children's book—but it is at least arguable that Thackeray was the fore-runner here, with his conscious decision to write children's (Christmas) books back a hundred years before Narnia. Or perhaps we should say Christmas (children's) books. The point is, as with Lewis, that what he wanted to say demanded a certain form, though it's arguable Thackeray played a greater part in designing that form than Lewis did. There is, for example, an influence of Narnia on Harry Potter (admitted, I think, by J.K. Rowling), but the Harry Potter books are school-stories with a fairy-tale apparatus incorporated as part of their real world—while the Narnia stories are about school-children out of school (except for the brief glimpses of Experiment House in *The Silver Chair*, and perhaps for Lucy's eavesdropping on her schoolfellows in *The Voyage of the "Dawn Treader"*), though the same apparatus is (differently) incorporated into Narnia.

Here, in looking at Lewis's antecessors, it may be time for an author's switch from literary critic to literary specimen. Unfortunately, in this context, I had only one friend of my generation who was brought up on *The Rose and the Ring*, from which he seemed principally to have derived an appreciation of Victorian carnival—that's only anecdotal evidence, of course, and he is no longer alive to give us more evidence or to serve as specimen. But I was brought up on *Prince Prigio* (though not on *Ricardo of Pantouflia*, which I did not read until adulthood). At an early age, I was terrified by the fight of the Remora with the Firedrake, one of my few childhood terrors recognizably derived from a fairy-story (if that is what *Prigio* is). I suppose I might have been terrified by the Earthquaker, though what I would have made of his being killed by a load of stupidity is hard to guess. But in the Firedrake and the Remora, Lang brought true faerie into his *conte*: yet, surprisingly, they do not overbalance it. It is not entirely clear why. Perhaps a look at the structure of *Prince Prigio* will produce at least a suggestion on the surprising balance Lang achieved there.

It will be recalled that, owing to the Queen's disbelief, the fairies were not invited to court for Prince Prigio's christening: they came anyway, and the last one to give a present gave the curse of too-cleverness. So when the Firedrake was harrying the kingdom, Prigio declined to attack it; his brothers did attack it, and perished, and he was therefore forsaken and abandoned. In that condition, he prowled the palace, found the other fairy gifts from his christening (Seven League Boots, Cap of Invisibility, Sword of Sharpness, and so on), flew off and set the Remora and the Firedrake against each other—thus destroying both—claimed his reward from King Grognio (Benson's comic interlude comes in here), restored his brothers (and various knights *et alii*) to life (Lewis borrowed the scene for *The Lion, the Witch, and the Wardrobe*), married the British Ambassador's daughter, wished to seem no cleverer than others, and they all (except the Remora and Firedrake) lived happily ever after.

It is known, from the date of the cheque for ten thousand purses that King Grognio wrote to Prince Prigio, in Falkenstein, in Pantouflia, that this adventure took place in July 1718, a date borne out by the appearance of Prince Charles Edward Stuart (1722–1788) in the sequel, a generation later. It may of course be in an alternative universe, inasmuch as Manoa, the City of the Sun, has diplomatic relations with both Pantouflia and Great Britain. In one way, this is a move apart from the contemporaneity of *The Rose and the Ring* (or, for that matter, of *Five Children and It*): it is not, however, a move into the once-upon-a-time mode of the fairy-tale, but into a distancing by history. The date may be noted to suggest a connection with another great (and satiric) set of travels, unaided by Seven League Boots on Flying Carpet, that took place about this time, in Lilliputia and elsewhere (and which, as has been noted, we know Lewis read in his childhood).

Prigio's son Ricardo, the eponymous hero of the second book, is far from being too clever: in fact, he is chiefly interested in having adventures. So King Prigio hides the various fairy gifts, but Ricardo goes on having adventures and having—in the absence of the gifts—to be rescued by the Princess Jacqueline. He had rescued her in his very first adventure, before he found the gifts. Eventually, he fights the Yellow Dwarf (borrowed from D'Aulnoy as the Remora was borrowed from Cyrano), and The Giant Who Does Not Know When He Has Had Enough, and Prince Charles Edward (before the other two), with Jacqueline in each case rescuing him by magic. However, she is herself taken captive by the Giant and turned over to the Earthquaker for safekeeping.

She is rescued from the Earthquaker by King Prigio, who flattens him with a load of pedant's stupidity, brought for the purpose from the moon, thus incidentally rescuing the City of the Sun, Manoa. The King of Manoa—the Inca—turns out to be Princess Jacqueline's father. The Inca becomes a Lutheran (why a Lutheran?), the High Priest an Archbishop, Ricardo marries his Jacqueline (with the Giant sending the two Gifts he had captured as a wedding present), and everyone but the Yellow Dwarf (and in our world Charles Edward) lives happily ever after. It is not so good a book as *Prigio*, but it is much more Langian than *Prigio*. It is comedic (belonging to the mythos of comedy); it is humorous; there are comic touches; it has touches of the fantastic. But it is not fantasy, not often comic, and with almost no touch of carnival.

That is not quite true of *Prigio*, perhaps because of Thackeray's influence. Where Thackeray was apparently largely original, Lang is derivative—though in this case derivative from Thackeray. In 1889, there was little reason for Lang's characters to have Italianate names, except perhaps that Thackeray's did. The cross old fairy who curses Prigio with too-cleverness must have been a close relation of the Fairy Blackstick. Benson is Lang's version of Thackeray's Gruffanuffs. And there is certainly a similarity of name between the Paflagonia of King Valoroso and the rest and the Pantouflia of Grognio (Prigio's father) and Prince Prigio and Ricardo. But it is a similarity of name only, for here is Lang at his slyest, the master of the *contes*, the self-mocker. Pantouflia? Draw on your *pantoufles*, Mr. Lang might say, and let us *pantoufle* together. That is to say, draw on your slippers (the kind, my dictionary tells me, with "ni tige ni talon") and let us talk together, intimately, quietly, slipper-talk, fireside talk, all in the family. For that is what the words mean. (But perhaps Lang told his slipper-kingdom stories to children: it is possible, and it might explain his achievement.)

Thackeray took advantage of the lingering aspects of carnival in the early Victorian Christmas, finding a way in which to present to the Victorian audience a work both comic and fantastic, but with the comic taking precedence. (Sometimes Christmas books may say best what's to be said?) Forty years later, with that route apparently closed, Lang side-stepped into comedy and humor, both creatures of order; and he treated the fantastic as though it were merely the fantastical. This requires a certain realism of technique and involves the humor of observation applied to the unreal—as with Prigio's alternately cheering on the Firedrake and the Remora, or the townee/schoolboy slanging of Ricardo by the Yellow Dwarf. And then, in a very short time, there seems to have been a fundamental change in the English attitude toward fantasy and the fantastic, at least in the line of authors we are following here.

The change in our line here is so great that, while the connection between Thackeray and Lang is obvious, the connection between Lang and E. Nesbit, is far less so, though she and Lang were in fact contemporaries and acquaintances—yet it is possible to take her three books considered here as the beginnings of a reaction against Lang or his attitudes. But to do this would be to oversimplify. In fact, the Flying Carpet got a very short rest after its use by Lang in 1889 and 1893, till its use in *The Phoenix and The Carpet* in 1904. The Fairy of the Desert was transmogrified from her (or its) unpleasant appearance and activity in *Ricardo of Pantouflia* (this Eastern influence keeps coming in) to become—or perhaps to give birth to—the Sand-Fairy, the "It" of *Five Children and It* (1902). The carpet, of course is the eponymous machina of *The Phoenix and The Carpet* (1904). Here it should be noted that E. Nesbit follows Lang in bringing these machines of the timeless fairy-story into a time specific—whether 1718 or 1902. It may be noted also that Thackeray, though contemporaneous with his story, is not time-specific in quite the same way as E. Nesbit—and, of course, he engages in a distancing by space, even if ironic, that she does not.

The analysis here is directed not at E. Nesbit generally, or even at all her stories with magic in them, but only this one set of three: *Five Children and It* (1902), *The Phoenix and The Carpet* (1904), and *The Story of the Amulet* (1906). Though Professor Lewis spoke more highly of her stories of the Bastables, it was these he emulated, and indeed these he read as a child. The five children, it will be recalled, are Robert, Anthea ("Panther"), Jane, Cyril ("Squirrel"), and "the lamb" (whose name when he is grown up will be Hilary St. Maur Devereux, but who is now fortunately only "the lamb"). They are real children, in a way that (to me) Peter and Susan and Edmund and Lucy are not, and certainly they are real children in a way that Bulbo and Betsinda and the rest of Thackeray's "young adults" in *The Rose and the Ring* are not and are not intended to be. Thackeray's satiric world was distanced by space and the absurdity of the naming, and Lang's by time and space and naming (but it is closer to England all the same, and Prigio marries the British Ambassador's daughter). E. Nesbit's creation is right here and now, yet it remains in the realms of fantasy, and follows the fairy-tale mode of proceeding from the here-and-now to the elsewhere-and-now (and even the elsewhere-and-othertime), before coming back again.

It may be instructive to concentrate here on three episodes, one from each of the three books in the set. In *Five Children and It*, the episode recounts the result of the wish to live in a castle, made between the time Robert arranged for the Psammead to grant a wish made by the others not in his presence, and the time Robert got back to the house to tell them he had made the arrangement. In *The Phoenix and The Carpet*, the episode recounts the visit of the Phoenix to the Phoenix Fire Office. In *The Story of the Amulet*, the episode recounts the merging of Rekh-mara with Jimmy—though it is tempting to take instead the visit of the Babylonian Queen to London, on which Jadis's visit in *The Magician's Nephew* was so evidently based. These have in common at least three things, apart from such obvious matters as their involving the same five children, and their appearing in a series of books by the same author. First, they are all in the realm of fantasy. Wishing for a castle does not commonly provide one. The phoenix is a fabulous bird that does not ordinarily visit London insurance companies, even those bearing his name. And ancient Egyptian priests are not frequently transported by magic amulets through time and merged with learned gentlemen who study at the British Museum. Second, all three (though the third the least) have their comic aspects. Of course, being besieged in the castle, like all the other ill-considered things the children wish for, turns out to be far different in experience from what it was in imagination. The Phoenix, coming to the Insurance offices in the belief they are his temple, and the employees his priests and acolytes, in fact converts the employees to his belief, and the pleasant fantasy is worked out with good humor and skill (better humor, perhaps, than with the Queen of Babylon, though the skill there is no less). But the merging of the Priest Rekh-mara and Jimmy? That is, at least partly, another story.

That there has been a good deal of humor in the building up of the character of Jimmy, and episodes of the comic in the story of Rekh-mara, is undoubted ("'For there is no secret sacred name under the altar of Amen-Ra.' 'Oh yes there is!' said a voice from under the bed."—

the Psammead, of course. [p. 613 in the Octopus one-volume ed., 1979]). But when Rekh-mara's soul and Jimmy's soul become one, each gaining his heart's desire, and the evil in Rekh-mara's soul becomes the scorpion that Robert kills, we have moved from the comic or even the humorous into the mythopoetic (even if the mythopoeisis is a little too much like Rider Haggard's for some tastes).

The Story of the Amulet, unlike the first two books of E. Nesbit's "trilogy" (if that word may be used here), is pretty much serious adventuring, though the Queen's coming to London and the sailors' singing about Tyre that rules the waves are at least comic interludes. It is here, in this story, that the great overarching wave breaks over Atlantis, here that there is a true granting of Heart's Desire, and here that the process of growing up (as when they see the pictures of themselves as adults while they are visiting Jimmy and the Amulet in the future) is given a serious treatment for the children—though the point is much the same as with the sudden growing-up of "the lamb" in the earlier volume. Neither is welcome—and that is not quite a throw-away line. They are not welcome because they have not come well—that is, in the natural order of things.

It may be that the children who read *Five Children and It* in 1902 were prepared for this greater seriousness in 1906. But it may also be (and it is well to remember) that the Englishness of English art (in Sir Nikolaus Pevsner's phrase) consists in the detailed observation of life around one, and in using this detailed observation to point a moral as well as to adorn a tale. It is possible that E. Nesbit's recovery of this particularly English sense and sensibility of humor has something to do with her association with William Morris and the Fabians. Be that as it may, there is a change in her creations between 1902 and 1906, as well as—and on top of—the obvious change between Lang's *Ricardo* (1893) and the first of the "Psammead" books. Part of what sets E. Nesbit apart from Thackeray and Lang, in these books, lies in the replacement of the comic and fantastical by a genuine fantasy that is humorous, though with some comic scenes. Lewis mentions the Bastables in *The Magician's Nephew*, but he does not emulate Nesbit's Bastable stories, which are (as he says) character studies of children written the only way children will read character studies.

Lang has "Englished" Thackeray's breakfast-table *jeu d'ésprit*—Prigio is recognizably an English schoolboy, of a particularly repellent type, and Ricardo is Prigio's son and the son of the British Ambassador's daughter. In Thackeray, the fantastic is the comic, and though there are shrewd touches (on occasion betraying something of Pevsner's

Englishness), these are generally unreal estates. In Lang, less so. Here, once again, it may be time to use critics as specimens. I disagree with Lewis that Lang achieved true fantasy with the death of the Yellow Dwarf, but here Lewis may be used as a specimen. The Remora terrified me as a child, and here I may be used as a specimen. The fact is, Lewis felt something with the Yellow Dwarf, as I with the Remora. Something of Lang's wide reading in the English medieval must have rubbed off on him. The Giant Who Does Not Know When He Has Had Enough, though scarcely a portrait drawn from life, is a lifelike portrait.

Just as Lewis, writing the Narnia books after the manner of E. Nesbit, created something quite different from Nesbit, so Lang, writing children's books after the manner of Thackeray, created something quite different from Thackeray. It was thirty-five years from Betsinda to Prigio, nearly fifty from "the lamb" to The Lion, but in both cases, in changing the original, the personality of the imitator was more important than the lapse of time. (For those adding up years, there were about ten years from Ricardo to Robert and Anthea and the rest.) In any case, by the time of E. Nesbit, the comic / fantastic of Thackeray and the comic / humorous fantasticality of Lang have been replaced by that strange creature, the humorous fantasy. The phrase "strange creature" is used advisedly. Grahame essayed something of the sort in *The Wind in the Willows* (1908), humorous in precisely that English sense, though occasionally comic, as with Toad and the Washerwoman, but it has generally not been widely done or well (though Alan Garner may be an exception, and even early Harry Potter). This brings us to Ratty and Moley and Toad and Badger in *The Wind in the Willows*.

"The Mole had been working very hard all morning, spring-cleaning his little home. First with brooms, then with dusters; then on ladders and steps and chairs, with a brush and a pail of whitewash; till he had dust in his throat and eyes, and splashes of whitewash all over his black fur, and an aching back and weary arms" (*The Wind in the Willows* in *The Penguin Kenneth Grahame,* p. 181). Here, at the very beginning of Grahame's great achievement, we come upon a paradox. This is quintessential Arcady, but Moley's house, Ratty's house with its bright fire in the parlour, the picnic basket with the comforts of home ("coldtonguecoldhamcoldbeefPickledgherkinssaladfrenchrollscresssad widgespottedmeatgingerbeerlemonadesodawater"), Toad's caravan (less so Toad Hall), and above all, Badger's house, all speak to the comforts of home.

There are dangers in the Wild Wood, dangers from which Ratty and Moley are rescued by Badger's House. I cannot forbear further quotation here (*Penguin Kenneth Grahame*, pp. 209–210): "He shuffled on in front of them, carrying the light, and they followed him, nudging each other in an anticipating sort of way, down a long, gloomy, and, to tell the truth, decidedly shabby passage, into a sort of a central hall, out of which they could dimly see other long tunnel-like passages branching, passages mysterious and without apparent end. But there were doors in the hall as well—stout oaken comfortable-looking doors. One of these the Badger flung open, and at once they found themselves all in the glow and warmth of a large fire-lit kitchen.

> The floor was well-worn red brick, and on the wide hearth burnt a fire of logs, between two attractive chimney-corners tucked away in the wall, well out of any suspicion of draught. A couple of high-backed settles, facing each other on either side of the fire, gave further sitting accommodation for the sociably disposed. In the middle of the room stood a long table of plain boards placed on trestles, with benches down each side. At one end of it, where an arm-chair stood pushed back, were spread the remains of Badger's plain but ample supper. Rows of spotless plates winked from the shelves of the dresser at the far end of the room, and, from the rafters overhead, hung hams, bundles of dried herbs, nets of onions, and baskets of eggs. It seemed a place where heroes could fitly feast after victory, where weary harvesters could line up in scores along the table and keep their harvest home with mirth and song, or where two or three friends of simple taste could sit about as they pleased and eat and smoke and talk in comfort and contentment.

There is much more I would like to quote (I can in my mind hear my father reading this to me when I was young), but this will do. One point here—this is not severely restricted description.

Let us look now at a children's writer Lewis certainly did not read as a child. George MacDonald's Curdie books—*The Princess and the Goblin* (1871, collected 1872) and *The Princess and Curdie* (1877, collected 1883)—came to my attention when I was thirteen through a reference in Lewis's *That Hideous Strength*. The Princess is Irene, who is eight in the first book and nine in most of the second, and she is not unlike Alice. Curdie is a miner's son, of no particular age (but recognizably a child), who rescues Irene (more than once, and there's more to the story than that, but that will do as summary). The King in the Curdie books, and especially in *The Princess and Curdie*, lives on bread and wine (this was the reference in *That Hideous Strength*), and the two books are, like much of MacDonald's work, sacramental and symbolic, rather than allegorical. In them the passage of time, though not the time itself, was important to MacDonald—that is part of his appreciation of differences in age. Think of Princess Irene's great-great-grandmother in *The Princess and the Goblin* (as summarized by Professor Roderick McGillis in his Introduction to the World's Classics edition of the Curdie books, 1990, p. xiii): "She [the great-great-grandmother] does not hesitate to present the child with difficult ideas. She tells Irene that she is 'her father's mother's father's mother,' and Irene responds: 'Oh, dear! I can't understand that.' The [great-great] grandmother then remarks: 'I didn't expect you would. But that's no reason why I shouldn't say it'."

This is a key to a new appreciation of childhood that came in Albert Lewis's time as a child (though I daresay it passed him by). The child cannot, it is true, understand the adult world, nor should the child be expected to. The child does not have adult attitudes, nor should the child be expected to—at least, not as a child. Whether he should be expected to grow into them is not clear—MacDonald doesn't think much of most adults, except the simple ones. From this perception (and perhaps from some intermixture of Rousseauvian virtuous savagery amidst the consciousness of Arcadia) comes the cult of the child, the Wise Child to replace or complement the Wise Woman or Wise Man, the Wise Child seen (though with the complication of dumbness) in its purer Scots form in George MacDonald's *Sir Gibbie*, and then later in its bowdlerized and sentimentalized form with Little Lord Fauntleroy.

The Curdie books are not the less a pastoral for their being a miner's pastoral. If they differ technically from Grahame's pastoral, it is chiefly in having an omniscient narrator rather than a (now-omniscient) recollector, and that is not important for us. Perhaps I should briefly recount what happens in the books, though here we are verging on dream rather than plot. We begin (in *The Princess and the Goblins*) with the Princess Irene, eight years old, in the absence of her King-Papa, exploring caverns below the castle, finding the goblins (or being found by them), and being rescued by Curdie Peterson, that is Peter's son, Peter being a miner. Curdie keeps returning to the mines in the caverns (or perhaps they are caverns in the mines) by night to earn extra money to buy his mother a red petticoat. Irene explores the castle and finds the room of her great-grandmother (or is she great-great- or even more?), at the top of the castle as the mines and the goblins are at the bottom. Meanwhile Curdie searches out the goblins, as much out of curiosity as anything else. Eventually Irene goes back to the caverns, Curdie rescues her again, returns her to her father, and the narrative more or less breaks off, not to be resumed for a decade. The book obviously influenced Lewis, especially—I think—in his caves and mines and most especially in the whole creation of the Gnomes and the Land of Bism. It has additional importance in the history of the development of German Romanticism out of Novalis, but that is not our story here. And, by the way, *The Princess and Curdie* is something of a different matter.

That is, Curdie rescues Irene and her King-Papa, but this time in a war with the neighboring kingdom of of Borsagrass, aided by the Uglies, including the dog Lina, who are really good and human, against the people of Gwyntystorm, whose hands he can feel to be bestial. There are more city pavements here than in *The Princess and the Goblins*, and it is Curdie who meets—and is given tasks by—the Grandmother. Eventually Curdie marries the princess and after the old king's death, they become king and queen. But they have no heirs, and the people of Gwyntystorm elect a king who goes on mining the precious metals under the city until the city collapses (Oxford World's Classics ed., pp. 341–42): "One day at noon, when life was at its highest, the whole city fell with a roaring crash. The cries of men and the shrieks of women went up with its dust, and then there was a great silence. Where the mighty rock once towered, crowded with homes and crowned with a palace, now rushes and raves a stone-obstructed rapid of the river. All around spreads a wilderness of wild deer, and the very name of Gwyntystorm has ceased from the lips of men." ("Heavy!" as one young reader remarked to me some years ago.)

And, as an aside (more or less on what we consider "age-appropriateness"), we have that late Victorian favorite, G.A. Henty. Though the young C.S. Lewis apparently did not enjoy reading Henty, there is certainly evidence that he read him. Also, the young W.H. Lewis read and enjoyed him. Here is a specimen passage from the first Henty book I ever owned (*Bravest of the Brave or With Peterborough in Spain*, London 1887):

> Hitherto his [Peterborough's] life had been a strange one. Indolent and energetic by turns, restless and intriguing, quarreling with all with whom he came in contact, burning with righteous indignation against corruption and misdoing, generous to a point which crippled his finances seriously, he was a puzzle to all who knew him, and had he died at this time [1704] he would have only left behind him the reputation of being one of the most brilliant, gifted, and honest, but at the same time one of the most unstable, eccentric, and ill-regulated spirits of his time. (p. 19 of the Chicago M.A. Donohue edition)

Besides being a first-rate description of a manic depressive, this gives an idea of the expected vocabulary and comprehension of the fourteen-year-olds to whom, so far as we know, Henty's books were directed. "Heavy!"

But they were certainly "corking good yarns!" In fact, G.A. Henty's books were the measure of the "corking good yarn" in Lewis's youth, though C.S. Lewis, who used the phrase, did not like them. The fact is, his taste was for "unreal estates" as his brother's was (like Henty's) for the real and historical. Since John Buchan's *Prester John* (1910) had an influence on Lewis, whenever he read it, we might now turn to that book:

> There were only two outlets from that cave—the way I had come and the way the river came . . . I sat down on the floor and looked at the wall of water. It fell ... in a solid sheet, which made up the whole of the wall of the cave . . . I began the climb [and] almost before I knew I found my head close under the roof of the cave . . . Just below the level of the roof [was] the submerged spike of rock . . . To get to my feet and stand on the spike while all the fury of the water was plucking at me was the hardest physical effort I have ever made . . . a slip would send me into the abyss . . .

And so, until

> after hard striving and hope . . . deferred, I found myself on a firm outcrop of weathered stone. In three strides I was on the edge of the plateau. [I stumbled] a few steps forward on the mountain turf and then flung myself on my face. When I raised my head I was amazed to find it still early morning . . . (*Prester John*, Popular Library ed., NY, n.d., pp. 230–34)

After a certain age, Lewis did not often openly confess his tastes, until he was older and then, I think, made them part of his *persona* as the "schoolboy [Dr.] Johnson"—perhaps we might look here at his great model. Dr. Samuel Johnson (1709–1784) is not so well known now as he used to be, apart from (or even perhaps including) students of English literature. He was a Conservative ("Tory") and Church of England scholar, essayist, literary historian, Christian apologist, versifier and occasional poet, novelist, science-fiction and fantasy writer, philosopher (though old-fashioned), satirist and controversialist—and the hero of Boswell's great and unique memoir *The Life of Dr. Samuel Johnson*, in which we hear him (in his own phrase) "talking for victory." W.H. Lewis described his brother's conversation with that phrase, and some scholars, Claude Rawson notably among them, have called Lewis the "schoolboy" Dr. Johnson (in an essay in the *Times Literary Supplement* in 1989).

Lewis observed in 1932 (in a letter to Arthur Greeves) that when he wanted light reading, he wanted "not so much a grown-up 'light' book (to me usually the hardest of all kinds of reading) as a boy's book." Did he ever put away childish (or schoolboyish) things? I think so—and then he took them down again from the shelf—corking good yarns and all that. Claude Rawson noted (in the *Times Literary Supplement*, August 11th–17th 1989) that "Lewis's enduring delight in the worlds of epic and saga almost certainly included a sense of their deep analogy to what Horace Walpole called the 'mimic republic' of schoolboys." The matter is complicated by the fact that some of Lewis's adult style came early in his life: Rawson adduces the following interchange at the age of eight, on returning from a holiday in France. Lewis "announced that he had 'a prejudice against the French.' When his father asked why, he replied, 'If I knew why, it wouldn't be a prejudice.'"

The point is, Lewis in his youth was in many ways very adult, and very like himself as an adult. A few years ago, Ruth James Cording put a little book together, *C.S. Lewis: A Celebration of His Early Life* (Nashville, 2000), based on materials at the Wheaton College Library. She quotes (p. 19) the famous statement by his tutor, W.T. Kirkpatrick, to Lewis's father: "Outside a life of literary study, life has no meaning or attraction for him. You may make a writer or a scholar of him, but you'll not make anything else." But before we get to Lewis in his mid-teens, we can look at him earlier. When he was only a year and seven months old, his older brother was sniffling, and the young Lewis turned to him and said, "Warnie wipe nose!" (p. 53). The next summer (he was two-and-a half), his mother took him into a toy store to buy a "penny engine" and the woman asked if she should tie a string to it. He replied indignantly (p. 56), "Baby doesn't see any string on the engines Baby sees in the station." This was before he grew tired of being Baby or Babbins and, not liking the name Clive, pointed to himself and said, "He is Jacksie" so that ever after he was first "Jacks" and then "Jack" Lewis. But in both these stories he is speaking in the third person.

That's another "childish thing" he did not put away—his friend Owen Barfield more than once remarked (both in print and to me) that some of Lewis's poems were along the lines of "this is a thing a man might say" rather than "I say." And also, as we noted earlier, as one other "childish thing" he did not put away, it is claimed that the wardrobe through which Lucy found Narnia was the wardrobe at the house called Little Lea, where the Lewis family moved in 1905. Indeed, his cousin Ruth Hamilton later told how they would sit in the wardrobe with Jack telling stories. That certainly may be true, and the Pevensies' scurrying into the wardrobe to avoid "grown-ups" in *The Lion, the Witch, and the Wardrobe*, has an air of reminiscence about it.

But the stories would not have been stories of faerie but of Animal-Land, or possibly Boxen. The origins of the trip through the wardrobe lie elsewhere, I think. Here is a passage from an essay in *Time & Tide* in 1946 (in *On Stories*, p. 121): "It was more as if a cupboard which one had hitherto valued as a place for hanging coats proved one day, when you opened the door, to lead to the garden of the Hesperides." And here is a passage from George MacDonald (*Phantastes*, 1858, Schocken ed. 1982, p. 5), which has—to me—quite a bit of the inside-to-outside feel of Lucy's entering Narnia:

> I saw that a large green marble basin . . . which stood on a low pedestal of the same material in the corner of my room, was overflowing like a spring; and that a stream of clear water was running over the carpet . . . And stranger still, where this carpet, which I had myself designed to imitate a field of grass and daisies, bordered the course of the little stream, the grass-blades and daisies seemed to wave in a tiny breeze . . . My dressing table was was an old-fashioned piece of furniture of black oak with drawers all down the front. They were elaborately carved in foliage, of which ivy formed the chief part. . . . on the further end a singular change had commenced. I happened to fix my eye on a little cluster of ivy-leaves. The first of these was evidently the work of the carver; the next looked curious; the third was unmistakable ivy. . . . Hearing next a slight motion above me, I looked up and saw that the branches and the leaves designed upon the curtains of my bed were slightly in motion.

One of the childish things Lewis left behind him was his childish imitation of his father's world of Ulster, for which he substituted, in adulthood, the world of faerie. Ruth Cording suggests that he read Henry Van Dyke's "The Blue Flower" in childhood, and it's true that he reports in *Surprised by Joy*, that he was a "votary of the Blue Flower"—a Romantic—before he was six years old (p. 7). I know of no place where Lewis mentions Van Dyke (1852–1933), and of course Van Dyke's "The Blue Flower" in *The Blue Flower* (1902) is directly from Novalis (1772–1801). Nevertheless, I think it likely this was the version he first read, if he read it as a child, and one may, I suppose (if one searches), find echoes in Lewis's writing of the other stories in this collection of Van Dyke's. In any case, there is little doubt that his mother read Kingsley's *Water-Babies* (1867) to him when he was very young, though he did not recall it till he re-read it in adulthood—*Water-Babies* being Colin Manlove's candidate for the book that invented Modern Fantasy. Lewis's childhood was clearly not entirely lived in the workaday political world of Ulster and Boxen, and it was the Ulster and Boxen part he largely put aside, not when he became a man so much as finally when he became a Christian.

The "Ulster" novel Lewis was writing in the 1920s is evidence that he was not yet working in the realms of faerie—which, if we read his diaries from 1922 to 1927 (*All My Road Before Me*), is exactly what we should expect. Let me re-echo here what I said before, that we really have relatively little evidence of what Lewis was like as a child. He loved railroad engines and trains (expected), got up early to see the trains pass (I did the same, aged five), wanted to be outside to play even in the rain (expected), liked to go in the water at the seaside or lakeside (expected but not entirely usual), read whatever he could get his hands on (until and if he decided he did not like it), spoke of himself in the third person (not expected!), was already a systematizer and historian (of his imaginary Boxen), had a thumb with only one joint so was—he says—clumsy in handwork (except drawing, painting, and writing), lost his mother when he was nine (and his grandfather Lewis also).

One of the stories in *The Strand* in 1908 was the classic "The Fog" by C. Morley Roberts (1857–1942). I have read "The Fog" more than once, most recently to see if there was any influence on Lewis—beyond what may be an obvious influence on "The Man Born Blind." I have seen none in Narnia. But note that *The Strand* is not a magazine for boys nor a fantasy magazine, and its stories not stories for boys or (mostly) fantasy stories, any more than Conan Doyle or Morley Roberts were writers of boys' books. But they wrote books boys read, and certainly the tone of "The Fog" is very much the tone of early H.G. Wells (which may or may not be fantasy, depending on how we define fantasy). Let's pause here and summarize this chapter.

We have looked at Lewis's decision to write a children's story, beginning with what "a children's story" meant to him. We have looked at Lewis's childhood and his childhood reading, and why he thought such a story "may say best what is to be said!" We looked at the children's story (or boys' books), especially at Thackeray, G.A. Henty, Andrew Lang, Kenneth Grahame, E. Nesbit, John Buchan. On this other point—Professor Claude Rawson has spoken of Lewis as the "schoolboy [Dr.] Johnson" and we have asked, in line with that, whether he wasn't still in some sense that schoolboy even at the age of fifty (or maybe a bit earlier) when he began the Narnia books. And we have looked at what from his Ulster and Boxen childhood he kept and what he put aside when he came to his adult years.

The children's book has a number of lines of descent, but one begins with the Christmas book and particularly Thackeray's Christmas books, and among them particularly his last, *The Rose and the Ring* (1854). This is comical and fantastical, and perhaps written over the children's heads to the adults behind, but not quite, and, of course, this was pretty much before the "Invention of the Child." And it is in places genuinely funny. Another line of descent begins with the "modern fantasy" of Kingsley's *The Water-Babies*—but despite the fact that Lewis's mother read this to him (or perhaps because of that), it is not really the line in which the Narnia books eventually appear. The true line for E. Nesbit's "Psammead" books, which are the model for Narnia, is (as I have pointed out recently in *The Rise of Tolkienian Fantasy*), from Thackeray in *The Rose and the Ring* (1854) to Andrew Lang in *Prince Prigio* (1889) and *Ricardo of Pantouflia* (1893), to *Five Children and It* (1902), *The Phoenix and the Carpet* (1904), and *The Story of the Amulet* (1906). And part of the progress along this line is from the comical and fantastical to the slyness and slipper-talk and mocking humor of Lang (which nevertheless can conceal neither his real taste for fantasy nor something real in his humor) to the humorous fantasy of the *Five Children*.

Lewis was witty but not, like his father, a comic. In his critical work, he praises what we have come to regard as the English humor of detail He praises the poet Layamon's description of Arthur, turning alternately red and white when he learns that he is the King. He praises the description of Mordred bleeding "both over the upper sheet and the nether sheet"—and observes "Best of all, we are told how much it cost (£20,000) to send the expedition in search of Sir Lancelot." Similarly, he rejoices in Gavin Douglas's prologues in the Middle *Scots XIII Bukes of Eneados*, with (for example) Douglas, on a frosty morning, leaving the window "a lytill on char" and crawling back under the "claythis thrinfauld." (This example is from *English Literature in the Sixteenth Century, Excluding Drama*, p. 88.) Not only did he recognize the trait; he obviously welcomed it. Moreover, it was a part of a lot of the stories and books in parts he read in *The Strand*—and it was a part of what Lewis wanted in the novels he read.

> If to love Story is to love excitement then I ought to be the greatest lover of excitement alive. But the fact is that what is said to be the most "exciting" novel in the world, *The Three Musketeers*, makes no appeal to me at all. The total lack of atmosphere repels me. There is no country in the book—save as a storehouse of inns and ambushes. There is no weather. (*On Stories*, p. 7)

Yet there were many novels (and short-story collections) available with both story and atmosphere, with the humor of detailed observation—and not just Trollope, his father's favorite. Somerville and Ross have it, especially with *The Irish R.M.* and *Further Adventures*, and *Mr. Knox's Country*. Thackeray has it with *Henry Esmond* and *The Virginians* (which are ancestors of Buchan's *Salute to Adventurers*), if not with *The Rose and the Ring*.

But it is not something Lewis seems to have used much in the Narnia stories, though he certainly used it in *That Hideous Strength*. What he does use in the Narnia stories is the comic vision he learned in his youth—a touch of caricature (in Professor Kirke, "Bless me! What do they teach them in these schools?" in *The Lion, the Witch, and the Wardrobe*)—the dogginess of the Talking Dogs in several of the Narnian stories and especially in *The Last Battle* (which touches on English humor)—the Monopods ("Dufflepuds") in *The Voyage of the "Dawn Treader"*—all likely to be throwbacks to *Punch*. There is no question that *Punch* was a huge influence in the Lewis household, and those who have read the collection of one hundred of Albert Lewis's dicta that the Lewis brothers put together in 1922 (*Pudaita Pie*, in the Marion Wade Collection at Wheaton College) will have seen how often Albert Lewis's comments ended with a genuine *Punch*-line.

This may help explain the discordant view of Narnia taken by Lewis's old friend Ronald Tolkien. He thought it something of a jumble, everything put in, as in the chorus of the old song "Widdecombe Fair"—"with Bill Brewer, Jan Stewer, Peter Gurney, Peter Davy, Dan'l Whidden, Harry Hawk, old Uncle Tom Cobbleigh and all, old Uncle Tom Cobbleigh and all." That jumble is characteristic of the comic or of comedy (even in Northrop Frye's definition of the *mythos* of comedy): the point is that the jumble is to be straightened out and resolved—everything will be drawn together and then everything will be set right. Even, in miniature, set right by a *Punch*-line.

But the jumble, in Tolkien's view, ought not to extend to the cast of characters, and, in his view, here—at least in *The Lion, the Witch, and the Wardrobe*—it does so extend. What he saw was the combination of classical mythology, fauns and satyrs and all, with Father Christmas, and then (especially in *Prince Caspian*) with dwarfs and other figures out of Norse mythology, and then a fairy-tale element, and Talking Beasts and other creatures out of children's literature—exactly what we might expect from story beginning with pictures (in this case, meaning in effect visions) following the logic of dream and vision rather than waking logic.

This takes us back to Novalis and the Blue Flower, and away from the ordinary—though associational—logic of childhood. Remember the famous dictum by Novalis: "Our life is not a dream—but it shall, and maybe must, become one" (*Novalis Schriften* 1977, vol. III, p. 281, aphorism no. 237). Novalis's doctrine of the dream is the basis for George MacDonald's use of dreams, as his doctrine of the Bergmann and the Earth is the basis for much that is in the Curdie books. The miner, the Bergmann, is the priest of Earth, the third cave into which the Bergmann leads Heinrich von Ofterdingen is a symbolic stopping place on the way to the Golden Age in which all time is at once, through the door of the timeless. This gives the clue to the importance of dream and *Marchen* (fairy-tale) in which Novalis finds Romantic truth.

In both dream and *Marchen*, as in the child's world, orderly operation of time is suspended (*Novalis Schriften* 1977, vol. III, p. 452, aphorism no. 959): "Dreams are often meaningful and prophetic because they are natural effects of the soul—and are thus based on the order of association. They are meaningful like poetry—but for that reason also irregularly meaningful—absolutely free." And this ties in with the nature of *Märchen*, which we translate (badly—it is really untranslatable) as fairy-tale or folk-tale. The time of a true *Marchen* is a time of freedom, when everything is miraculous and mysterious, a time before time. The true *Marchen* must be prophetic depiction, and the genuine poet of *Märchen* (or teller of *Märchen*) is a seer of the future as well as an ideal and ironic child (summarizing *Novalis Schriften* 1977, vol. III, pp. 280–81, aphorism no. 234).

The freedom Novalis finds in dream derives from what we may call the associational and non-linear progress of dream. As we have noted, childhood also has something of that freedom—but childhood also has a different (associational) logic. Moreover, that freedom is, in Novalis's view, the freedom of the Golden Age—which is Arcadian. It may be ironic that the Curdie books are miner's pastoral in the harsh land of Scotland, but they are pastoral and they are children's books. And when Novalis says that life is not a dream but should and must become one, he is also saying that we must be free of time, not only as a dream is free, but as a *Marchen* or childhood or Arcady is free. The ironic child is the prophet; the prophecy is the *Marchen*. Here we begin to see a possible key to considering the Narnian stories as Comedy as well as comedy, and a true connection of fairy-tale (if defined as *Marchen*) with children's stories.

[2]
Creating Narnia:
Background and Beginnings

C.S. Lewis's first world was the world of Ulster; his first created world was the world of Boxen, and neither of them seems to have a huge similarity to Narnia. To be sure, the hills of Holywood, just unreachable on the near horizon in his early years, play a part in the Lewis landscapes in many of his books, including Narnia, and one could doubtless argue that the story of Lewis's Narnia over the past century is simply "From Holywood to Hollywood"—with, perhaps, a great deal of what that implies. Certainly the first stirrings of Narnia are likely to be found in those hills, in the landscapes of Lewis's youth.

And the seascapes. Actually, boats and ships (and maps) are what continue in a direct line from the early days in Belfast and its environs into Boxen and finally into Narnia. The landscapes and seascapes are in the Ransom stories also, though it is floating islands more than boats on the seas of Perelandra, and the Martian oceans are dry (but the handramits are not) on Malacandra. Where the Ransom stories differ from both Boxen and Narnia is in the maps (the systematizer again)—they do not have them, while Boxen and Narnia do.

The point of one of the Albert Lewis stories told in *Pudaita Pie* is that he could not understand why his children would want to take a picture of a house (or, it could easily be added, a landscape) without people (in this case himself) in the picture (no. 84). Pictures should be story-pictures and stories involve humans. It is, of course, a characteristic Victorian view (a Medieval and Pre-Raphaelite one also). At first glance, it might be thought that Narnia is a little different. For one thing, it is not a land for humans (though it is a land for humans to rule over), and thus—one would think—not so much for human stories.

For another, in *The Last Battle*, Lewis refers to the hundreds of years when nothing much happened in Narnia, which makes it not so much—at that time—a land for stories at all. Almost all the Narnian stories involve the children from our world, not only because the stories are being told in our world, but because it is when things happen that the children are needed—or is it that the children are needed when things are to happen or are happening (to bring resolution)? Or is it that the children are needed in order for things to happen? In any case, the children are there when things happen, and when they are not there, apparently, "things" do not happen.

But this is not to say that the pictures don't involve sentient and reasoning beings, though Mr. Tumnus the faun is not human, nor is Jadis (a daughter of Lilith, but not of Adam), nor is the Lion Aslan (at least, not in that world). They do indeed involve sentient talking and presumably reasoning beings, and they are thus story-pictures. The names in Narnia, too, by the way, are, in Tolkien's view, a jumble: Aslan is Near-Eastern (a version of a word for "lion" in Turkish); Tumnus the faun is Italic or even Celtic—only dubiously Roman and certainly not Greek; and Jadis, though the name could be many things including Near-Eastern (it is a variant of the word for "witch" in Turkish), is by character very much from that part of the Near-Eastern world and of the Near-Eastern mythological world. The names of the fauns who dance for Caspian in Prince Caspian (p. 78) are Mentius, Obentinus, Dumnus, Voluns, Voltinus, Girbius, Nimienus, Nausus, Oscuns—names (with Tumnus) if not from *The Lays of Ancient Rome* then at least from that world. I am far from having Lewis's expertise on Italy before the hegemony of Rome or on Latin literature, but that certainly seems to be where the Faunish names are from, and the list is part of the same schoolboy extravagance as the list of the White Witch's crew in *The Lion, the Witch, and the Wardrobe* (pp. 132, 148): Ogres and wolves and bull-headed men, Minotaurs, Ghouls, Boggles, Spectres, spirits of evil trees and poisonous plants, the People of the Toadstools, Cruels, Hags, Incubuses, Wraiths, Horrors, Efreets, Sprites, Orknies, Wooses, Ettins. Never mind, for the moment, that wolves and sprites and wooses can be good—here they're not, and in any case, there is a schoolboy pleasure and extravagance in the listing. (And he certainly ransacks the lumber room of his childhood and school days for the names!)

The Pevensie children (at least), we are told, were brought to know Aslan in Narnia that they might know Him better in our world. This would suggest that the creation of Narnia in the childhood days of Digory Kirke and Polly Plummer came about as part of the same scheme of things of which Lucy's passage through the Wardrobe was a part—in other words, Lucy through the Wardrobe in *The Lion, the Witch, and the Wardrobe*, was implicit in Digory and Polly and Uncle Andrew and Jadis and Frank and Strawberry and the pool in the Wood between the Worlds in *The Magician's Nephew* (though in the process of Lewis's creation, of course, Lucy came before Digory and Polly and the rest). Now the relationship between Narnian time and our time is odd (though events seem to come in the same order, even if the tale of years is different), but we know that, in Lewis's mind, this was not necessarily the case. "Not all times that are not present are therefore past or future" (*That Hideous Strength*), and time in both *Perelandra* and *That Hideous Strength*, on the one hand, amd *The Dark Tower*, on the other, has thickness or breadth as well as length.

This may be interpreting as theology which is in fact close to fairy-tale—but then, theology and mythology are linked, including the mythology of the fairy-tale. We will need to ask eventually, I think, if the things that happen in Narnia are determined by the character of the children (and of their times) in this world. The clearest example in the affirmative on the times is in *The Magician's Nephew*, which occupies a special place in the Chronicles of Narnia, because, in a sense, Digory and Polly are friends of "Jacks" Lewis. All the books—except *The Last Battle*, which occupies another but very different special place—are affirmative examples on the character of the children.

Only—what about the difference between Susan (Susan the Just) in *The Lion, the Witch, and the Wardrobe,* and in *Prince Caspian*, and for that matter in *The Horse and His Boy*, on the one hand, and Susan who is no longer a friend of Narnia in *The Last Battle*? Are they the same Susan? Are there alternative time lines, in one of which Susan is still a Friend of Narnia? And if it's "Once a king [or queen] in Narnia always a king [or queen] in Narnia!"—then why isn't Susan there at the End of Narnia, or did her queenship pass away when the Giant squeezed the sun and Narnia (but not the true Narnia) passed away? Or is that part of the story that's too wonderful to tell, at the end of *The Last Battle*? But for the moment, let all that pass.

The poster child (so to speak) for what happens in Narnia's being determined by the character of the children from our world might well be Eustace. There would have been no need for the dragon that took care of the Lord Octesian (or perhaps, but less likely, was the Lord Octesian) if Eustace had not been the sort of boy (in our world) who would have greedy dragonish thoughts (in that world). On the other hand, the thought would not be described as greedy and dragonish if there were not dragons there—*hic dracones* in the words of the old maps. Also, of course, the greedy dragonish thoughts in all of us—in our world generally, this Earth of ours—provide the meaning for what happens in Narnia, make this a true history.

For the moment, we can take what may seem a detour (as it may seem to us in Lewis's own life, as viewed from 2016) and look at Boxen and his next (surviving) attempt at story, the beginnings of his "Ulster" novel in the 1920s. Then we can set against these what we know of his imaginative reading (Jeffrey Farnol, for example, as well as James Stephens) and his attempt at *The Tragedy of Loki, or Loki Bound*, Greek in form and outcome, Norse in content, and envisioned as an opera, perhaps with music by Arthur Greeves (*Letters*, ed. Walter Hooper, Vol. 1 [Family Letters 1905–1931] esp. pp. 75–78).

We have already spoken of Boxen, but we can look a little more closely and in detail here. The earliest Boxen story (in this case, play), betraying, by the way, that young Jacks (age not yet eight) had been reading *Hamlet*, is "The King's Ring, a Comedy" (in *Boxen: The Imaginary World of the Young C.S. Lewis*, pp. 25–34). One of the characters is Mr. Icthus-Oress (Ichthyosaurus), who joins King Bunny, Sir Peter Mouse, Sir Big, Sir Goose, and other Mouse-Land (Animal-Land) worthies: he got his name from fighting an "Icthus-Oress," according to young Jacks's notes. The most interesting information provided in the notes is that the ancient Mice believed that at sunset the sun cut a hole for itself through the earth (p. 34)—one sees the influence of scholarly notes in Jacks's readings (a conclusion supported by the illustration of King Bublish I "from an old MS" in "History of Mouse-Land" in *Boxen*, p. 39).

In a later Boxen story, "The Chess Monograph"—to be dated sometime in 1908–1910—we find one of the more pleasant Boxonian inventions, chessaries, which are institutions for the lodging of chessmen (p. 50). The originator of the chessary was that distinguished chessman (shades of George MacDonald Fraser), G.H. (Gengleston Herbert) Flaxman. Previously, the chessmen in the various countries in the Boxonian world (Animal-Land, India, Dolfin-Land, Prussia, Pongee, and many more too numerous to mention) were treated like the Jews in England in medieval times (and these were the Boxonian medieval times). Though the first chessary was built under armed guard in the semi-civilized land of Clarendon (had Lewis been reading Lord Clarendon's *History of the Rebellion?*), the great chessaries were in Murry (capital of Mouse-Land, on the Jemima, a great port city famed for ship-building) and Fuczy (capital of Squirrel-Land, on Lake Fuczy, famous for its corn). The gathering of the chessmen in Clarendon seems almost a forecast of the gathering of the Jewish people in Israel after the Balfour Declaration (or perhaps the proposals for a Jewish homeland wherever located).

Now who would have thought that young Jacks, who in later days was known for his almost entire lack of interest in politics or even current events, would have absorbed so much of the current world political situation when he was ten? One might even think that the name of Lord Big, the frog who was Littlemaster in Boxen (more specifically in Animal-Land), had something to do with the name of Sir Arthur Bigge (1849–1931), Private Secretary to Queen Victoria (1895–1901) and to King George V (1910–1931), though it is true that when Sir Arthur was raised to the peerage it was as Lord Stamfordham rather than as Lord Bigge.

But to me the significance of the chessaries in Murry on the Jemima and Fuczy on Lake Fuczy is much beyond this: the chessary and the position of the chessmen in society shows considerable "combinative" or "associational" imagination—childhood imagination, to be sure, as these words suggest, but real and strong. The Jemima almost certainly comes from Beatrix Potter, Murry is from Irish history, Fuczy probably out of Ruritania (or, perhaps, Graustark), but the chessaries (and G.H. Flaxman?) are, so far as I know, Jacks's invention.

Here we should perhaps dispose of a false lead (but largely true statement) in Lewis's *Surprised by Joy*: in a footnote there (p. 15) he writes "For readers of my children's books, the best way of putting this would be to say that Animal-Land had nothing whatever in common with Narnia except the anthropomorphic beasts. Animal-Land, by its whole quality, excluded the least hint of wonder." The problem is that "wonder" is not the only quality of Narnia. Let me take a round-about here. In a largely neglected note (or rather brief letter, May 13th 1951) in the first volume of the quarterly *Essays in Criticism* (1951, p. 313), Lewis accepts Professor Ian Watt's argument that the story of Robinson Crusoe is one of the great Western myths, like Faust or Don Quixote. In the sense in which Lewis is using "wonder" in that note in *Surprised by Joy*—the wonderful or the marvelous—there is none in *Robinson Crusoe*, though to Crusoe himself there are moments of wonder, like the discovery of Friday's footprint. My point is that Animal-Land is not devoid of myth, even if, in this sense of "wonder," it is devoid of wonder. Nor is it devoid of imagination. The stories of Boxen are told in the manner of English history (even to dates), but they are imaginative history—as well as feigned history—and they are part of a myth.

For want of a better name, we can call it a Myth of Edwardian Belfast, or Edwardian Ulster. But there is a better name. When Lewis came to essay his first novel, in 1924–25, it was a novel incorporating a great deal of his Ulster life. Ronald Bresland, in his *The Backward*

Glance: C.S. Lewis and Ireland (Belfast, 1999), refers to a remark of Lewis's (p. 68) to the effect that he could not describe a set of Ulstermen better than by saying they were a perfect realization of a child's dream of what a "grown-up" should be. The myth that Lewis was creating or "realizing" in Boxen was a child's myth of grown-ups, and since it was an Ulster child, they were Ulster grown-ups, and it was an Ulster myth. Think of Thomas Andrews, the Ulsterman who created the *Titanic* and went down with the ship, confident he was doing the right thing, a practical man and a Romantic. He could be one of Lewis's Ulster grown-ups. Of course, Lewis's Ulster is not simply the city of men who go down to the sea in ships (or down in the sea in ships), but that is, I believe, part of it, and plays a part in his myth-making.

We are using the word *myth* here, and quite probably we ought to look a little more at what that word means. What is a myth? I (and in this I am not entirely unlike Lewis) grew up on Bulfinch and *Heroes of Asgard*, Sidney Lanier's version of Arthur, and other Victorian redactions of the world's mythology. One learned, as I have elsewhere observed, to recognize the mythological. One also learned to recognize the mythic. To list a few—Davy Crockett, Sherlock Holmes, Alfred the Great and the cakes, Robert Bruce and the spider, Daniel Boone, George Washington, Abraham Lincoln, Babe Ruth, Bobby Jones, Robinson Crusoe, Natty Bumppo, Ahab and Moby-Dick (and even the Old Man and Moby Minnow), Hamlet, Henry V, Falstaff, other Shakespearean characters, Faustus, Tamerlane: the figures of literature intermingled with the figures of history, and some, like Richard III, who were both (though it was not the same Richard III in both).

Mythic—but not thereby mythological. A transformation of types into archetypes—that was part of it, archetypes (as we might say) of mythic proportions. Conan Doyle did not set out to create a myth with Sherlock Holmes. Melville did not set out originally to write mythic books—indeed, he set out to write histories: it was not until *Moby-Dick* that the myth-making bent obvious in "Bartleby" and (later) in *Billy Budd* was melded with his experiences at sea to produce a myth of the sea. About Fenimore Cooper there is more doubt, but, in my reconstruction, the forest landscape (which provides much of the mythic quality) is an add-on to Natty Bumppo, not there at the beginning (and an add-on, I believe, from Classical Paganism).

It is, I think, the atmosphere—the taste of the story—that gives the status of mythology to a story centered on a being of mythic proportions. Now, if story of the mythic and mythological is indeed what constitutes myth, much of Sir Walter Scott is myth; and of Dickens, at least

Pickwick and *A Christmas Carol*; Surtees with his grocer of Great Coram Street; Melville with Ahab and Moby-Dick; Doyle with his Sherlock Holmes and Haggard with his She-Who-Must-Be-Obeyed. But did Haggard create a myth in *King Solomon's Mines*? It involves a mythos of Dark and Secret Africa, and a past alive in the present. So also with *She*. But She-Who-Must-Be-Obeyed is a mythic figure in a way that the far less important Gagool of *King Solomon's Mines* is not. Is *She* therefore myth while *King Solomon's Mines* is not? Does true myth require the great mythic figure—the god or goddess? However we may answer that question, it seems we are confronted with difficulties.

Myth is frequently defined as a form—generally considered a pure or pattern form – of story. That definition is at the root of Northrop Frye's four *mythoi:* comedy, romance, tragedy, satire. But I do not think it is at the root of what Lewis finds to praise in George MacDonald or Rider Haggard, which is where much of his comment on myth takes place. What he is praising in both seems to be a sense of the presence of Myth in their world-creation. That is, when one reads MacDonald, one senses that "thought beyond their thoughts to those high bards were given"—there are unexplained depths within depths—and over all, the spirit of Novalis's "Life is not a dream but it must and should become one." Of Haggard's *King Solomon's Mines*, we can say, in answer to the question I asked above, *yes*, this is myth-making, this is story: as Lewis says, Haggard (at least here and in *She*) had the myth-making gift pure and undiluted—but we can also say there is an atmosphere to the myth, and this is what we come back for.

To put it in Novalis's terms, dreams, like *Märchen*, show the real patterns of human behavior, which we enshrine or embody in myth—but they also have the visual or atmospheric characteristics of dream or vision. It is not an argument against MacDonald's creation of myth to say that he writes with the associative logic of dream. Does this creation of myth require both mythic figure and mythic pattern? I would answer *yes,* for if it does not, then we have removed one of the common meanings of the word *myth* from our consideration. But perhaps it is not all mythic larger-than-life figures, but only the true archetypes—the Scout, the Trickster, the Father of his Country, the Wizard—that are required for the creation of myth.

Perhaps the separation between mythic pattern and mythic figure is not a true separation. In Jung's terms, perhaps one is the dream and the other the hypnogogic visual appearance, and both are present in all true myth-making. What about the quality of *Pickwick* or *Moby-Dick*? Both these could be taken as the name of a principal character or of the book itself. And we may begin by asking what myth we are talking about in each case: How are we using the word *myth*? And what is the myth a myth *of*? The answer is easier for *Moby-Dick*, despite whatever difficulties we may have with a sacramental or symbolic text. The myth of *Moby-Dick* is the myth of (the hunt for) the great sea-creature that destroys the hunter, and frequently those close about the hunter. It is the myth of the sea-serpent that destroyed ships in the Middle Ages. It is the myth of Leviathan. (And not far from the myth of the *Titanic*.) And *Pickwick*? Is there a pattern to *Pickwick*? A story? Are its strengths not rather the strengths of Old England, of Sam Weller, that "angel in gaiters," of the pathos of "But after all, Samivel, she died," of the Fat Boy, of Picwicaresque adventures through the England of coaching days and coaching taverns—a "mythology for England" one might say, but not a *mythos*, not a story pattern.

And yet, is that the whole truth? Don Quixote would not have taken a coaching journey through Spain, nor yet D'Artagnan through France. But a journey from pillar to post, Land's End to John o' Groat's, tavern to tavern, as the rolling English drunkard made the rolling English road—*Yes*. That is a kind of pattern story. Moreover, it is the pattern story of a particular people, a peculiar people (one might say), sanctified to the open road. Perhaps it goes back to the wonderment of Angles and Saxons and Jutes at the Roman high roads, as I think Ronald Tolkien suggested (and I daresay it is implicit in Chesterton).

There is indeed, I believe, a particular kind of atmosphere or taste (flavor) in Myth. Lewis makes this point in connection with *King Solomon's Mines*, the film version of which not only drags in an entirely extraneous young lady, but ends with fire rather than the silent ages of the cave—quite the wrong atmosphere. And Novalis remains of interest here, also, for his insistence that dream and *Marchen* have the associative logic of space rather than the causal logic of time. The more I think on this point, the more I am convinced it helps to explain why atmosphere seems to me an inherent part of Myth, atmosphere functioning as a kind of (or in line with) associative logic. Granted that times as well as places have atmospheres, or at least that places have certain atmospheres at certain times (as with a Myth of Edwardian Belfast), it remains the case that hypnogogic visual impressions have atmosphere, dreams have atmosphere, the *Märchen* that embody primary story-patterns carry their atmosphere with them down through the ages—and there are recognizably different atmospheres to different mythologies (as Lewis himself observed long ago, in *Surprised by Joy* and elsewhere). We will look later at the atmosphere of Narnia.

When one reads Haggard, one is conscious of ineluctable age, the past alive in the present, things handed down from generation to generation, a world (like MacDonald's) with a particular taste, not quite like any other taste (and certainly not like MacDonald's). And while Haggard fell so in love with his creation Ayesha that his power of story declined, nevertheless his earlier *King Solomon's Mines* is a great story of its kind and stands as a major achievement of what Lewis apparently meant by the myth-making gift, and so does *She*. Of other writers we have mentioned, Conan Doyle had some gift for story—*The Lost World* is a classic (in *The Strand* in Lewis's youth, by the way)—but much more for incident, and a considerable gift for atmosphere. Do you remember Vincent Starrett's words: Sherlock Holmes and Dr. Watson will "live for all who love them well; in a romantic chamber of their heart; in a nostalgic country of the mind; where it is always 1895" (concluding lines of *The Private Life of Sherlock Holmes*, 2nd ed., Chicago 1960)? This is not a matter of plot but of *milieu*, not of incident but of atmosphere or taste. And as Kenneth Grahame portrayed the English squirearchy in Badger, somehow the young Jacks Lewis portrayed the "grown-up 'Ulsterness'" of grown-up Ulster in his anthropomorphic Boxonians.

The ferry between Belfast and Liverpool (where his unfinished 1924–25 novel begins) is part of Boxen also. The politics of the 1924–25 novel are already in *Boxen*. In fact, what seems to me to have happened between (say) 1912 and (say) 1924 was that Lewis became newly aware of the world of wonder, in a sense aware of the two worlds of romance and realism, coming out of the "ancient unity" of novel. *Boxen* is romance and realistic novel, a Defoe-ian unity of "[mythic] novel" (as his critical interchange with Ian Watt on *Robinson Crusoe* might suggest). In 1923, in revulsion perhaps against the death of Mrs. Moore's brother, "the Doc," with its sense of horror and of powers and principalities of evil, he began to write a realistic novel, involving a doctor, Scrabo Easley, who may in part have been modeled on "the Doc."

But events—including his appointment to Magdalen—intervened, and he completed and published instead his narrative poem *Dymer*—which despite the artificiality of the structure and metre inclines rather to the side of wonder and marvel than the workaday Ulster "grown-up" world. And then we have the beginnings of his academic career and especially his academic writing career, his father's death and the severing (in large part) of ties with Ulster, his curious *Pilgrim's Re-gress: An Allegorical Apology for Reason and Romanticism* (1933), his settling at The Kilns in Headington outside Oxford, the influence of his colleagues at Oxford, his brother's retirement from the army, and of course his reconversion throughout this time to Christian belief. The Ulster experience lingers (it shows in places in *That Hideous Strength*, for example in his remark about the assured masculine laughter of bachelor uncles), but the center has not held, and something (or rather Someone, and not a rough beast, slouching) is coming toward his Bethlehem to be born.

This brings us to one further background element to Narnia, the poet William Butler Yeats, whom Lewis met in the early 1920s. Owen Barfield told me that Lewis all his life considered himself an Irishman, and while we know that, we sometimes forget we may look to all of Ireland, rather than just Ulster, for the earlier parts of the Narnian background. Now Yeats is in part the model for Merlin in *That Hideous Strength*, but he is more. He is the living (in Lewis's lifetime) and Irish exemplar of what George MacDonald exemplified earlier and from Scotland—in part, myth-making (*mythopoesis*) as a literary form, and in part, overwhelming consciousness of the mythological. Not so much the mythic. As a matter of record, neither Yeats nor Lewis's other Irish model, James Stephens, were much involved with the great mythic figures, the archetypes. Stephens tended toward abstractions or allegorical figures or *personae* rather than true archetypes, and while Yeats himself embodied an archetype, the Magician, his fictions are of another kind. (In George MacDonald, there are few enough archetypes, though Sir Gibbie the dumb child-seer [*gybi*] is one, and the Great-Grandmother in the Curdie books another.)

When he came to write the Narnia books, it may be Lewis showed himself more the child of James Stephens than of Yeats, but his distrust of Magic that came in part from Yeats (and the death of "the Doc") lives on in his picture of Uncle Andrew, still more of Jadis, in *The Magician's Nephew*. Perhaps, since he told Chad Walsh these children's books were "after the manner of E Nesbit," and since we know he read Andrew Lang, we are looking in the wrong places for the background and beginnings of Narnia. But we have already looked at the Five Children and Pantouflia, the site of *Prince Prigio* and *Ricardo of Pantouflia* (and at Thackeray's Paflagonia also). What we are doing here is trying to fill out the picture of the background for Lewis's Narnia, looking to all the round world's four corners (only Narnia is not a round world).

Here we might look for clues at a few fragmentary Narnian manuscripts that appear in Walter Hooper's *Past Watchful Dragons: The Narnian Chronicles of C.S. Lewis* (1979). These include 1. an "Outline of Narnian history so far as it is known" (pp. 41–44), compiled after the books were finished and not of much use to us here; 2. a long fragment seeming to be an earlier sketch for Digory and the origins of Narnia (pp.

48–65), with an Aunt Gertrude and a fairy godmother Mrs. Lefay (possibly written around 1945, though it was read to Roger Lancelyn Green in 1949); and 3. a version of Eustace's diary in *The Voyage of the "Dawn Treader"* (published 1953), the version probably only very slightly earlier than the finished version (pp. 68–71). There are also (p. 46) what seem to be brief notes on the plot for what became *The Voyage of the "Dawn Treader,"* (and three other plots), this voyage seeming to be a much more "scientifictional" story than the book itself. Of all of these, the two most suggestive (to me, and thus the most useful for our purposes here) are the brief note and what Walter Hooper calls the Lefay fragment. The reason they are useful lies in what they suggest. And what they suggest is Lewis beginning a story from picture and out of the furniture of his mind—which we could have guessed—but perhaps in a way we could not have guessed.

In the notes on the voyage, one thing that is important is that the voyage is to carry the voyagers back in time, to islands that no longer exist in our time, islands out of the *Odyssey* or the *Navigatio Sancti Brendani*. The children who are voyaging have been kidnapped because a king needs the blood of a boy from the far future, but given the chance, they prefer to stay with the kidnappers rather than those who are "rescuing" them. Now something of this blood for a king from a kidnapped human comes in passing into *Out of the Silent Planet* (1938), and it must have been a theme in Lewis's mind for a while—perhaps from his youth. In the Lefay fragment (which ends with directions that sound like they're about to take Harry Potter to Diagon Alley on his own), Mrs. Lefay (shades of Morgan Le Fay in the Arthurian stories and in *That Hideous Strength*) is apparently Digory Kirke's good fairy godmother, and at the beginning of the fragment Digory has the gift of speech and understanding with trees and animals—which he loses by sawing a branch off a tree. This is much more the modern "realization" of traditional fairy-tale than any of the existing Narnian stories. One has the impression that this fragment also came from pictures (*viz*, the description of Mrs. Lefay) and perhaps partly from *Punch,* again out of and through the furniture of Lewis's mind. What is particularly noteworthy is that there is nothing arguably Christian in either plot note or fragment.

We might also ask, why Digory? I do not pretend to have any special knowledge on this, except that Digory (or Diggory or Degory) is a name more common in Devon and especially Cornwall (and even more the parish of Launceston in Cornwall) than elsewhere in England (and may Lewis's friend, the historian of Cornwall, Kenneth Hamilton Jenkin, forgive me for saying Cornwall "in England")—even more common in Cornwall generally than in Devon.

I suppose Lewis was familiar—either through Jenkin or Tolkien or even through his friend Leonard Rice-Oxley—with at least one famous Oxford Digory. This was Digory Whear, a Cornishman, the first (Camden) Professor of History in the University of Oxford, appointed October 1622, formerly Fellow of Exeter College (Tolkien's undergraduate college). Digory Whear (1573–1647) was creator of Oxford's new Schola Historica, author of *De Ratione et Methodo Legendi Historias*, later (in 1633) expanded as *Relectiones Hyemales De Ratione et Methodo Legendi Utrasque Historias,* translated into English by Edmund Bohun in 1694, and employed as a textbook (in Latin) at both Oxford and Cambridge throughout the seventeenth and early eighteenth century. But if the name Digory memorializes Digory Whear, it was presumably in Lewis's mind either from his visit to Jenkin in Cornwall in 1944, or Jenkin's visit to Oxford around 1949 (this may be more likely), or perhaps from conversation with Tolkien and Rice-Oxley in the early 1930s, when both were members (with Lewis) of the "Cave."

That was a gathering of English dons and scholars (including an occasional Professor) with a view of the study of English differing from the accepted Oxford view. Rice-Oxley was noted chiefly for his book *Oxford Renowned* (1925, 2nd ed. 1934, 3rd ed. 1947, 4th ed. 1950, etc.), and as an Oxford historian was well-acquainted with Digory Whear. Lewis knew Rice-Oxley from the Cadet Battalion days at Keble—Rice-Oxley had published a booklet called *Oxford in Arms: With an Account of Keble College* (1917)—and had met him again in 1924 as a fellow-Examiner for the Locals (*All My Road Before Me*, p. 345). Of course, the name Digory may come from some other source, and the portrait is clearly a portrait of a Lewis (older) contemporary, not of anyone back in the days of James I (and Elizabeth I and Charles I). But it is quite an uncommon name. (There is, by the way, a Diggory Betts in one of Henty's boys' books, *By Right of Conquest*.)

The first story of Lucy in Narnia—*The Lion, the Witch, and the Wardrobe*—is dedicated to Lewis's God-daughter Lucy Barfield, daughter of Owen (1898–1997) and Maud (1884–1981) Barfield—and *The Voyage of the "Dawn Treader"* is dedicated to her brother Geoffrey. *Prince Caspian* is dedicated to Mary Clare Havard, daughter of Dr. Havard (R.E. "Humphrey" Havard of the Inklings). *The Silver Chair* is dedicated to Nicholas Hardie, son of Colin Hardie (1906–1998, of the Inklings). *The Horse and His Boy* is dedicated to Lewis's stepsons, David and Douglas Gresham. All of these are children of Lewis's friends (in the case of David and Douglas, Joy's children). *The Last Battle* has no dedication. *The Magician's Nephew* is the odd book out, being dedicated to The Kilmer Family, presumably Kenton and Frances Kilmer and their family. Only with Lucy Barfield (for Lucy Pevensie's first adventure in *The Lion, the Witch, and the Wardrobe*) and the Gresham boys (for *The Horse and His Boy*) is there any apparent connection between the story and the person (or persons) to whom it is dedicated, so I do not expect to find one here. But that point is open for further investigation.

This directs us back (for the time being) to what is indicated by the brief plot note and the Lefay fragment. There is nothing especially Christian about either story, just as there is nothing especially Christian about the story of Bree and Hwin and Cor (Shasta) and Aravis in *The Horse and His Boy*, or the story in *Prince Caspian* or in *The Voyage of the "Dawn Treader"* or in *The Silver Chair*. That is, I think, because there is nothing specifically Christian in Lewis's visions—the pictures it all began with. A vision of a hundred years of winter and no Christmas is arguably a Christian vision, at least in Lewis's mind, but a picture of Father Christmas is *per se* no more Christian than a faun in a snowstorm with umbrella and parcels on his way to afternoon tea (*l'après-midi d'un faune*, as I have said before).

So far from the stories having begun as a way to sneak Christian myth past the watchful dragons, it almost looks as though the original pictures were Christianized in order to make them into a story (or set of stories). Of course, Lewis said they began with the pictures, and he presumably knew what he was talking about. What he did not say was that the Christian story came naturally. Which brings us to three questions.

First, were there watchful dragons? Second, what was it that was being got past the watchful dragons? Third, why was or is that something in Narnia? For the moment, we will take the watchful dragons as real and really there, though we will come back to that (and to *why dragons?*). Apart from some Freudian interpretations of Narnia that seem to me far on the weird side (to put it mildly), there seems little doubt in most people's minds that what was being smuggled past the watchful dragons was the Christian myth, or perhaps Christian doctrine. That certainly is the implication of Lewis's original statement (*On Stories*, p. 47):

> I saw how stories of this kind could steal past a certain inhibition which had paralyzed much of my own religion in childhood. Why did one find it so hard as one was told one ought to feel about God or about the sufferings of Christ? I thought the chief reason was that one was told one ought to. An obligation to feel can freeze feelings. And reverence itself did harm. The

whole subject was associated with lowered voices; almost as if it were something medical. But suppose that by casting all these things into an imaginary world, stripping them of their stained-glass and Sunday school associations, one could make them for the same time appear in their real potency? Could one not steal thus past those watchful dragons? I thought one could.

I am immediately reminded (probably by the stained glass) of Dorothy L. Sayers, in her introduction to her radio plays on the life of Christ, *The Man Born to be King* (1943). There she writes of our "reassuring sensation that 'it can't happen here'. And to this comfortable persuasion we are assisted by the stately and ancient language of the Authorized [King James] Version, and by the general air of stained-glass-window decorum with which the tale is usually presented to us" (p. 6). And then in a footnote (p. 6n) to "stained-glass-window" she writes "'In which saintly figures color one's view of outward things'—*Times* Cross-word clue to the words STAINED GLASS. Et ille respondens ait: Tu dicis." ["And he answered him and said, Thou sayest"—Luke 23:3]. More of what Miss Sayers had to say in that Introduction seems to me relevant here.

First, she points out (pp. 3–4):

> that in writing a play on this particular subject, the dramatist must begin by ridding himself of all edificatory and theological intentions. He must set out, not to instruct but to show forth; not to point a moral but to tell a story; not to produce a Divinity Lesson with illustrations in dialogue but to write a good piece of theatre. . . . We are none of us, I think, under any illusions about our ability to do what the greatest artists who ever lived would admit to be beyond their powers. Nevertheless, when a story is great enough, any honest craftsman may succeed in producing something not altogether unworthy. . . . But the craftsman must be honest and must know what work he is serving. I am a writer and I know my trade; and I say this story is a very great story indeed, and deserves to be taken seriously. I say further . . . that in these days it is seldom taken seriously. It is often taken, and treated, with a gingerly solemnity: but that is what honest writers call frivolous treatment. Not Herod, not Caiaphas, not Pilate, not Judas ever contrived to fasten upon Jesus Christ the reproach of insipidity; that final indignity was left for pious hands to inflict. (p. 21)

So perhaps it is not Christian doctrine or Christian myth *per se* that is being taken past the watchful dragons, but the mythic quality and the "real potency" and strength (virtue in the Roman sense) of that story, and I think the atmosphere of wonder. (Aslan is not a tame lion, and God is not a tame god?) They were the something (the very complex something) that was being smuggled past the watch. If that is the case, then there are two ways of answering the question, "Why was that (very complex) something in Narnia?"

First, why was it in Lewis's mind to be put in Narnia? Second, why did he choose to put it there? It's well enough to seek sources and analogues, which we are doing and which will help us find out about the something that was in Lewis's mind. But we should also see why Lewis selected these particular parts or exemplars of the mythic quality and potency to put them into Narnia. Both these forms of the question will be asked and the answers taken up in more detail in subsequent chapters on the individual books, but we can take a general overview here.

If we take Lewis's word for it—and we should—the faun came first, then the Queen on the Sledge, then the Lion, in the visions for *The Lion, the Witch, and the Wardrobe*. There may be something of the Snow Maiden or the Spirit of the Snow in the White Witch—at least in the original vision—and Lewis has not told us when he first saw the Queen on the Sledge. But it was before Aslan came bounding in. By Lewis's reconstruction, Aslan came after the faun and the Witch, and indeed Aslan is first mentioned in *The Lion, the Witch, and the Wardrobe* on p. 64, after we have seen Mr. Tumnus (illustration, p. 8) and Jadis (the Queen on the Sledge, illustration, p. 21). Since Aslan is mentioned before we know he is a lion, but the name means lion, we know it is Aslan around whom (or Whom) Lewis is constructing the story. Where did Aslan come from, and why did Lewis pick him (Him?) as the fulcrum of his story? The second part may be easy enough, but where did Aslan come from? After all, in children's books about dressed animals, there are rarely lions. But, of course, in the pages of *Punch*, there are plenty—after all, in those days, in those pages, the lion is the symbol of England as especially of the English monarchy (the American example of the Cowardly Lion in *The Wizard of Oz* is not relevant here).

I believe the Lion was there in Lewis's mind a very long time, from the days of the bound volumes of *Punch* at Little Lea. But Lewis was not an Englishman, and he was not a monarchist. In one of their early conversations on February 4, 1923 (*All My Road Before Me*, p. 190), Nevill Coghill told Lewis that the only thing he would be willing to fight for was Monarchy, agreeing with Hobbes (after Lewis's questioning) that civilization and monarchy went together—a proposition which Lewis did not then agree with. It was Tolkien, I think, with his Mythology for England, who brought Lewis to his appreciation of England and thus of Monarchy, and thus, if perhaps indirectly, to the Lion, who is the King of the wood and the son of the Great Emperor-Beyond-the Sea, the King of the Beasts, the Lion, the great Lion (*The Lion, the Witch, and the Wardrobe*, p. 75).

No doubt Aslan as the Christ symbol is the engine of story for all the Narnia books, but if we did not know about Tenniel's illustrations in *Punch*, we should not have thought the Lion a likely symbol—or engine of story—for Lewis. In much the same way, to look again at the name of Narnia, we should not at first have thought it likely that Macaulay's *Lays of Ancient Rome* were significant, given some of Lewis's strictures on Macaulay. But the dressed animals in *Punch* (and probably some of the tales in Andrew Lang's vari-colored Fairy Books) and the footnotes to Macaulay started a ferment in Lewis's mind that worked throughout forty or fifty years into Narnia. (Possibly also there is some influence from Lang's version of the *Thousand Nights and a Night*, which Lewis read but says he did not very much like.) In any case, though Aslan is referred to by Mr. Beaver as the King of the woods, that is the last we hear of that, and when He becomes the milk-white Lamb at the end of *The Voyage of the "Dawn Treader"*—then the business of the King of the wood is long forgotten.

Now was Lewis seriously trying to get his something—the mythic quality, the potency of story, the atmosphere of wonder—past the same watchful dragons that Miss Sayers found guarding the way? Was he trying to restore these things to the *Greatest Story Ever Told* (the title, it may be remembered, of a best-selling 1949 retelling of the life of Christ by the American popular author Fulton Oursler 1893–1952, which is not so full of these things, though it's a good effort)? I think we need to grant him that—after all, he said that was what he was trying to do. Did he pick the best way of doing it? Probably that's not entirely a useful question, though I think it has some value in answering our questions about where his "something" came from and why he put it in the way he did., and we will ask it again a little later in a different form.

The fact is, the parameters of Lewis's imagination were set early in his life: the last—but one—great revision or addition came probably with George MacDonald when Lewis was sixteen. We have learned lately that things learned early in life can come back later when the channels in the brain are again unblocked—Lewis's Christianity might be a case in point—and the last great revision and addition (in 1936) seems to have brought back some earlier vision of the Lion. For the last great addition and revision came with Lewis's reading Charles Williams's *The Place of the Lion* (originally published 1933). Here is what Lewis wrote (February 26, 1936) to Arthur Greeves (*Collected Letters of C.S. Lewis*, Vol. II, 1931–1949, San Francisco 2004, p. 180):

I have just read what I think a really great book, *The Place of the Lion*, by Charles Williams. It is based on the Platonic theory of the other world in which the archetypes of all earthly qualities exist: and in the novel . . . the archetypes start sucking our world back. The lion of strength appears in the world and the strength starts going out of houses and things into him. . . . But man contains and ought to be able to rule all these forces: and there is one man in the book who does, and the story ends with him as a second Adam, 'naming the beasts,' and establishing dominion over them.

Lewis recommended the book to his brother and to Tolkien, loaned his copy to Barfield and then to Cecil Harwood—the book had been recommended to him by Nevill Coghill. And then, on March 11th 1936, he wrote a fan letter to Williams, in which he said (p. 83):

I have just read your *Place of the Lion* and it is to me one of the major literary events of my life—comparable to my first discovery of George MacDonald or G.K. Chesterton or William Morris. There are layers and layers—first the pleasure that any good fantasy gives me: then, what is rarely (tho' not so very rarely) combined with this, the pleasure of a real philosophical and theological stimulus: thirdly, characters: fourthly, what I neither expected nor desired, substantial edification.

We'll talk more about Morris along the way (he is particularly important in connection with *The Magician's Nephew*—notably in the Wood Between the Worlds), but what is particularly important for us just now is what Williams brought to Lewis's Idea of the Lion, and thus in the end into Narnia. In *The Place of the Lion*, Quentin and Anthony see first a lioness and then (though they deny it to themselves) a lion—indeed, The Lion. They hear thunder, but (as Foster—who has trained himself to see these angelicals—tells them, p. 52) it is not thunder, but the roaring of the lions. Foster tells them further (p. 53)

that this world is created, and all men and women are created, by the entrance of certain great principles into aboriginal matter. We call them by cold names; wisdom and courage and beauty and strength and so on, but actually they are very great and mighty Powers. . . . In the animals . . . each is shown to us in his own becoming shape: those Powers are the archetypes of the beasts, and very much more . . . Now this world in which they exist is truly a real world, and to see it is a very difficult and dangerous thing . . .

One can hear Professor Kirke, saying "It's all in Plato" (and I don't think Professor Kirke's Platonism is merely coincidental). The Lion, Aslan (which is more or less the word for Lion), the Witch Jadis (which is more or less the word for Witch), are both something like Platonic forms, and not human. Mr. Beaver (*The Lion, the Witch, and the Wardrobe*, p. 77) is very definite that Jadis descends from Adam's first—non-human—wife, Lilith, but not from Adam or indeed any human, and of course, by Foster's argument in *The Place of the Lion*, she, as an "imitation-human" or "apparent-human," is not a true archetype, not among the animals that are each a representation of a Power in its own becoming shape. But Aslan is. The Lion is the shape, so to speak, of Strength. But even more important, for our purposes, the Lion exists as a great and mighty Power in a true world that is not our world.

Lewis converted the Platonic myth to the Christian myth (as Williams had done before him, and Plotinus—and some of the Church fathers – sixteen centuries before Williams) and in that conversion lies, first, the whole story of Narnia (implicit in the Christianizing of Aslan), and second, a reference—if no more—to the sense of wonder and an overturning of the quotidian world that Lewis felt in reading *The Place of the Lion*. That sense of wonder, I believe, brought back at least his memory of the "Knights in Armor" bound-volumes-of-*Punch* days of wonder in his youth. An indication can be seen in the nature of the four children when they are in Narnia after the Witch is defeated (*The Lion, the Witch, and the Wardrobe*, p. 181).

The Two Kings and Two Queens govern Narnia well "and long and happy was their reign . . . And they themselves grew and changed as the years passed over them. And Peter became a tall and deep chested man and a great warrior and he was called King Peter the Magnificent. And Susan grew into a tall and gracious woman with black hair that fell almost to her feet and . . . she was called Queen Susan the Gentle. Edmund was a graver and quieter man than Peter, and great in council and judgment. He was called King Edmund the Just. But as for Lucy. she was always gay and golden-haired . . . and her own people called her Queen Lucy the Valiant." And listen to their conversation as they seek the White Stag (p. 182).

"Then said King Peter (for they talked in quite a different style now, having been Kings and Queens for so long) 'Fair Consorts, let us now alight from our horses and follow this beast into the thicket; for in all my days I never hunted a nobler quarry.' 'Sir,' said the others, 'even so let us do'." We are back in the days of *Sir Nigel* (and *The White Company*) in Lewis's youth. Or consider how Father Christmas gives Peter his gifts of the sword Rhindon and the shield that was (p. 104) "the color of silver and across it there ramped a red lion, as bright as a ripe strawberry the moment when you pick it. The hilt of the sword was of gold . . ." We are back also in the medieval days of Boxen, as well as of Froissart and the Hundred Years' War in our world (the days of *Sir Nigel*). But even if we do not feel the wonder of the time, we can see that Lewis now feels it. He has studied medieval literature—particularly for *The Allegory of Love*—and he is beginning (or perhaps more than beginning) to find his points of personal reference in the Middle Ages, including his personal references for wonder (wherever they may have been originally).

Lewis's first published critical writing on literature (that I have seen) was his 1929 letter to the *Times Literary Supplement* on James I (of Scotland)'s poem *The Kingis Quair*, a letter which is pretty much repeated in *The Allegory of Love*, pp. 235–36). Let me quote:

> The author, after reading Boethius too late at night, falls into a meditation upon Fortune, and reflects "In tender youth how sche was first my fo, / And eft my frende . . ." and well he might, if, as the story tells us, he was once a solitary prisoner, and is now a free man and an accepted lover. It is at this point that a brilliantly original idea occurred to him, a novelty that struck with such unpredicted resonance on his mind that the easiest imaginative projection sufficed to identify it with the matin bell striking that same moment in the objective world. As he says, "me thocht the bell / Said to me, Tell on man quhat the befell." In our own language, the author, who had long desired to write but spent much ink and paper "to lyte effect," had suddenly perceived that his own story, even as it stood in real life, might pass without disguise into poetry.

Now the point here—though this quotation is useful for several of our purposes—is not Lewis's view or understanding of *The Kingis Quair*, a poem written by James Steuart (1394–1437), King of Scotland (1406–37), imprisoned in England 1406–24, married Joan Beaufort (1406–1445), cousin of Henry V and Henry VI, and aunt of Henry VII of England. The point is that Lewis was in the 1920s and 1930s (and even 1940s) re-immersed in the England (and Scotland) of the Middle Ages, till it was part of the furniture of his mind, as it had been back when he was writing about the Boxonian Middle Ages. But wonder—even awe—has been added, at least in his mind.

One problem for our consideration here, of course, is that what Lewis was trying to do, as also Miss Sayers, was to convey the sense of wonder, the potency, the atmosphere of greatness, the mythic quality, the strength, the virtue of the story. Miss Sayers chose to try to do this directly. Lewis chose to do it through the—if you like—objective correlatives, the references, the times and forms that had the potency and mythic quality for him. Her success could be measured by her new realism and the paradigm-shift, the new lens, it gave her readers (or, originally, listeners). His success must be measured by the appropriateness of the form and the paradigm-shift, the new lens, it gave his readers. What he was seeking to get past those watchful dragons was not Christian doctrine *per se* but the wonder and potency, the greatness and the atmosphere, the strength and the virtue of the Christian myth. We know pretty much what was in Lewis's mind—furniture and pattern. Did it work?

Obviously, in one sense, it must have worked—the *Chronicles of Narnia* have sold in the millions, and someone must be reading them. If the watchful dragons were patrolling to keep out re-telling of the Christian story, the patrol was unsuccessful. But if they were patrolling to keep the message—or the excitement of the message, the greatness and the atmosphere, the strength and the virtue of the Christian myth— away from those who had not always listened to it, if they were patrolling against a use of children's story as evangel, it is something more of an open question whether Lewis got past those dragons. As a plain question, have the Narnia books served to spread the Christian gospel? And if we cannot answer that question, let us ask, in lieu of that, another question: if Lewis was using his Narnia stories as a way of imparting wonder and strength and excitement to the Christian myth, were his means well chosen? Or, asking another way, does the great moment of recognition come when the reader recognizes Aslan as the type of Christ? Or does it come when, later on, the reader, coming later to the New Testament, recognizes that the Narnian story has been, all along, a version of the "Greatest Story Ever Told"—and that having known Him through Narnia has been prepared to know Him here?

My own history as a reader in Narnia rather militates against my successfully answering this question in any of its forms—except, perhaps, whether the means were well chosen. After all, when I read my first Narnia book, *The Lion, the Witch, and the Wardrobe*, I was already a full member of the Episcopal Church. But I think I can see an area in which my history may make me useful as a specimen. I recognized that Aslan was a type of Christ as soon as I heard about his Father, the great Emperor-Over-Sea, who was clearly (to me) a representation of God the Father. What Narnia, both on a first reading and subsequently, gave me was an additional way of viewing the Christian story, a way connected with Lewis's own vision. Of course, I too read bound volumes of *Punch* (with Tenniel illustrations) when I was in school, and (like Warnie) read G.A. Henty at home—and my father had read *Prince Prigio* to me, and I remember Beatrix Potter from my early years—so some of the furniture of his mind was mine also. And this meant that some of what Lewis envisioned as giving additional (or new) meaning to the Christian story-pattern was for me something of a matter of auld acquaintance. Of course, this also had the result of making me a critic in places where he simply wanted me (or anyone else) to be a recipient.

I asked myself, even on my first reading, whether it was quite the thing for Lewis to be talking about the Deep Magic and the Deeper Magic Before the Dawn of Time: to me (and of course fourteen is a very critical age) this business of "Magic" was "atmospherically" wrong. Now I had by this time read *The Place of the Lion* and Charles Williams's other six novels, including my then-favorite, *The Greater Trumps*, and I had a reasonably clear idea in my mind (given my age) of what was Magic and what was—well, something else, the something else I felt in Lewis's interplanetary books, and in Olaf Stapledon, and in G.K. Chesterton, something I now know to be akin to Myth. What Narnia did, for me, was to continue my education in things spiritual to the point where I could more fully understand what Lewis meant (in *That Hideous Strength*) when he talked about Solomon as that bright solar blend of King and Magician. In a way, far from Christianizing Magic (which Williams had already begun to do for me), Narnia led me to see that Magic could be regarded as inherent in the Story all along.

I can recall reading at some time a comment that, in his interplanetary stories, Lewis had baptized the universe and filled it with the glory of Maleldil. Maleldil the Young and the Old One are the progenitors in the Ransom stories of Aslan and the Great Emperor-Over-Sea in the Narnian stories. Lewis was not treading strange ground here. And in Narnia what Lewis has been baptizing is pretty much what he was baptizing in the interplanetary stories, the Pagan myths, including (in this case) Magic. One thing I note here in passing. In his *Times Literary Supplement* letter on *The Kingis Quair*, comparing James I's "Tell on man quhat the befell" to Sir Philip Sidney's "Fool! Look in thy heart and write!" Lewis set out the path he followed in his inaugural lecture, *De Descriptione Temporum* (pp. 24–25 in *They Asked for a Paper*, London 1962): "And because this is the judgement of a native, I claim that, even if the defence of my conviction is weak, the fact of my conviction is an historical datum to which you should give full weight. That way, where I fail as a critic, I may yet be useful as a specimen." As I may also, as I am following his path here— tell what happened to you; look in your heart and write; what does your experience tell you (and us)? That is behind Lewis's *An Experiment in Criticism* (1961), and it is behind my experiment here.

There is a story making the rounds that Lewis's present publishers wanted to publish new Narnia books, perhaps in competition with Harry

Potter, de-emphasizing the Christian "parts" of the Story, which strikes me as something like de-emphasizing the Divine "parts" of God. (Yes, I know God is a Spirit without "parts or passions," but that isn't what that means.) Douglas Gresham is supposed to have put his foot down and said "No!" Right on! The fact is, the Christian Story is the pattern-story (or Myth) for Narnia. The characters are from Lewis's pictures or visions or dreams (and from his friends' children), but it is Aslan who ties them together, and what he ties them together with (or in) is the Greatest Story Ever Told—presumably because that was the Story in Lewis's mind as he wrote the books.

On Lewis's story-writing I have something of a disagreement with my friend Walter Hooper: he thinks Lewis a natural story-teller. I think Lewis was a natural historian, but his brother Warnie had much more of his father's gifts as raconteur. Of course, it was the great neglected writer and critic John Buchan who reminded us that there are only a certain number of stories and that the great age of the English novel came when the novelists were "realizing"—fleshing out, "novelizing"—the patterns of the *Märchen*. But Lewis's genius (not always fully embodied) seems to me to have lain in the imaginative leap by which a story already known could be seen in a new light, what Thomas Kuhn called paradigm-shift. That is what he essayed with Cupid and Psyche in *Till We Have Faces*. That is what is at the root of Fairy-Land as totalitarian (Nazi-model) modern state in *The Dark Tower*. That is behind his draft *After Ten Years*." That is, perhaps, behind his translation of the Christian Story into a world otherwise not entirely unlike Boxen, a world called Narnia.

Of course, Lewis was a Christian when he wrote the Boxen stories— but here we might look briefly at his view of Christianity and Ulster, if not exactly of Ulster Christianity, and then of the "Romantic." The text is *The Pilgrim's Regress: An Allegorical Apology for Christianity, Reason, and Romanticism* (1933). In the opening of the book, John, the hero, as a young child, is taken to the Steward, to learn about the Landlord's rules, and the black pit full of snakes that awaits those who break the rules, and then his Uncle George is turned out of his old farm by the Landlord, without notice. There's a lot about masks (which is part of the allegory), and some pretty good dialogue, but what is more noticeable is the countryside, which seems to be Ulster. What is most noticeable, however, is the rejection of Ulster in favor of—well, something else.

In his Afterword to the Third Edition (1950), written about the time Lewis was writing *The Lion, the Witch, and the Wardrobe*, there is a discussion of the "Romantic" object of desire (p. 158 in the *Collected Works of C.S. Lewis*, Inspirational Press 1996 ed.):

When Sir Arthur Conan Doyle claimed to have photographed a fairy, I did not, in fact, believe it: but the mere making of the claim—the approach of the fairy to within even that hailing distance of actuality—revealed to me at once that if the claim had succeeded it would have chilled rather than satisfied the desire which fairy literature had hitherto aroused. Once grant your fairy, your enchanted forest, your satyr, faun, wood-nymph and well of immortality real, and amidst all the scientific, social and practical interest which the discovery would awake, the Sweet Desire would have disappeared, would have shifted its ground, like the cuckoo's voice or the rainbow's end, and now be calling us from beyond a further hill.

With Magic in the darker sense (as it has been and is actually practised) we should fare even worse. How if one had gone that way—had actually called for something and it had come? What would one feel? Terror, pride, guilt, tingling excitement . . . but what would all that have to do with our Sweet Desire? It is not at Black Mass or séance that the Blue Flower grows? As for the sexual answer [which Dymer and John were both involved in], that I suppose to be the most obvious false Florimel of all. On whatever plane we take it, it is not what we were looking for. Lust can be gratified. Another personality can become to us "our America, our New-found-land." A happy marriage can be achieved. But what has any of the three, or any mixture of the three, to do with that unnameable something, the desire for which pierces us like a rapier at the smell of a bonfire, the sound of wild ducks flying overhead, the title of *The Well at the World's End*, the opening lines of *Kubla Khan*, the morning cobwebs in late summer, or the noise of falling waves.

It appeared to me, therefore, that if a man diligently followed this desire, pursuing the false objects until their falsity appeared [this is the story of John in *The Pilgrim's Regress*] and then resolutely examined them, he must come out at last into the clear knowledge that the human soul was made to enjoy some object that is never fully given—nay cannot even be imagined as given—in our present mode of subjective and spatio-temporal experience. This desire was, in the soul, as the Siege Perilous in Arthur's castle—the chair in which only One could sit. And if nature makes nothing in vain, then the One who can sit in the chair must exist.

Now, if one agrees with Lewis here (and I do), one will conclude that what must be conveyed in any even partly successful attempt to set forth the unnameable something must be done by "poetic" description, by allusion, by an objective correlative, if you like, by what Coleridge called sacramental rather than symbolic writing—not by "objectifying" it, not by "actualizing" it. And Coleridge, by the way, had something to say about moralizing. Owen Barfield has convincingly argued (*What Coleridge Thought*, 1971, ch. 1 and 2) that Coleridge was essentially concerned with morals. He has also convincingly argued the metaphysical logical priority of inward-directed imaginative power (*What Coleridge Thought*, pp. 64–67), so that the centrifugal force of sensibility is simply a particular perspective on the centripetal inward-directed imagination, a kind of "separative projection." That is, sensibility—directed outward—is a way of seeing imagination, directed inward, as projecting oneself on the outward world. We may tell the well-known story of Mrs. Barbauld as Coleridge told it, so to speak, on himself (see Robert Penn Warren, *Selected Essays,* pp. 335–36):

> Mrs. Barbauld once told me that she admired *The Ancient Mariner* very much, but that there were two faults in it—it was improbable and had no moral. As for the probability, I owned that might admit some question, but as to want of a moral, I told her that in my own judgement the poem had too much; and that the only, or chief, fault, if I might say so, was the obtrusion of the moral sentiment so openly on the reader as a principle or cause of action in a work of such pure imagination.

Coleridge goes on to say that a work of pure imagination should perhaps have no more moral than a story out of the *Thousand Nights and a Night*, "of the merchant's sitting down to eat dates by the side of a well, and throwing the shells aside, and lo! a genie starts up, and says he must kill the aforesaid merchant, because one of the date shells, it seems, put out the eye of the genie's son." But one suspects Coleridge of jesting here, one might even say of putting poor Mrs. Barbauld on. In fact, a poem of pure imagination—and this is Robert Penn Warren's point—must necessarily have a moral, however the author (or the Muse) may choose to point that moral. Moreover, if the world is a copy, sacramentalism is precisely the right way to look at the world of appearances, shadows or shades, and symbols do precisely participate in the unity they represent. As Lewis reminded us in "The Weight of Glory," we have never met a mere mortal.

In this connection, we should look at the poet Ruth Pitter's note on Lewis's poetry (on a 1948 letter of his), a note written five years after Lewis's death (*Collected Letters of C.S. Lewis*, II, p. 882).

> Now I wonder, is his poetry after all not? About how many poets or poems would readers agree 100 percent, or even 50 percent? "The peaks of poetry are shiftingly veiled, and different readers catch differing glimpses of the transcendental." I should like to know more about the actual process of conception in his case. Did his great learning and really staggering skill in verse inhibit his poetry? Did he ever (like most of us) catch some floating bit of emotional thistledown and go on from that, or did he plan on a subject like

an architect? (Producing perhaps short epics?) He had a great stock of the makings of a poet: strong visual memory, strong recollections of childhood: desperately strong yearnings for lost Paradise and hoped [-for] Heaven ("Sweet Desire"): not least a strong primitive intuition of the diabolical (not merely the horrific). In fact his whole life was oriented and motivated by an almost uniquely-persisting child's sense of glory and of nightmare. The adult events were received into a medium still as pliable as wax, wide open to the glory, and equally vulnerable, with a man's strength to feel it all, and a great scholar and writer's skills to express and to interpret. It is almost as though the adult disciplines, notably the technique of his verse, had inhibited his poetry, which is perhaps, after all, most evident in his prose. I think he wanted to be a poet more than anything . . . But if it was magic he was after, he achieved this sufficiently elsewhere.

Remember that we suggested earlier a limitation implicit in his remarks about writing a sonnet.

In short, we may conclude that there were indeed watchful dragons—and some of them at least were in Lewis. (Many, I think.) We may suggest that one particular strength in his Narnian story (or stories) comes from the strength of childhood (and the things of childhood, the images of his childhood, even of Ulster and Boxen) in him and in his mind—with his adult abilities to learn and write—and it comes from the strength also of the position that the Christian story had taken in his mind. The objective correlatives are those important to him, the Romantic glimpses are his, the success of Narnia as generally understood lies (so far as we are concerned here) in his success in seeing the Christian Story in these terms. (Not a success that came easily to him, I think.) When it becomes most actual, most objective, or most allegorical, we are furthest from this part of Narnia's success. The neater the tying up of the story, the further we are from the suggestive, from the atmosphere, from the pictures, the visions, the dreams, from the allusiveness, the illustrative, the Romantic, the Romance—from any type or kind of the Larger Life.

[3]
The House in the Country
and the First Larger Life

The prayer ("For an Anniversary of One Departed" in the *Book of Common Prayer*) runs, "Almighty God, we remember this day before thee thy faithful servant [N.], and we pray thee that, having opened to him the gates of larger life, thou wilt receive him more and more into thy joyful service, that he may win, with thee and thy servants everywhere, the eternal victory; through Jesus Christ, our Lord. Amen."

But there is, I believe, more than one larger life, and more than one set of gates. This chapter is aimed at the larger life of the imagination, called here the First Larger Life. It begins with one of the pictures it all began with, the magnificent Lion, who brought the story with Him that linked the other pictures.

In a letter to a girl named Anne (May 5th 1961, in Hooper, *The C.S. Lewis Companion*, 1996, p. 426), Lewis said that Aslan is a lion because Christ was once called the Lion of Judah, and because the lion is the king of the beasts (compare Aslan as "the King of the wood" in *The Lion, the Witch, and the Wardrobe*), and because he was having dreams (visions?) of lions about the time he was beginning the Narnia books. (This last point, of course, begs a further Why?). The controversial Lewis scholar Kay Lindskoog entitled the published version of her Master's thesis on Narnia *The Lion of Judah in Never-Never Land*. In my youth, as it happens, and until I was in my thirties, as for much of Lewis's adult life, the "Conquering Lion of Judah" was the Emperor Haile Selassie of Ethiopia. (The Ras Tafari Makonnen [1892–1975] became His Imperial Majesty Emperor Haile Selassie I in 1930). But there is indeed a reference to the Lion of Judah, a prophecy of the Christ, in the Book of the Prophet *Hosea* (5:14–6:2):

For I will be unto Ephraim as a lion, and as a young lion to the house of Judah: I, even I, will tear and go away; I will take away and none shall rescue him. I will go and return to my place, till they acknowledge their offence, and seek my face: in their affliction they will seek me early. Come, let us return unto the Lord, for he hath torn and he will heal us; he hath smitten and he will bind us up. After two days will he revive us: in the third day he will raise us up, and we shall live in his sight.

But in fact Aslan is a lion because Aslan is (a) Lion—that is what the name means. I give Kay Lindskoog full scholarly marks for her clever title and her reference to *Hosea*—and perhaps even for reminding Lewis himself of the good side of the rather mixed Biblical symbolism of the Lion ("The young lions do lack and suffer hunger, but they that seek the Lord shall not want any good thing," for example, in Psalm 34:10, as a *per-contra*). And of course, if we want to look to Lewis's scholarly endeavors in Medieval and Renaissance English Literature, there is a supervisory lion at the beginning of Spenser's *The Faerie Queene*. But I remain convinced that the old representations of the British Lion with the monarch's face (especially the face of the Martyr King Charles I in the 1649 *Eikon Basilike*), and Tenniel's lions in *Punch*, are closer to this Lion than anything in *Hosea*. Be that as it may, we have another question here, a question of origins that needs further elucidation. Why Narnia? And why Lucy of Narnia—Lucy the Valiant of Narnia?

I mentioned earlier my search for the reference to Lucia da Narni in my summer reading in 1952, which I had decided I found in *The Prince of Foxes* (1947) by Samuel Shellabarger (1888–1954). Shellabarger (B.A. Princeton 1909, Ph.D. Harvard 1914) was an historian and biographer of some repute (*The Chevalier Bayard* 1928, *Lord Chesterfield* 1935), before he turned to popular historical novels in the last years of his life. Now I have no way of knowing if Lewis read *The Prince of Foxes* (though it certainly would seem to me to be something Warnie would have read). But I can testify that, having read it, I was not ill-prepared for Queen Lucy the Valiant of Narnia. You see, one of the subplots in this romance of the life and times of Cesare Borgia has to do with the plans of Ercole d'Este, Duke of Ferrara, to supply his city's need for holiness by bringing there (by Andrea Zoppo, called Orsini) the Blessed Lucia da Narni. There are thus several scenes involving Lucia da Narni, including scenes making her something like Joan of Arc. Here the Blessed Lucia da Narni, she of the Stigmata, confronts Cesare Borgia (*The Prince of Foxes*, pp. 373–374), to rescue from him Andrea Zoppo, called Orsini.

Still unnoticed, she had come forward while Borgia was announcing the close of his entertainment. "I have a message for you," she said quietly. He frowned at her, puzzled. Then, observing her bandaged hands, he inferred who she was and frowned in another fashion. . . . "I have a message for you," she repeated. The calm power of her eyes disconcerted him. He unleashed the lion power of his own to overbear it, but found himself blinking. "Message from whom?" he snapped. "From our Lord God." At that moment, on the lips of anyone else, the words might have sounded childish or mawkish. Spoken by her, they had an unearthly ring that froze everyone, including Borgia, to a breathless attention. Rallying, however, the Duke forced a smile. "I am honored that Almighty God condescends to address me, though I must take your word for it. What's the divine will?"

She answered in the same remote voice; "Our Lord has spoken to me. He bids me tell you that the man Andrea is now clear of guilt, and that the time of his death is not yet. Our Lord wills that he grow for a while in this world to the end that he may bear worthy fruit. You will give heed to this." Borgia's smile widened. "Is that all? . . . Signori [to the others there], it seems I was premature in requesting your applause. The comedy has an epilogue . . . I ask Your Reverence again, is that all?" "No. For I must tell you that, if you disobey the message I bring, you will die tonight. Therefore, take heed."

Whatever he might be, Cesare Borgia was not a coward. . . . Moreover, he belonged to the enlightened select of the age, who had freed themselves from old wives' superstitions. . . . But neither courage nor skepticism helped him at this point. He was forced by the fact—no less hard for being intangible—of spiritual force; or, if spiritual is the wrong word, by something akin to the force which a lion feels in the presence of its tamer. Absolute faith, absolute assurance, has the faculty of communicating its conviction, at least temporarily, to other minds. It was the power of Joan of Arc; it was the power of Lucia da Narni. Therefore, at the moment, not only the others at table, but Cesare Borgia himself, believed what Lucia said.

No, as I say, I do not know if Lewis ever read *The Prince of Foxes*—and I'm virtually certain he did not see the 1949 movie with Tyrone Power. (George Sayer might have known, but I did not ask him, nor did anyone else, to my knowledge.) But I certainly did read *The Prince of Foxes*, and reading the passage in which the valiant and holy Lucia da Narni faced down the evil of Cesare Borgia, made it easier for me to see in the young Lucy at the beginning of *The Lion, the Witch, and the Wardrobe* the eventual Queen Lucy of Narnia, the Valiant. At least Professor Shellabarger's novel provides something to make the distant figure of a fifteenth-century recipient of the Stigmata into a real person, who could take a real place in Lewis's mind. Of course, he may have learned something about the life of Lucia da Narni elsewhere, and he may not have read *The Prince of Foxes*, and of course the whole Lucia da Narni/Lucy of Narnia business might be factitious and coincidental. I don't think so.

That said, we can go on to look in greater detail at *The Lion, the Witch, and the Wardrobe*. We have already noted the "pictures of origin" and something of the origins of those pictures. Let us look more at the book Lewis wrote. *The Lion, the Witch, and the Wardrobe* bears the sub-title, *A Story for Children*—and of course this is the children's story (not just part of that story) "after the manner of E. Nesbit." that Lewis was writing in 1948–49. Actually, Lewis began it back in the days when he and Warnie and Mrs. Moore and Maureen gave shelter to children evac-uated from London at the time of the Blitz, and the opening recalls those days. "Once there were four children whose names were Peter, Susan, Edmund, and Lucy. This story is about something that happened to them when they were sent away from London during the war because of the air-raids. They were sent to the house of an old Professor who lived in the heart of the country, ten miles from the nearest railway station and two miles from the nearest post office" (*The Lion, the Witch, and the Wardrobe*, p. 1). We know the original names were Anne, Martin, Rose, and Peter, with Peter the youngest (Hooper, *Companion*, p. 402). Quite possibly those were the names of real evacuees. (Jill, as in Pole, in *The Silver Chair*, certainly was, Jill Flewett Freud).

Ransom's cottage in *Perelandra* is only three miles from the station, which Lewis walks. Professor Kirke lives much further into the country, in a huge house, not within walking distance of a station: he is (in the original [1940?] version) a relation of the children's mother, and in both versions he is a Professor. This is—for want of a better word—curious, much more curious for an Englishman or Irishman than for an American (or Continental European). The difference is that the title Professor is far less common in the British Isles than in the United States. It would almost make one think Lewis had a particular Professor in mind when he chose the name Digory (which was by the time of the Lefay fragment, around 1949). Tolkien was a Professor as early as 1925 (Lewis not until 1954), but he was scarcely old and bearded like Professor Kirke. (Nor was Lord David Cecil, in 1948 chosen Goldsmith's Professor of English Literature.) The name of Lucy comes almost certainly from Lucy Barfield (b. 1935), only daughter and middle child of Owen and Maud Barfield, and from Lucy (we have argued) comes Narnia. While we can find a Peter among the children of Lewis's friends (Peter Havard, b. 1939), he seems an unlikely model, though Susan's name could have something to do with Susan Baker (b. 1930), daughter of Lewis's (and Barfield's) Oxford friend Leo Baker (1898–1986).

The description of Professor Kirke (pp. 1–2) is reminiscent (to me, at least), though I have been searching to find what it is reminiscent of: "He himself was a very old man [well, no, scarcely above fifty at the time of the Blitz, if we follow the clues in *The Magician's Nephew*] with shaggy white hair, which grew over most of his face as well as on his head . . . but . . . he was so odd-looking that Lucy (who was the youngest) was a little afraid of him . . ." Now, somewhere, at some time, I thought to myself, I have read a description very like that, and it had something to do with a Professor (which can be, of course, a Continental European title as well as an American).

So I thought and I searched, especially in books that had made a profound impression on me and that I knew Lewis also read. And I found it—Eureka? Well, no, not exactly, but I know now where my picture of Professor Kirke comes from. Let me make a slight detour here, by way of a clue in the robing scene for the coming of the *Oyéresu* to St. Anne's in *That Hideous Strength*, a scene I have long been sure came from the robing scene in G.K. Chesterton's *The Man Who Was Thursday*. Was there a very old Professor in *The Man Who Was Thursday*? And was there a man whose hair (not smooth hair) ran into his beard in *The Man Who Was Thursday*?

The answer to both these questions is *Yes*—though, to be sure, the two are not the same man. But here (*The Man Who Was Thursday*, Boni and Liveright Modern Library ed., p. 80) is "a very old man, Professor de Worms, who still kept the chair of Friday [in the Council of Days], though every day it was expected that his death would leave it empty . . . His face was as long as his long grey beard, his forehead was lifted . . ."—and here also (pp. 75–76) is Tuesday: "out of this collar there sprang a head quite unmanageable, a bewildering bush of brown hair and beard that almost obscured the eyes like those of a Skye terrier." Now both Professor de Worms and the hairy Pole Gogol are in fact police detectives in disguise. Professor Kirke is not a police detective in disguise, to be sure, but like Tuesday and Friday (and every other member of the Council of Days), he is other than he seems. And at least looking to the very old man, Professor de Worms, may provide the beginnings of a shadow of an explanation why Lewis calls Professor Kirke a very old man, when even the most elastic interpretation of *The Magician's Nephew* cannot make him much more than sixty (and he is probably less than fifty) at the beginning of *The Lion, the Witch, and the Wardrobe*—scarcely "very old." But with Professor de Worms in mind .

. .

And looking at Gogol's "bush of brown hair and beard" may give us a clue to Professor Kirke's hair "which grew over most of his face as well as on his head." I'm not saying that Lewis had not met hairy Professors in his life time, and of course "Kirk[e]" could be from W.T. Kirkpatrick, his tutor at Great Bookham in Surrey from 1914 to 1917, though Kirkpatrick scarcely had bushy hair and beard. And of course there were bearded Professors in Lewis's earlier days at Oxford, and into the 1930s. But I think it likely that the vision of Professor Kirke comes partly from the vision of Tuesday and Friday from the Council of Days. Moreover, Professor Kirke's great and grand house is not only George MacDonald's house in the North: it is also the great and grand house into which the Man Who Was Thursday and his companions on the Council of Days are led for the robing toward the end of Chesterton's book.

In quite another way from those already mentioned, it is significant that the way into Narnia lies through the wardrobe in the spare room ("Daughter of Eve from the far land of Spare Oom where eternal summer reigns around the bright city of War Drobe"). We will get shortly to another wardrobe through which a young girl (Amabel) in an E. Nesbit short story ("Amabel and The Aunt"), enters a strange land. But let us continue with Chesterton.

The "feeling" of this first entry into Narnia (first in Lewis's order of writing) is not—to me—unlike the feeling of *The Man Who Was Thursday*. There is comedy, high spirits (I might even say "highjinks"), the great certainties of Chesterton ("païens ont tort et chrestiens ont droit"), high adventure and homely comparison, all the motion from and between the "cloud-capped palaces" and the "south suburbs at the Elephant." But here I would like to stop and look briefly at two novels for which Lewis showed a marked partiality in his mid-teens. These two perhaps unexpected novels (to which I also am partial) may show Lewis in a light we rarely see shining on him, and may help us with our follow-up here.

On February 2nd 1915 he writes to Arthur Greeves (*They Stand Together*, p. 65), "I am glad to hear that you have read *[The History of Henry] Esmond*: it is one of my favorite novels, and I hardly know which to praise most, the wonderful, musical, Queen Anne English, or the delicate beauty of the story. True, I did rather resent the history, and still maintain, that when a man sets out to write a novel he has no right to ram a European War down your throat—it is like going back to Henty! Did you ever try that arch-fiend?" (But Warnie enjoyed reading Henty.)

On November 22nd 1916, a week before his eighteenth birthday, he writes Arthur (*They Stand Together*, p. 152) about "the most glorious novel (almost) that I have ever read. . . . It is Nathaniel Hawthorne's *The House of the Seven Gables* . . . although there is nothing supernatural in the story itself there is a brooding sense of mystery and fate over the whole thing." And then a slight correction a week later (on his eighteenth birthday),"I shouldn't have said 'mystery'—there really is no mystery in the proper sense of the word, but a sort of feeling of fate and inevitable horror . . . I really think I have never enjoyed a novel more' (p. 153). He describes the scene with Judge Pyncheon dying alone in the house, in his chair, and the corpse sitting in the chair as the room grows darker, and the ticking of his watch, and says "I intend to read all Hawthorne after this. What a pity such a genius should be a beastly American."

I should note that—although *Esmond* and *Seven Gables* seem to me unexpected as Lewis favorites—he was reading a considerable number of previously unread novels in his father's library, under the influence of Arthur Greeves. Some of these—notably Scott's Waverley novels—became lifelong favorites; in fact, it might almost be said that almost all the nineteenth-century novels Lewis read under Arthur's influence became lifelong favorites.

Now these are story-novels, it is true, but they are also novels of atmosphere, and we recall his comments (just short of age sixteen) on Malory's (fifteenth-century) *Morte D'Arthur* (quoted from Sayer, *Jack*, pp. 103–04):

> he felt that Malory was not a great author; rather, the book was great because it was based on genuine folklore. "Malory has the gift of lively narrative, and," he wrote to Arthur, "the power of getting you to know characters by gradual association." Although Malory never sits down to describe a man's character, by the end of the first volume, Lancelot, Tristan, Belin and Pellinore are "real life people." Even the names of the chapters, such as "How Launcelot in the Chapel Perilous got a cloth from a dead corpse," bear with them a fresh sweet breath from the old-time faerie world wherein the author moves.

It looks as if Lewis found *Henry Esmond* and *The House of [the] Seven Gables* bearing the same breath, if not quite so very sweet.

I read *The House of the Seven Gables* a year earlier in my life—I was a week short of seventeen—and I had no idea, of course, that Lewis had read it. In my case, it was my second Hawthorne novel, and my reaction likewise was to the atmosphere, but also to its general "New-Englandness" and then (which is probably not relevant here) to the curiosity of the fact that my immigrant ancestor knew the Pyncheons (though the branch that went to Springfield in the person of Captain John Pyncheon). When I read *Henry Esmond* later, my reaction, again, was to the (very different) atmosphere, but also (as with Hawthorne) to the artistry of the book. I still think *Henry Esmond* is almost a Platonic form of the novel—perhaps, in many ways, the closest thing to a perfect novel ever written, at least in English.

But let me here quote the (1963) introduction to the Everyman edition, by M.R. Ridley (p. viii):

> Thackeray brought off an astonishing *tour de force*. He assumed a manner of writing different from his own; he maintained it equably through a long novel, with hardly a falter or false note, and apparently without strain. . . . (p. x) I should like to end this Introduction with another word about the style of the book, not considered as a literary *tour de force*, but simply as the work of a master of the English language at any period. For I believe that the real glory of *Esmond*, its essential elixir of immortality, is not in its firm structure, not its clear characterization, not its brilliant picture of a period, but, simply, its style.

And here I would say, of *The Lion, the Witch, and the Wardrobe* (a far less perfect work, as Lewis would have said), that the real glory of this first-written Narnia story, is not in its structure, certainly not in its characterization (which would be a distraction were it attempted), not its picture of another world (or of this one), but, simply, its style.

It may be good at this point to quote (from George Sayer's *Jack: A Life of C.S. Lewis*, p. 75, quoting a letter of December 1912) a passage in which Albert Lewis is describing the difference between his style and his younger son's on the one hand, and Warnie's on the other. "Warren, he said, would be classically severe, with one adjective too few rather than one too many. On the other hand, his and Jack's style 'strives for the witchery of words which can be to the human ear the ripple of the sea beneath the sea, or the roar of the ocean as the hurricane drives it.'" Though Jacks was only fourteen when this was written, and Warnie seventeen, the difference continued throughout their lives.

We can see that Lewis, in his Narnian stories (and especially *The Lion, the Witch, and the Wardrobe*), like Thackeray (in *Henry Esmond*), is writing—or attempting to write—in a style, a manner of writing, not his own. If what he says about the form of the fairy-tale represents what he was trying to achieve in Narnia, then we have a writer one of whose greatest strengths is description choosing a manner of writing that minimizes description and emphasizes story. He does not—at least not in

The Lion—achieve the fairy-tale, the *Marchen,* the Myth. He does achieve—what is much closer to his ordinary manner—a children's story in the manner of E. Nesbit.

Yet he also achieves—perhaps through objective correlatives—something of the atmosphere of the fairy-tale, something of that style, a kind of literary tour de force, yes, but also real. This in despite of the Beavers, Fauns, Father Christmas, Sons of Adam, Daughters of Eve, Witches and all. And here I think I should go into this matter of the objective correlative. The term is T.S. Eliot's (though borrowed from Washington Allston, the nineteenth-century painter). The objective correlative (from Eliot's 1919 essay on Hamlet, collected in *The Sacred Wood*) is defined as "a set of objects, a situation, a chain of events which shall be the formula of that particular emotion; such that when the external facts, which must terminate in sensory experience, are given, the emotion is evoked."

In other words, what Lewis is doing in *The Lion, the Witch, and the Wardrobe* is not perhaps quite what the authors he admired were doing in *Henry Esmond* or *The House of [the] Seven Gables.* Thackeray sank himself into another time, another world, so much that he could write originally rather than imitatively in the idiom of that time, that world. Hawthorne sank himself—or was sunk—into another time, another world, so much that he could write originally in the idiom of that time, that world, as well as in his own—for *Seven Gables* is a book that links the two. Note that in both cases, the time (all of Thackeray's, part of Hawthorne's) was a century and a half before, and note that the two authors were contemporaries. Note also (though it is presumably no more than a kind of coincidence) that two of the authors with a great effect on the youthful Lewis were classmates in the Class of 1826 at Bowdoin College in Maine, Longfellow and Hawthorne. But the importance of the great house in *Henry Esmond* (Castlewood) and in *The House of [the] Seven Gables* is not a coincidence. Let us briefly describe Hawthorne's book (for those who have not read it or been assigned to read it and taken the *Cliff's Notes* way out).

The House of [the] Seven Gables is, as Hawthorne explains in his preface, a romance, which he defines as "a legend prolonging itself" and connecting a bygone time with the present. There is the sense that events and personalities recur throughout time and even throughout the generations; the task of the first chapter is to establish the origins of the legend. The tale of Colonel Pyncheon and Matthew Maule proves the central event of the novel, although it occurs more than a century before the majority of the novel takes place. The events leading to the origin of the *House of the Seven Gables* include patterns and characteristic behavior that future characters will show in very similar ways.

This romantic sensibility that Hawthorne employs is therefore very deterministic (this is what the young Lewis was referring to as the feeling of fate and inevitable horror); the sins of Colonel Pyncheon will be visited and revisited upon his descendants, while Matthew Maule's descendants will bear similar burdens It has been pointed out that the house itself was like a great human heart with a life of its own, full of rich remembrances. A green moss of flower shrubs called Alice's Posies (after an Alice Pyncheon) had grown upon one of the gables. In the front gable there was a shop door that had once contained a small store

The house here is central to the story. The abandonment of the old Castlewood and the building of the new Castlewood in Virginia is central to *The History of Henry Esmond, Esq, Colonel in the Service of Her Majesty Queen Anne*. "Frank formally and joyfully yielded over to us the possession of that estate which we now occupy, far away from Europe and its troubles, on the beautiful banks of the Potomac, where we have built a new Castlewood, and think with grateful hearts of our old home. In our Transatlantic country we have a season, the calmest and most delightful of the year, which we call the Indian Summer: I often say that the autumn of our life resembles that happy and serene weather, and am thankful for its rest and its sweet sunshine" (p. 427). Here is the great house, set down in the sunshine of—we might say—Arcady. Of course, the house at Little Lea was central to Lewis's life—as he said in *Surprised by Joy*, he was the child of that house. But we may want to look a little more at the whole business of the house in the country— what I have elsewhere spoken of as dwelling places in Arcady (in *The Rise of Tolkienian Fantasy*).

First, on the matter of Arcady (or Arcadia), there is a passage worth quoting here at length, in which Lewis speaks of Sidney's Arcadia (*English Literature in the Sixteenth Century*, p. 336): its applicability should be evident.

> We can paint Arcadia all "humble vallies comforted with refreshing of silver rivers," all trees that "Maintaine their flourishing olde age with the onely happinesse of their seat, being clothed with continual spring because no beautie here should euer fade." We can people it with lovers who "Stoppe their eares lest they grow mad with musicke" and who, on seeing their mistresse in an orchard, exclaim "The apples, me thought, fell downe from the trees to do homage to the apples of her breast." We can mention the war horse "milk white but that vpon his shoulder and withers he was fretted with red staines as when a few strawberies are scattered into a dish of creame," his mane and tail "Ddied in carnation" and his harness "artificially made"

like vine branches. Such is the Arcadia we know from popular tradition before we open the book. And all this is really there. But it is not there alone. Against these passages we can quote almost as many of a sterner and graver kind. "Judgment," says Euarchus (as if he had been reading Burke), "must undoubtedly bee done, not by a free discourse of reason and skill of philosophy, but must be tyed to the laws of Greece and the municipall statutes of this kingdome."

Lewis goes on (pp. 336–37) to give more examples, many in a style recognizable from the mighty conclusion to Ralegh's *Historie of the World*.

There are, in fact, several reasons for the word Arcadian to apply to Narnia. The first is the common meaning or significance of the word—what everyone knows about Arcady before reading about it: the pastoral, the countryside, the green and pleasant land with animals. The second is what one finds in Sidney's *Arcadia*: the Arcadian epic (drawing from both Sannazaro's Menippean Satire and the epic adventure story of Heliodorus). Possibly the pageant detail of English pastoral, and specifically of Sidney's Arcadia provides another reason. Also, there is, in the Arcadia, as in English pastoral generally, a kind of judgment after pastoral, which is linked with the fundamentally hierarchical, elegiac, and complex nature of pastoral. One may find examples not only in Sidney but in Milton's *Lycidas* and even *L'Allegro*—even *Comus*—and in Spenser's *Shepheardes Calender*. Even in Crashaw's great anthem, *In the Holy Nativity of Our Lord God: A Hymn Sung as by the Shepherds*. This underlying combination of hierarchy, elegy, and complexity is revealed and realized in the trial and judgment in the Arcadia, and even in late exemplars of pastoral (as William Empson has reminded us) like *The Beggar's Opera* and *Alice in Wonderland* and *Through the Looking Glass*—and here. And once we are sure that we are in Arcadia, we can look at the matter of the dwelling-places in Arcady, or, in simpler diction, houses in the country.

We'll begin with Warnie's favorite and Jacks's arch-fiend. Henty has a whole book (*George Andrews*) whose theme is furnishing a house, and several whose theme is establishing or providing a home; there is a significant amount of architectural description in quite a number of his books; while Terence O'Connor is fighting in *With Moore at Corunna* and *Under Wellington's Command*, his cousin Mary is refurbishing the family homestead so they can marry and move into it; quite a number of subordinate characters settle down in snug cottages on the estates of those they have followed in war, frequently doing little or no work, but telling tales of great days to the children of the next generation. There are most certainly dwelling-places in Arcady.

And if Henty described buildings at some length, and placed a considerable emphasis on dwelling-places, we are forced to conclude—however unlikely we may think it—that this is what his readers wanted, reading while they themselves were in the Arcadia of childhood. Not all of his millions of volumes sold could have been bought by uncles and aunts for unwilling recipients. In fact, Henty was controversial in his time because some thought he gave his juvenile readers too much of what they wanted.

And then, recall how Kipling's *Stalky* begins: "In summer all right-minded boys built huts in the furze-hill behind the College—little lairs whittled out of the heart of the prickly bushes, full of stumps, odd root-ends, and spikes, but, since they were strictly forbidden, palaces of delight" (p. 13, Puffin edition). Such a hut in the furze-hill was Stalky's (and M'Turk's and Beetle's) refuge from the world of the Olympians—alias the Masters. But they find a better refuge from the Masters (p. 17):

> Beetle wormed into the gorse, and presently announced between grunts of pain that he had found a very fair fox track. This was well for Beetle, since Stalky pinched him à tergo. Down that tunnel they crawled. It was evidently a highway for the inhabitants of the combe; and, to their inexpressible joy, ended, at the very edge of the cliff, in a few square feet of dry turf walled and roofed with impenetrable gorse.

And then (also p. 17):

> He parted the tough stems before him, and it was as a window opened on a far view of Lundy, and the deep sea sluggishly nosing the pebbles a couple of hundred feet below. They could hear young jackdaws squawking on the hedges, the hiss and jabber of a nest of hawks somewhere out of sight; and, with great deliberation, Stalky spat on to the back of a young rabbit sunning himself far down where only a cliff-rabbit could have found foothold. Great grey and black gulls screamed against the jackdaws; the heavy-scented acres of bloom round them were alive with low-nesting birds, singing or silent as the shadow of the wheeling hawks passed and returned; and on the naked turf across the combe rabbits thumped and frolicked.

And what is Stalky's reaction to this? "'Whew! What a place! Talk of natural history; this is it,' said Stalky, filling himself a pipe. 'Isn 't it scrumptious? Good old sea!' He spat again approvingly, and was silent."

Fenimore Cooper wrote almost an entire novel centering on building an estate and planting its grounds, and whose scenery, for all its origins in the formal garden, is one of his most notable achievements (and who is stepfather to Tolkien's forests). Grahame's *The Wind in the Willows* is our quintessential Arcady, but Moley's house, Ratty's house, as I have said, the picnic basket with the comforts of home ("coldtonguecold-hamcoldbeerpickledgherkinssaladfrenchrollscresssandwidgespotted-meatgingerbeerlemonadesodawater"), Toad's caravan, and above all, Badger's house, all provide us a picture of the comforts of home. And so do Number Five Study and the "Pleasant Isle of Aves" in *Stalky*, and "Volaterrae" (Dan and Una's hideaway) in *Puck of Pook's Hill*. We have noted the dwelling-places in Arcady in Henty. Inns are dwelling-places in the Arcady of the open road—and we know the dangers of the open road. For, after all, there are robbers on the road and wolves in the pastoral (else why do we need the pastor?), just as there are dangers in the Wild Wood, dangers from which Ratty and Moley are rescued by Badger's House.

Whoever the author (and whether he or she was dwelling in Arcady or looking down from Olympus), whatever the age of the children in Arcadia, their Arcadia (all Arcadia) is beset with perils, so an agreeable dwelling-place is all to the good. There is a link between child and countryside, as well as between schooldays and golden days: the link is the link of Arcady; but the house in the country is very close to being essential. There is also in these Arcadias a strong sense of the past somehow immanent in the present, not always a golden past but at least a past streaked with gold, whether it is as a buried city in *The Wind in the Willows* or the Dorincourt estates in *Little Lord Fauntleroy*. And notice that the Dorincourt estate has a great and grand house to end all great and grand houses (except perhaps that in *The Man Who Was Thursday*).

So it is not accidental that the way to the land of Arcady (or Narnia—or, in "The Aunt and Amabel," the place called Whereyouwantogoto, or the door Anodos takes in *Phantastes*) lies through a door in the house in the country.

It is not, as we have suggested, accidental that it is a wardrobe door, and here, though skeptical about the exact linkage, we may look at "The Aunt and Amabel," one of the short stories in *The Magic World* by E. Nesbit (published in 1912). If you haven't read "The Aunt and Amabel," it's probably worth telling you that eight-year-old Amabel does something she believes was a good and thoughtful act, but her aunt thinks otherwise, and Amabel is punished. She winds up spending the day in the spare room where there is a large wardrobe. She discovers a train timetable. On it she sees a station named Bigwardrobeinspareroom. After climbing into the wardrobe, she winds up at a place called

Whereyouwantogoto. The business about the city of War Drobe in the far land of Spare Oom (in *The Lion, the Witch, and the Wardrobe*) may echo this.

One of the girls evacuated from London in 1939–40 is supposed to have asked Lewis what was in an old wardrobe (possibly the one now in the Wade at Wheaton). Could she explore it? I have heard it suggested that her question may have stayed in Lewis's mind. We also have cousin Claire (Hamilton) Clapperton's reminiscence of Lewis going into the wardrobe to tell stories to his cousins as a child. The fact is, children, like cats, like to go into cozy places, boxes or under tables or in wardrobes or closets, or under the covers. The impulse probably needs no explanation—and of course Lewis liked to tell (or write) stories as a child, and later in his teens, no matter where he was.

Here is a sometimes overlooked description of Lewis in his early mid-teens, by his study-mate at Malvern, (Air Chief Marshal Sir) Donald Hardman (quoted in Sayer, *Jack*, pp. 84–85). "He was a bit of a rebel; he had a wonderful sense of humor and was a past-master of mimicry. I think he took his work seriously, but nothing else . . . When I knew him I can only describe him as a riotously amusing atheist. . . . I can remember going [on] long walks with him on Sundays when he was in the gayest of moods . . . storytelling and mimicking people—one of his chief butts being the worthy master in charge of the O.T.C." He was, in short, something of a raconteur, like his father. Now, as to whether he told well-plotted stories . . .

But it is time to get back to *The Lion, the Witch, and the Wardrobe*. Lucy has gotten to the big house (with her siblings), into the wardrobe (first without any of her siblings), and thus into Narnia (also without any of her siblings). And she meets the faun Tumnus ("Mr. Tumnus" she calls him). Now what Sir Donald has told us of Lewis should come to mind here. He was a humorist, a mimic, a raconteur who would give a humorous turn to the stories he told. He was, in fact, something of a wit, as we remarked earlier. Now Tumnus is a perfectly good Classical (possibly Umbrian or Etruscan) name, like the names of the fauns (including Dumnus) in *Prince Caspian*. But a little girl from 1940 England straying through a wardrobe into the Classical world (but one where a faun carries an umbrella and parcels), and calling the faun Mr. Tumnus, and going home with him to a tea of boiled egg, sardines on toast, buttered toast, toast with honey, and then a cake with sugar-icing—well, that is humorous and deliberately so. And indeed, if the original picture of the faun with an umbrella had been in Lewis's mind since 1914–15, and represents a humorous idea of what a faun would do in the afternoon if he were in Georgian England (had Lewis heard—he must have heard of—Debussy's tone poem, *L'Après-midi d'un faune?*).

Now not all humor, of course, is mocking. In fact, it may be worth looking at this point in a little more detail. It is in the detailed observation of daily life that Stephen Potter considered the essence of the English sense of humor (Stephen Potter, *Sense of Humour*, New York 1954, pp. 3–34), and that Nikolaus Pevsner called a key part of Englishness in Art. For Pevsner, Englishness in the arts is defined 1. by the belief that the intention of art is to teach and 2. by the belief that the most effective teaching is done through the detailed observation of daily life (Pevsner, *The Englishness of English Art*, London 1956, p. 24 and *passim*).

This is clearly allied to what Potter has called the humor of observation, whose chief exemplar he finds in Boswell's *Life of Johnson*. Humor is thus, in this sense, a creature of both realism (for the observation) and immediacy. Of course, it shades off into the comic, as we will see. But it is important to remember that while this humor may be funny (as in the patter songs in Gilbert and Sullivan), it is usually far removed from anything like comic slapstick ("slapstick comedy"). Here we might pause to look at Potter in a lyrical passage (Potter, *Sense of Humour*, pp. 12–13). One of the rewards of the academic student of English literature

> is the appreciation of first bursts; and there was never such a first burst as happened to the English in the fourteenth century. Humour came suddenly to our literature without warning. . . . No Eng. Lit. disciple will ever believe there is a greater innovator in any art than Chaucer in his. There is the language he chose, the dialect of that language, the making rhythm out of that language, the attitude to his writing . . ., the eye turned intently to the contemporary reality of life . . ., the recognition of the sacred importance of detail, the recognition that character is . . . a fusion into small unpredictable traits . . . no need to add humour to these attributes which together make up Humour itself.

On the other hand, by the comic is meant not a reference to comedy *per se* and certainly not to Comedy (the mythos) in Northrop Frye's sense, but to the risible, to things that we laugh at or (if no more) smile broadly at. As I have noted, it includes jokes, slapstick, shaggy dog stories, wordplay, Groucho Marx's eyebrows and leer, "'Enery the Eighth," Vaudeville—and it also at least borders on certain forms of humor, and particularly the humor of exaggeration, in "tall stories" and "yarns" of the Davy Crockett sort—raconteur's humor. And both the fantastic and the comic are designed to give a particular kind of pleasure, which we might speak of as the pleasure of release—release from our quotidian environment, release from the daily grind. Both may be considered in some sense romantic, meaning that the feeling and intention behind them are the feeling of the Romantics and the intention of the romances.

Mikhail Bakhtin has linked the grotesque of the comic to the grotesque of the Gothick: we might say that, in Montaigne's phrase, the comic and the fantastic are the types "dignes qu'en s'amuse" (see Bakhtin, *Rabelais and His World*, p. 65). The release of the Gothick in particular, as well as of the fantastic in general, could be taken as a kind of polar opposite from the release of the comic—negative as opposed to the positive release of the comic, as Wolfgang Kayser has suggested (ibid., introd., p. 46). Briefly summarizing my argument in *The Rise of Tolkienian Fantasy*, I suggest that a work of literary imagination whose locale is the countryside will be either Comedy or Romance (using Northrop Frye's definitions), indeed will probably have elements of both.

I would further suggest that the nineteenth-century invention of Childhood made possible, first, the avuncular tone of Lear and Lewis Carroll, and John Ruskin, the fatherly tone of Kipling (in *Puck of Pook's Hill* and *Rewards and Fairies*), the motherly (but still parental) tone of E. Nesbit, the fatherly tone of Tolkien's stories for his children (even, in the case of *The Lord of the Rings,* his grown-up children), and the Godfatherly (a version of avuncular) tone of C.S. Lewis in the Narnia books. It is not accidental that children playing in the countryside of Victorian England themselves linked childhood and pastoral. And I think it likely that the necessary association of pastoral with countryside acted in the English creative genius to amalgamate pastoral with Redemptive Comedy, to produce the English phenomenon of pastoral-with-judgment long before Northrop Frye developed his taxonomy (the *mythoi* of Comedy. Romance, Tragedy, Satire) or Nikolaus Pevsner defined the Englishness of English Art, or Stephen Potter defined humor.

There is a little of Ruskin's *The King of Golden River* in Narnia—the comic spirit, the "antic hay" one might say. That goes with the slapstick, the wordplay, the events and language reminiscent of *The Rose and the Ring* or *Prigio* or the *Five Children*, the Lewis who was mimic and raconteur in his mid-teens, the "riotous" atheist turned now turned believer, but still "riotous." Of course, the *bouleversement* characteristic of the classic nineteenth-century boys' books, the subversiveness of Arcadia, the topsyturvydom of W.S. Gilbert, and the whole extravagance of Irish-English doubtless also play their parts. The important thing to note, before we go on, is that *The Lion, the Witch, and the Wardrobe* is both a humorous and in places a funny book. The Witch tells Edmund he is "'much the cleverest and handsomest young man I've ever met. I think I would like to make you the Prince—some day, when you bring the others to visit me.' 'Why not now?' said Edmund. His face had become very red and his mouth and fingers were sticky. He did not look either clever or handsome whatever the Queen might say" (p. 34).

Or the "other lion" when Aslan rescues the captives from the Witch's house (p. 172)—"'Did you hear what he said? Us lions. That means him and me. Us lions. That's what I like about Aslan. No side. No stand-off-ishness. Us lions. That meant him and me.' At least he went on saying this till Aslan had loaded him up with three dwarfs, one Dryad, two rabbits, and a hedgehog. That steadied him a bit."

Some may find the humor (or comedy, or "comicality") a little slapstick, or a little ponderous, or a little avuncular, or a little too much in the music-hall ("Vaudeville") direction, or a little Victorian. And there is always something of the problem with Lewis that one had with Ronald Reagan—how much was his, and how much was simply remembered lines—in Reagan's case from old films, in Lewis's from books or magazines read long ago? In the end, it is doubtful whether that question matters. If John Buchan is right, and the great English (and American) novels are fundamentally *Märchen* on an epic scale, originality is something of a distraction—and still more in children's stories or fairy-tales, where the story should not vary from night to night of telling.

Nor is it important that we may not enjoy the slapstick or the music-hall or the avuncularity—my experience is that those who read the books as children do enjoy them. And in any case, they show Lewis himself, as he was in life, and remains here. I know he said he didn't enjoy the music-hall the way his father and brother did (in *Surprised by Joy*), and I'm assuming he was telling the truth—but he did enjoy the nights out, and the humor he remembered as part of the enjoyment of the general bustle and excitement and sense of a night out. And the remembering of a pleasure is what brings the pleasure to its full strength—remembering is part of the pleasure, and more than part—as we know from Ransom's conversation in Hyoi in *Out of the Silent Planet* ("'But the pleasure he must be content only to remember?' That is like saying 'My food I must be content to eat'," p. 73, Macmillan paperback ed., 1965).

We all pretty much know the story of Lucy in Narnia in *The Lion, the Witch, and the Wardrobe* by now, but it may be a good idea to note particular parts of it as we go along. After coming into Narnia through the wardrobe, she meets the Faun Tumnus, homeward bound to his afternoon tea, carrying his parcels and his umbrella. He invites her into his (very domestic) cave, prepares the tea, while she looks at a little bookshelf with books on it with names like *The Life and Letters of Silenus*, or *Nymphs and Their Ways*, or *Men, Monks, and Gamekeepers: A Study in Popular Legend*, or *Is Man a Myth?* The latter two titles are take-offs on popular 1930s–1940s (or earlier) titles in our world dealing with the possibilities of the unseen or mythic world; the former two are simply transpositions from this-worldly titles (say, *The Life and Letters of Sir John Fastolf*) into that world. In either case, the trick (and the humor) is the same—like the idea of two devils in the Hellish bureaucracy corresponding with each other, as in *The Screwtape Letters*—once again a (humorous) transposition of one world into another.

So Lucy has her tea with "Mr." Tumnus, and he confesses he was going to kidnap her for the Witch ("My old father, now . . . that's his picture over the mantelpiece. He would never have done a thing like this." p. 15). He doesn't, of course, and sends her back to the Lamp-post, so she can find her way back to this world—but not before she gives him her handkerchief that he has been using to dry his tears at what a bad Faun he's been. She comes back instantaneously to this world, and the other children think she has been pretending, particularly because Narnia is not there for them then, when they look in the wardrobe. A little later on, Edmund follows her into the wardrobe and into Narnia, they are separated, and he falls in with the Witch, eats her enchanted Turkish Delight, then finds Lucy, they come back—and Edmund betrays her by telling the others they have just been playing. Peter and Susan worry that Lucy is going mad, they take their worries to the Professor, and here is his reaction (pp. 43–46):

> Then he cleared his throat and said the last thing either of them expected. 'How do you know,' he asked, 'that your sister's story is not true? . . . There are only three possibilities. Either your sister is telling lies, or she is mad, or she is telling the truth. You know she doesn't tell lies and it is obvious that she is not mad. For the moment then, and unless any further evidence turns up, we must assume that she is telling the truth' . . . 'But there was no time,' said Susan. 'Lucy had no time to have gone anywhere, even if there was such a place . . .' 'That is the very thing that makes her story so likely to be true,' said the Professor. 'If there really is a door in this house that leads to some other world (and I should warn you that this is a very strange house, and even I know very little about it)—if, I say, she had got into another world, I should not be at all surprised to find that that other world had a separate time of its own . . .'"

Eventually, of course, the magic was traced to the fact that the wardrobe had been made from the wood of the tree that had grown from the core of the apple (the Apple of Youth) that Digory had brought back from Narnia (by Aslan's permission) for his mother—that is, we are given to believe (after Lewis had rationalized and systematized the story) that the magic was in the wardrobe, and in the house only because the wardrobe was in the house. That makes sense—but I would doubt it was part of the original vision. Ruth Pitter has given us a picture of Lewis as a poet whose poetry—read, imaginative writing—was limited by his skill in versification, one might even say, by his search for a form. She certainly knew Lewis better than I, and would have been able to give more examples and more details, but I think I can see how this opposition worked out in the Narnia stories. For me, the mystery (or mysteriousness), the romance, the visionary quality, the mythic quality, if you will, were better (and more traditionally) conveyed by having the magic in the house. The door to the other world (which is a common enough motif) ordinarily is attached to a place (like the Wood between the Worlds in *The Magician's Nephew*), rather than to an object. (But note that the object as door has come to be much more familiar now, in the days of Harry Potter.)

When all four children come through the wardrobe (in Chapter VI of *The Lion*, "Into the Forest"), they find that "the Faun Tumnus" has been taken away by the Witch's Secret Police, with a notice posted reminiscent of twentieth-century secret police in Nazi Germany or the Soviet Union. In the American editions up to 1994, the chief of the Witch's police is Fenris Ulf, but in the British editions, and all editions after 1994, it is Maugrim. Fenris Ulf, Fenris the Wolf (Fenrir), is the great wolf of the Norse myths. Maugrim's name is reminiscent of the wolf Isengrim in the medieval Reynard the Fox, with Mau- (Mal-) for evil in place of Isen- (for iron?). The change back to Maugrim in the American editions was unwelcome to more than one reader familiar with Fenris Ulf (and Peter as Sir Peter Fenris-Bane). We will come back to that. In the meantime, we find out that poor Tumnus got wind of his arrest before it happened, and passed Lucy's handkerchief on to the Beaver as a token, for when Lucy came back. And then comes one of the passages representing (for me) Lewis at his most characteristic (p. 64):

Then signaling to the children to stand as close around it as they possibly could, so that their faces were actually tickled by its whiskers, it added in a low whisper—"They say Aslan is on the move—perhaps has already landed." And now a very curious thing happened. None of the children knew who Aslan was any more than you do; but the moment the Beaver had spoken these words everyone felt quite different. Perhaps it has sometimes happened to you in a dream that someone says something which you don't understand but in the dream it feels as if it had some enormous meaning— either a terrifying one which turns the whole dream into a nightmare or else a lovely meaning too lovely to put into words, which makes the dream so beautiful that you remember it all your life and are always wishing you could get into that dream again. It was like that now.

What is so characteristic of Lewis? First, there is the realism (and "realization") of the Beaver's whiskers touching the children (and note the use of "it" rather than "he" for the Beaver). Second, there is the reference to how the reader may have felt in a dream—the kind of simile that so strengthened the broadcast talks that make up *Mere Christianity*, and, of course, in this case, a simile based on Lewis's own experiences in his youth (and described in *Surprised by Joy*). And third, the dream simile is a double strength, for it also links Narnia with dream, and thus brings us (though we may not know it, and probably do not or did not know it at the time) into the whole mysterious and Romantic world of dream, Heinrich in the Cavern in Novalis, "our life is not a dream but should and must become one," Xanadu in Coleridge's vision, Anodos through the door of the timeless in *Phantastes*. For if death brings us into the second larger life (which is immortality), one road to the first larger life (which is imagination) comes through death's image, sleep, and from sleep, vision and dream. Where exactly does dream fit in, or does it? It does.

Where it fits in, of course, depends on what we believe about dream. For all that Freud and Jung have written (and in Narnia Freud is a distraction), and for all the German Romantics and their heirs, the most important passage for our general purposes antedates their work by the better part of three millennia: "Friend / many and many a dream is mere confusion / a cobweb of no consequence at all. / Two gates for ghostly dreams there are: one gateway / of honest horn, and one of ivory. / Issuing by the ivory gates are dreams / of glimmering illusion, fantasies / but those that come through solid polished horn / may be borne out, if mortals only know them."

The reason that this exceeds in importance virtually the sum total of everything written since, for our purposes in Narnia, is that the literature of Antiquity, of the Middle Ages and Renaissance (linked together here as Lewis linked them together), of the seventeenth century, of the Augustans and the Romantics, all the literature Lewis loved as an Old Western man, was crafted with this in mind, at least in the back of the mind. Note well that visio, the dream through the gates of horn, is still a dream, a ghostly dream.

Dante in the *Divine Comedy* has a vision *nel mezzo del cammin per una selva oscura*, Langland in *Piers Plowman* a "ferly" bi a bornes side: these are visions of the countryside. In fact, medieval visions are frequently pastoral visions. The reason is in part, I suspect, that the Middle Ages were pastoral ages. Some later ages, and especially the Victorian Age, cherished that pastoral time, and—the life of the person recapitulating the life of the people—looked to childhood as pastoral, as the golden age for the person lost to the people as a whole. As indeed it is (but then we are the heirs of those Victorians). Of course, Homer's ivory-gated "fantasies" are not our fantasy: the dream-vision, whether through gate of horn or gate of ivory, whether lying or veridical, is not fantasy, because it is not providing truth-in-despite-of-fact, nor is it elvish craft, nor is it feigned to be believed. What comes through the gate of horn may be borne out, if mortals can only understand it: that is *visio*. What comes through the gate of ivory may be vain fancy or phantasm, the gods cheating on us, but whatever it is, it is not something we are creating or imagining. "If you ever go to Narnia, you must be sure to have a look at those caves. . . ."

We have earlier noted a connection between George MacDonald and dream. What of Kenneth Grahame's connection? Are Grahame's title *Dream Days* (his book before *The Wind in the Willows*), and the use of dream-endpieces there, and the connection between dream and pastoral in him merely fortuitous? I think not. There is perhaps a kind of Barfieldian ancient unity between pastoral and dream. Nevertheless, when we look at the matter-of-factness of the narration, within the compass of the romantic introduction (or, in some cases, endpieces) for his *Golden Age* or *Dream Days* stories, we may reasonably say this is characteristic of Kenneth Grahame, more even than of MacDonald, and if the ancient unity overshadows it, it is not hid in the shadows. The Grahame view of Arcady, for all that it is an Arcadian view, is clear-eyed and matter-of-fact. And that is perhaps partly MacDonald's doing, in *Sir Gibbie*, for example. And Lewis here seems to be following his master (or his masters, or his Master). There is nothing fuzzy at the edges about Lewis's Narnia, even if its all-inclusiveness repelled Tolkien and puts us in mind of Widdecombe Fair.

So it is not coincidental that Lewis uses the dream-simile as the name—or is it the Name?—of Aslan is introduced. Nor is it coincidental that, shortly thereafter, Mr. Beaver ("Mr." because, like "Mr." Tumnus, he is now part of the children's world, in which adults, even if beavers or fauns, are "Mr.") quotes two old rhymes. One is "Wrong will be right when Aslan comes in sight, / At the sound of his roar, sorrows will be no more, / When he bares his teeth, winter meets its death / And when he shakes his mane, we shall have spring again" (pp. 74–75). The other is, "When Adam's flesh and Adam's bone / Sits at Cair Paravel in throne / The evil time will be over and done" (p. 76). There's also a prophecy (possibly not in verse and certainly not quoted directly) to the effect that when two Sons of Adam and two Daughters of Eve sit in the four thrones at Cair Paravel, it will be the end of the Witch's reign and her life (p. 77). Now these two prophecies in verse, at least, are very curious indeed. Parts read like (possible) genuine verse prophecies, or, to put it more exactly, both start like genuine verse prophecies— "Wrong will be right . . . " and "When Adam's flesh and Adam's bone . . ."– and then tail off in a manner more reminiscent of *Drayneflete Revealed* or *1066 and All That* than of the genuine article. Now Lewis, whatever might be said of his poetry generally, was a highly skilled versifier, and if he wrote verse-prophecies for Narnia that have a touch of parody in them, then I daresay there was a reason. (He was a satirist, after all.)

When I was perhaps six years old, and living in Hampton, Virginia, in an area now called Southampton, my father came home on leave (he was a lieutenant in the Army Transportation Corps), and lo! and behold! I found a map drawn on old paper with directions to a buried treasure that seemed to be located in the sandy brushy area at the end of Clyde Street (we lived at 112A Clyde Street), between the last houses and the water of Hampton Roads. We went, my father and mother and older sister and I, on an excursion, found the spot designated on the map, and digging down in the sand, found a little wooden box (I think of the kind that a toothbrush came in that you got from the dentist), with a sliding top, and in the box were new copper pennies (this was the year after the "steel penny"). Now I knew this wasn't a genuine old map—though it had dragons on it—but it was a "make-believe" set up by my father, and part of the pleasure was in the intermingling of fantasy—pirates, treasure map, *hic dracones*—with an actual excursion to the bottom of Clyde Street, and the finding of an actual (though modern) treasure.

And this seems to me to be related to what Lewis is doing with rhymes of prophecy he knows (and shows) to be make-believe. At this point, this is still very close to the spirit of Andrew Lang in *Prigio* and *Ricardo of Pantouflia*. If not *Marchen*, this is at least *conte*. I'm not saying the infelicities (almost parody) of "when Aslan comes in sight" or "When he bares his teeth winter meets its death" are deliberate signposts on the borders of make-believe, but they come from a spirit and outlook in Lewis telling stories (even if in his mind only) to his god-daughter or to young evacuees that was not unlike my father's spirit and outlook in creating a story for his son. Perhaps it has something to do with the spirit of the times—my father was three years younger than Lewis and I am two years younger than Lucy Barfield, and all of this takes place in the 1940s, with the Second World War in the background.

So Edmund sneaks out from the Beavers' house, and slips and slides and sloshes and slouches through the snowstorm and then the freezing cold to the Witch's castle with its courtyard of beings frozen in stone, and brings her the news that his brother and sisters are nearby, while Peter and Susan and Lucy, finding him gone, want to search for him, and Mr. Beaver tells them he is already in the Witch's service ("He had the look of one who had been with the Witch and eaten her food"—p. 81) so there's no use in looking for him, they had better leave quickly. And Mrs. Beaver placidly goes on preparing for their journey as though it were to the end of the world—ham, tea, sugar, loaves of bread, bread-knife, matches, handkerchiefs, and wishing she could bring her sewing machine.

They come to the Beavers' hiding-place of old times (the past alive in the present). And then, when they come out in the morning, there is Father Christmas with his sleigh—not the eight tiny reindeer of our "Night Before Christmas" but "they were far bigger than the Witch's reindeer . . . And on the sledge sat a person whom everyone knew the moment they set eyes on him. He was a huge man in a bright red robe (bright as holly-berries) with a hood that had fur inside it and a great white beard that fell like a foamy waterfall over his chest. Everyone knew him because, though you see people of his sort only in Narnia, you see pictures of them and hear them talked about even in our world—the word on this side of the wardrobe door. But when you really see them in Narnia it is rather different. Some of the pictures of Father Christmas in our world make him look only funny and jolly. But now that the children actually stood looking at him they didn't find it quite like that. He was so big, and so glad, and so real, that they all became quite still. They felt very glad, but also solemn" (pp. 102–03, and here I think of Lewis on the true meaning of the medieval *solempne*).

You will notice what has happened here. It is as though, just for this time, the world of Narnia incorporates everything on that side of the passage, as though the world of Narnia has in it many countries, perhaps even many worlds. As the stories go on, Narnia becomes more and more the country, and its adjoining countries, but here, at the beginning (in Lewis's mind), it has in it Father Christmas and the Dryads and Naiads and the Wolf Fenrir and the Giants and the Trolls, efreets, and others out

of *The Thousand Nights and a Night*, all the panoply and rout and rabble of the myths and legends of all mankind. Father Christmas, of
course, is the figure better known in the United States as Santa Claus
(Sinter Klaas, St. Nicholas). He is, by the way, as you know, the central
figure in one of Tolkien's books, *The Father Christmas Letters* (Boston,
1976).

These letters begin when eldest son John Tolkien is two or three and
continue until daughter Priscilla (the youngest) is almost to her teens—
the last, to "Dear children," reads in part "Now I shall have to say good-
bye, more or less. I shall not forget you. We always keep the names of our
old friends, and their letters, and later on we hope to come back when
they are grown up and have houses of their own, and children . . ." Along
the way the children heard Father Christmas wondering "When is
Michael going to learn to read and write his own letters to me?"
(Christmas 1925), and next year they heard about the time when North
Polar Bear turned off the tap for the Aurora Borealis ("Rory Bory Aylis"),
and there was "the biggest bang in the world" and it "shook all the stars
out of place, broke the moon into four—and the Man in it fell into my
back garden. He ate quite a lot of my Xmas chocolates he said he felt better and climbed back to mend it and get the stars tidy" (Christmas 1926).
By 1933 the letter is to Christopher and Priscilla, and Father Christmas
tells them about the worst attack of Goblins for centuries.

In that letter Father Christmas refers to himself as "your old great-
great-great-etc. grandfather at the North Pole"—which hints, curiously, at
North American tribal mythologies (which also include the Aurora
Borealis and Polar Bears—at least in the versions my father told me). The
letter from Ilbereth the Elf, though his name is Elvish (cf. Elbereth), shows
a sketch of Ilbereth not devoid of Pigwiggenry. The 1926 letter shows the
North Pole in its arctic expanse looking rather like a Chesley Bonestell
rocket ship on Mars. Even the picture of Father Christmas in bed in his
bedroom shows the chill outside, but the polar landscapes are more than
merely chilly. In one of the letters, the Red Gnomes who live in the caves
under the North Pole promise Father Christmas and North Polar Bear that
they will get rid of the Goblins who seem to have taken up residence there.
The caves are good, with appropriate cave-drawings on the walls.

My reason for this excursus is that Lewis knew Tolkien's Father
Christmas letters from the 1930s on, and he follows Tolkien in the red
clothes rather than the Medieval and Renaissance English green. But
whereas Tolkien's Father Christmas has the same willing make-believe
quality as my father's treasure map or the Narnian verse prophecies, here
Lewis turns the tables to the point where Father Christmas is practically

an eldilic (angelic) appearance, in his hugeness, his "Man Who Was Sunday" quality, his appearance as a Platonic form or (almost) a planetary angel—perhaps an interplanetary angel.

He rather overbears the other characters, except Aslan, and in giving the three children who are present their Gifts (Christmas? three sets of gifts? what exactly is going on here?), he is a stand-in for Aslan, indeed for the Christ who is part of his name. And is it accidental that Peter receives sword and shield, the gifts of power, the High King's gifts, and Susan receives the horn whose sound carries through the worlds to summon (also bow and arrows), and Lucy receives the healing "juice of one of the fire-flowers that grow in the mountains of the Sun"? Am I being too inventive when I see here the King's Gifts ("Gold I bring to crown him again"), the Gift that summons across time and space, a Gift of Divinity ("Frankincense to offer have I / Incense owns a deity nigh"), and a Gift for Anointment (but for the living not the dead, better than "Myrrh is mine, its bitter perfume . . .")? Well, perhaps that is fanciful— but one thinks of three sets—three kinds—of Gifts, at Christmas . . .

As we all know, when the Witch sets out with Edmund for the Stone Table (and here we seem to be back in Norse myth), the winter begins to break up. "There was no trace of the fog now. The sky became bluer and bluer and now there were white clouds hurrying across it from time to time. In the wide glades there were primroses. A light breeze sprang up which scattered drops of moisture from the swaying branches and carried cool delicious scents against the faces of the travelers. The trees began to come fully alive. The larches and birches were covered with green, the laburnums with gold. Soon the beech trees had put forth their delicate transparent leaves. As the travelers walked under them the light also became green. A bee buzzed across their path" (pp. 117–18). And, as this is happening with Edmund (and the Witch's Dwarf and the Witch), "miles away the Beaver and the children were walking on hour after hour into what seemed a delicious dream" (p. 119). A dream.

When they reach the Stone Table, and Peter draws his sword against Fenris Ulf (I stick to the name I remember, rather than Maugrim), and plunges it in, and then "came a horrible confused moment like something in a nightmare" (p. 128). And, earlier, as Edmund has been carried along prisoner in the Witch's sledge, "as they went on, hour after hour, it did come to seem like a dream" (p. 110). But now, still like a dream, it is a delicious dream of pastoral and a coming out of nightmare—and yet, Edmund still, as a traitor, belongs to the Witch, by the Deep Magic written on the Table of Stone, indeed "written in letters as deep as a spear is long on the trunk of the World Ash Tree" (p. 138).

Let us go back for a minute to what Lewis was reading as a child, first "The Saga of King Olaf" (*The Works of Henry Wadsworth Longfellow*, reprinted Wordsworth, Ware (Herts), UK, 1994, pp. 364–386), then "Tegner's Drapa" (pp. 190–91). And I daresay he read others of Longfellow's poems in that collection, perhaps (I should think) "Hiawatha" with its *Kalevala* meter (quite possibly his father had the same Riverside collection of Longfellow's poems as my father and grandfather had, which is the one reprinted by Wordsworth). We know the impression made by "Tegner's Drapa"—though we may not know all of it.

Remembering that Lewis was always a voracious and retentive reader, and remembering also that he was one who easily formed pictures (and remembered them), let us look at the less well-known later stanzas of "Tegner's Drapa" (p. 191)—"So perish the old Gods! / But out of the sea of Time / Rises a new land of song / Fairer than the old. / Over its meadows green / Walk the young bards and sing . . . / Ye fathers of the new race, / Feed upon morning dew, / Sing the new Song of Love. / The Law of Force is dead. / The Law of Love prevails"—no more shall Thor the Thunderer challenge the Christ. And looking at the "Saga of King Olaf" he was reading with a chance look through the pages of the book, we find the same theme. Recall the description of Olaf in Thyri's chamber – "Then King Olaf entered / Beautiful as morning, / Like the sun at Easter / Shone his happy face; // In his hand he carried / Angelicas uprooted, / With delicious fragrance / Filling all the place."

And then, at the end (p. 386), is heard the voice of St. John, to the Abbess Astrid—"The dawn is not distant, / Nor is the night starless; / Love is eternal! / God is still God, and / His faith shall not fail us; / Christ is eternal!" Lewis may have been enjoying the rhythms of "King Olaf" and found the *Drapa* a deeper poem, caught by the sunward-sailing cranes and the cry "Balder the Beautiful is dead!" But the theme is the same—Christ replaces the old gods, and with Christ and in Christ is the Spring. As the old hymn has it, "Earth her joy confesses, clothing her for spring; / All fresh gifts returned with the returning King / Bloom on every meadow, leaves on every bough, / Speak his sorrow ended, hail his triumph now. / Welcome Happy Morning! Age to age shall say!" (And "Hiawatha" at the end shows the priests of Christ replacing the old religion—although there the splendors of nature belong to the old gods, as Hiawatha departs, with the evening sun leaving "upon the level water / One long track and trail of splendor," departs "in the glory of the sunset, / In the purple mists of evening, / To the regions of the homewind, / Of the northwest wind Keewaydin , / To the Islands of the Blessed, / To the kingdom of Ponemah, / To the land of the Hereafter" (p. 272).

So Aslan gives Himself willingly to be executed in Edmund's place, and by the Deeper Magic Before the Dawn of Time, comes back to life, the Table cracks, Death itself starts working backwards—and Aslan romps with Susan and Lucy and rushes off to the Witch's house, bounds over the wall, and begins to restore the statues to life (in a scene directly out of *Prince Prigio*). "Creatures were running after Aslan and dancing round him till he was almost hidden in the crowd. Instead of all that deadly white [of marble], the courtyard was now a blaze of colors; glossy chestnut sides of centaurs, indigo horns of unicorns, dazzling plumage of birds, reddy-brown of foxes, dogs, and satyrs, yellow stockings and crimson hoods of dwarfs; and the birch-girls in silver, and the beech-girls in fresh transparent green, and the larch-girls in green so bright that it was almost yellow. And instead of the deadly silence the whole place rang with the sound of happy roarings, brayings, yelpings, barkings, squealings, cooings, neighings, stampings, shouts, hurrahs, songs and laughter" (*The Lion, the Witch, and the Wardrobe*, p. 166).

Then Giant Rumblebuffin knocks down the gates to clear the way out of the Witch's house, asks for a "handkerchee" and on Lucy offering hers, he picks her up for the "handkerchee" (and this is the third appearance of the handkerchief *motif*). But, that settled, they all go off to assist Peter and Edmund and Lucy in their fight against the Witch, with the Lion flinging Himself on the Witch, and then she is dead (pp. 172–73). The Witch's army runs, Lucy brings out her cordial from the valleys of the Sun, heals Edmund and others, and then they march Eastward to the shore of the sea, by Cair Paravel, where "in the Great Hall of Cair Paravel—that wonderful hall with the ivory roof and the west door all hung with peacock's feathers and the eastern door which opens right onto the sea, Aslan solemnly crowned them and led them onto the four thrones . . ." (pp. 178–79).

That night there is high revelry in Cair Paravel, and then the "two Kings and two Queens governed Narnia well and long and happy was their reign" (p. 180). And so "they lived in great joy and if ever they remembered their life in this world it was only as one remembers a dream" (p. 181). Until they go a-hunting and come upon the Lamp-post and so suddenly return to the spare room in the Professor's house. "And that is the very end of the adventures of the wardrobe. But if the Professor was right it was only the beginning of the adventures of Narnia" (p. 182).

And it was Aristotle, long before Kipling, who taught us the formula, "that is another story." Which is like Lewis's lead-on here. But what I want to turn to now is the great hall at Cair Paravel with the ivory roof and the peacock's feathers, and to the name Cair Paravel itself. What is the line in Masefield's "Cargoes"—"Quinquereme of Nineveh from distant Ophir / Rowing home to haven in sunny Palestine / With a cargo of ivory,/ And apes, and peacocks, / Sandalwood, cedarwood, and sweet white wine." The emphasis—and the objective correlative—is Biblical (and the comparison is through history, with the past of the quinquireme alive in the present of the dirty British coaster). But Caer is the Welsh (or Celtic) word for Castle. And what of Paravel? Well, it rhymes with caravel, the ship. And it is reminiscent of Caer Pedryvan (would that be the Caer of Peredur?) in the *Mabinogion* and the Arthurian stories, and Paravel is reminiscent of Perlesvaus (which is Perceval or Peredur).

In other words, the points of reference for Cair Paravel and its hall in Lewis's mind would seem to be Celtic legend and the Bible. An odd mix, one might say, except that the whole history of the Holy Grail has exactly that twin linkage, which may tell us something about Cair Paravel. And of course the subsequent return of the Four Children as *reges quondam regesque futuri*—once and future kings (and queens), as King Arthur was *rex quondam rexque futurus*.

On the matter of the handkerchiefs, was there a connection between Lucy Barfield and Lucy's handkerchiefs (and Mrs. Beaver and the handkerchiefs) in *The Lion, the Witch, and the Wardrobe*? We know Maud Barfield urged Lewis to remind his young readers never to go into a wardrobe and close the door (a reminder he must have put in not much short of half a dozen times): there was at least that much real connection between Lucy Barfield and Lucy in the book—greater than any comparable connection except perhaps that between David and Douglas Gresham and Prince Cor and Prince Corin in *The Horse and His Boy*. In any case, one thing we can be sure of. The pictures that led to Narnia led primarily to *The Lion, the Witch, and the Wardrobe*—though the picture on the wall at the beginning of *The Voyage of the "Dawn Treader"* had been glimpsed before.

The process of creation (or subcreation) of *The Lion, the Witch, and the Wardrobe* comes from (and echoes) a wide range of sources (and analogues). And for the most part, the parameters of the books that follow have pretty much been set, except for the true odd-book-out, the one from the time of Lewis's own youth (or a little earlier perhaps), *The Magician's Nephew*. What have we found thus far on *The Lion*? It has its origins in E. Nesbit; it is a kind of pastoral; it is Arcadian; and it can be traced in some ways to a huge amount of Lewis's childhood and boyhood experience, including childhood and boyhood reading— Hawthorne (*Seven Gables*) and Longfellow, Thackeray (*Henry Esmond*) and Chesterton, and most especially, Lewis's long-time longing not so much for a form as for atmosphere.

Oh yes, and it is comic and funny and comedic and humorous, sometimes in a music-hall way, sometimes emulating Thackeray in *The Rose and the Ring*, sometimes Andrew Lang in *Prince Prigio*, sometimes E. Nesbit. It links realism and dream and at least has the hint of a shadow of a suggestion that this is connected with dream and dream can be real—and of course not only are things not always what they seem, but places may be sometimes there and sometimes not there. We will come back to say more on this later on. In the meantime, we will be looking in the next chapter at four of the books, each in light of a particular theme or *motif*.

Specifically, we shall be looking particularly at the idea of the past alive in the present in *Prince Caspian*, at the character development of Eustace Clarence Scrubb (". . . And he almost deserved it") in *The Voyage of the "Dawn Treader*," at the question "What exactly is the real world?" in *The Silver Chair*, and the cry "For Narnia and the North" in *The Horse and His Boy*, and we will center the discussion of each book on that particular issue, at the same time trying to do justice to the book itself, not merely as an illustration of the central point.

[4]
Writing the "Chronicles" and Realizing the World of Dragons

And so we come to *Prince Caspian: The Return to Narnia*, dedicated to Mary Clare Havard, daughter of Dr. Robert Emlyn Havard ("Humphrey" to the Inklings), Lewis's (and Tolkien's) family doctor. This is the story noted in the "Plots" list in *Past Watchful Dragons* as "Inverted—Ordinary fairy-tale K[ing], Q[ueen] and court, into wh[ich] erupts a child from our world" (p. 46). Of course, it is all four children who "erupt" into Narnia, and the court of King Miraz and Queen Prunaprismia in Narnia is not an "ordinary fairy-tale court" unless we would also include the court of King Valoroso XXIV of Paflagonia in *The Rose and the Ring* or the court of King Prigio of Pantouflia in *Ricardo of Pantouflia* as an ordinary fairy-tale court.

I hear the voices of Charles Dickens ("prunes and prisms") and per-haps of George Meredith (*The Shaving of Shagpat*) or one of the other nineteenth-century English writers of "Eastern" novels, or at least of the *Thousand Nights*. Can we take a "Queen Prunaprismia" entirely seri-ously, or is this yet again a "humorous fantasy" in the line running from Ruskin (*The King of Golden Mountain*) to Thackeray and Lang and E. Nesbit? Clearly not entirely seriously, and clearly humorous fantasy.

But despite this, the story of the "eruption" of the children into the other world (which turns out to be Narnia) begins to have a mythic qual-ity, even if the myth is the myth of Robinson Crusoe. The children, catching hands as they feel the pull, are pulled from the station platform at the railroad junction which is their last stopping place together at the end of vacation before they go off to their separate schools. (And we remember that in E. Nesbit's story of "The Aunt and Amabel" the wardrobe in the spare room was a railroad station.) "The four children found themselves standing in a woody place—such a woody place that branches were sticking into them and there was hardly room to move" (*Prince Caspian*, p. 3). And then, "'Oh Peter!' exclaimed Lucy. 'Do you think we can possibly have got back to Narnia?' 'It might be anywhere,' said Peter. 'I can't see a yard in all these trees. Let's try to get into the open—if there is an open." So they struggle out of the tulgy wood, and there they are, at the wood's edge, above a sandy beach, lapped by a calm sea (pp. 3–4). For the next few pages they are simultaneously four children wading at the beach and Robinson Crusoe exploring his island. For they *are* on an island. But there is a stream flowing down to the beach, so they have water to drink—and then they follow the stream into the island. And there we leave them for now.

The word "Chronicles" is in quotation marks in the title of this chapter: that's what the books are commonly called. But as we shall see in Chapter 7, in the distinction made by Lewis's Magdalen friend and associate, Robin Collingwood, the "Chronicles of Narnia" are in fact the History of Narnia, while the fragment "The Outline of the History of Narnia so far as It is Known"—in *Past Watchful Dragons*—is really Chronicle. Without the children from our world present to give it meaning, the whole series of Narnian events over twenty-five (Narnian) centuries, is only Chronicle, not History. How much of that meaning is rooted in our world's myths we shall see, as we go on.

After stooping under branches and climbing over branches, the children on their island begin to smell the apples, then they find the apple trees—and then they "found themselves in a wide open place with walls all around it. In here there were no trees, only level grass and daisies, and ivy, and grey walls. It was a bright, secret, quiet place, and rather sad; and all four stepped out into the middle of it, glad to be able to straighten their backs and move their limbs freely" (p. 11). "'This wasn't a garden,' said Susan presently. 'It was a castle and this must have been the courtyard'" (p. 12). It was, and after Peter points out the dais for the thrones, just like the dais in their castle at Cair Paravel, Susan says (in a "rather dreamy and sing-song voice"), "'In our castle of Cair Paravel . . . at the mouth of the great river of Narnia. How could I forget?'" And of course it is their castle at Cair Paravel, a thousand (Narnian) years later (pp. 12–23).

They find their old treasure chamber, down sixteen steps (as Lucy had counted them those many years before—shades of Sherlock Holmes!), and they reclaim their gifts, Peter his sword Rhindon and his shield, Lucy her tiny crystal bottle of cordial from the flowers of the sun, Susan her bow and arrows, but not her horn (which "must have got lost when we blundered back into that other place—England, I mean," p. 24). Of course it is Queen Susan's horn, lost for the ages and found by Dr. Cornelius (whom we will meet shortly), that has summoned the children back to Narnia. Or, at least, that is the proximate cause of their return.

But before they find that out, they rescue the dwarf Trumpkin (a very Dickensian dwarf—or possibly Surteesian), and hear about Miraz and Prunaprismia, and Prince Caspian, and his nurse, and Dr. Cornelius, his tutor. Why Caspian? Well, there comes to my mind a book of what you might call humorous sketches that I read about the time I read the Chronicles of Narnia. The (very slim) book is called *Reginald*, it was published as a collection in 1904 from sketches published previously in the *Westminster Gazette*, and it reproduces some of the catch-phrases and fads of those days. The author was Hector Hugh Munro (1870–1916, called "Saki").

If one looks at the very first sketch (also called "Reginald"), one finds Reginald engaged in horrifying and infuriating virtually everyone at the McKillop's garden party, and in a great silence fallen on the party, "'What did the Caspian Sea?' asked Reginald, with appalling suddenness'" (*The Short Stories of Saki*, Modern Library ed., p. 6). That was a joke-becoming-a-catch-phrase of the time when Lewis was busily furnishing his mind with *Punch*, though I can't say for sure he read the *Westminster Gazette*. But he surely heard the phrase. Now, one can suggest other points of origin, and many of the Late Narnian names are of this sort (Rilian, Erlian, Tirian)—but Caspian came first, and I think it came from the old joke.

I called Trumpkin the Dwarf a Dickensian character (or Surteesian—the reference being to the novels of Robert Smith Surtees 1803–1864, author of the Handley Cross novels—see Chapter 3 in my *Rise of Tolkienian Fantasy*, Open Court, 2005). He doesn't cry out "Prunes and prisms!" (although we do have Queen Prunaprismia), but there are "Beards and bedsteads!" (p. 33) and "Whistles and whirligigs!" (p. 65), and "Thimbles and thunderstorms!" (p. 92), and "Giants and junipers!" (p. 104) and "Bottles and battledores!" (p. 130), and "Cobbles and kettledrums!" (p. 144) and "Wraiths and wreckage!" (p. 149) and "Crows and crockery!" (p. 184)—that's enough for this book, though Trumpkin comes back in person in *The Silver Chair* (and *in absentia* in *The Voyage of the "Dawn Treader"*).

Lewis seems to have been carried away by the exercise, and one wonders a little if Lewis isn't putting something of himself into Trumpkin here: one recalls his discussion of *phusis* in *Studies in Words* (quoted from 2d ed. 1967, pp. 33–34), where he writes that the word and its cognates have two major branches of meaning, the second being "'to grow (transitively, as one "grows" cucumbers or a beard, and intransitively as beards or cucumbers grow), to become.'" This passage led Ronald Tolkien, in a letter to his son Christopher, to lament (*Letters of J.R.R. Tolkien*, p. 302) that he had written for Lewis a long analysis of "the semantics and formal history of *BHÛ- with special reference to φύσις and all that remains is the first nine lines of PHUSIS (pp. 33–34) with the characteristic Lewisian intrusion of 'beards and cucumbers'"— which almost, I think, sounds like Trumpkin (minus the alliteration, though that is important). We have "Beards and bedsteads!"—what about "cossets and cucumbers!" or even "kickshaws and cucumbers!" And there are characteristic pieces of Lewisian verse not unlike these.

It turns out that the red dwarf Trumpkin and the black dwarf Nikabrik, and the badger Trufflehunter, have found the boy Caspian, thrown by his horse Destrier, when he has fled his home at Dr. Cornelius's urging, after his uncle Miraz, the usurper, and his queen have had their first son. First Caspian's nurse (who has dwarf blood) and then his tutor (who is a half-dwarf) have told him about Old Narnia and aroused his longing for that (made him a votary of the blue flower?— well, not quite that, but set him seeking the past alive in the present, the Old Narnia in the New). Then when it is evident (to Dr. Cornelius) that Miraz will put Prince Caspian out of the way, he arrangers for Caspian to flee (with Queen Susan's horn and a pack of food) and Caspian by his accident finds the Old Narnia. The rebellion of Old Narnia begins.

Miraz learns of Caspian's flight when Destrier returns riderless; Doctor Cornelius escapes and brings Caspian warning (they are sheltering is Aslan's How, built up over the Stone Table); they send messengers to the other two great places of Narnia, the Lamp-post and the shore where Cair Paravel lies in ruins and the forest grown up over it.

They are attacked; Caspian winds the horn in a breathing-space, while on his way down to the mouth of the great river Trumpkin is captured and his captors take him down to the shore (by good fortune his desired destination) to give him to the ghosts. Which they do, but of course the ghosts are not ghosts now. They are Peter, Susan, Edmund, and Lucy Pevensie, and they rescue Trumpkin after his "executioners" have bound him hand and foot to throw him into the water. Then, with many questions and halts and byways, Trumpkin tells the four children the story of Caspian the Tenth and the rebellion (or counterrevolution?) of Old Narnia.

After which, Trumpkin remarks that he will have to go back to Caspian and tell him no help has come, to which Lucy asks, "'But don't you yet see who we are?'" To which Trumpkin replies, "'I suppose you are the four children out of the old stories . . . And I'm very glad to meet

you of course. And it's very interesting, no doubt. But—no offence—
. . . you know, the King and Trufflehunter and Master Cornelius were
expecting, well, if you see, help . . .'"

But after Edmund has disarmed him in a fight with broadswords, and
Susan has outshot him, and Lucy has healed his wound from his last battle, he realizes that the four children are help, and they begin their trip
through a Narnian landscape changed by a thousand years, to find
Aslan's How. They row to the mouth of Glasswater and up the creek,
expecting to find it an easy stage across the little Rush to the hill of the
Stone Table. But of course the Rush has formed a deep gorge over the
thousand years, and the land is all changed ("but not what you would
call changed" as Merlin said to Ransom in *That Hideous Strength*), and
Aslan has to lead them to the How.

Though it is important to the story, it is not so important here that
first Lucy sees Aslan, but the others cannot see and will not follow, they
go amiss, then Aslan appears again to Lucy and she finally gets the others to follow her, then Edmund (who has before this voted to go the way
Lucy says) sees him, then Peter and finally Susan, and then Trumpkin
(though when he actually sees Aslan is unclear). Then they are at the
How and all have seen and believed (pp. 149–150). "'Now,' said Aslan,
'The Moon is setting. Look behind you: there is the dawn beginning. We
have no time to lose. You three, you sons of Adam and son of Earth, has-
ten into the Mound and deal with what you will find there.' The Dwarf
was still speechless and neither of the boys dared to ask if Aslan would
follow them. All three drew their swords and saluted, then turned and
jingled away into the dusk. Lucy noticed that there was no sign of weari-
ness in their faces: both the High King and King Edmund looked more
like men than boys."

And I am reminded of Lewis's description in the Ulster novel of how
the adults in his youth perpetually jingled. Also, both the High King (in
Celtic story, and in the person of Brian de Boru at Clontarf in 1014) and
King Edmund (Ironside, in England, 1016) are figures in the History of
the British Isles—and by the way, the four children were first in Narnia
in the (Narnian) years 1000–1015. They are, so to speak, millennial children.

And then there is "Look behind you: there is the dawn beginning."
When I look in my heart and write, I find this brings to mind the famous
lines (by Arthur Hugh Clough 1819–1862), "And not through Eastern
windows only / When daylight comes, comes in the light. / In front the
sun climbs slow, how slowly, / But westward look! The land is bright."
We know Lewis was familiar with those lines (one of the ghosts quotes

them in *The Great Divorce*), and I think the whole poem might be taken as an objective correlative here. The fourth and final stanza I have already quoted—here are the first three: "Say not the struggle nought availeth, / The labor and the wounds are vain,/ The enemy faints not nor faileth, / And as things have been, things remain; // If hopes were dupes, fears may be liars; / It may be, in yon smoke concealed, / Your comrades chase e'en now the fliers— / And, but for you, possess the field. // For while the tired waves vainly breaking / Seem here no painful inch to gain, / Far back, through creeks and inlets making, / Comes silent, flooding in, the main. . . ." The girls, Susan and Lucy, watch the boys jingle off.

"The light was changing. Low down in the East, Aravir, morning star of Narnia, gleamed like a little moon. Aslan, who seemed larger than before, lifted his head, shook his mane, and roared. The sound, deep and throbbing at first like an organ beginning on a low note, rose and became louder, and then far louder again, till the earth and air were shaking with it. It rose up from the hill and floated across all Narnia. Down in Miraz's camp men woke, stared palely in one another's faces, and grasped their weapons [and I recall some lines— ". . . through their paly flames / Each battle sees the other's umber'd face // . . . and from the tents / The armourers . . . / Give dreadful note of preparation . . ." in *Henry V*, Act IV, Prologue]. And in Narnia: "Down below that in the Great River, now at its coldest hour, the heads and shoulders of the nymphs, and the great reedy-bearded head of the river-god, rose from the water."

> Beyond it, in every field and wood, the alert ears of rabbits rose from their holes, the sleepy heads of birds came out from under wings, owls hooted, vixens barked, hedgehogs grunted, the trees stirred. In towns and villages, mothers pressed babies close to their breasts, staring with wild eyes, dogs whimpered, and men leaped up groping for lights. Far away on the northern frontier the mountain giants peered from the dark gateways of their castles. (*Prince Caspian*, pp. 150–51)

And as Merlin promised he could do in *That Hideous Strength*, as Tolkien did in *The Lord of the Rings*—which was being read to the Inklings as Lewis was writing *Prince Caspian*—Aslan's roar has awakened the trees.

This is a long way, imaginatively, from the Old Wives' couplet "At the sound of his roar / Sorrows will be no more." It is the same roar, but Aslan has changed, grown larger, and the compass of the story larger with him. Not for nothing just now was Lewis reading and rereading the literature of the Golden Age of English Poetry for his *English Literature in the Sixteenth Century, Excluding Drama* (1954).

And then when Peter ("by election, by prescription, and by conquest, High King over all Kings in Narnia") challenges Miraz to single combat, he writes (or rather Dr. Cornelius writes for him in a learned and clerkly hand), "it is our pleasure to adventure our royal person on behalf of our trusty and well-beloved Caspian in clean wager of battle to prove upon your Lordship's body that the said Caspian in lawful King under us in Narnia both by our gift and by the laws of the Telmarines . . . Wherefore we most heartily provoke, challenge and defy your Lordship to the said combat and monomachy" (pp. 172–73), we are in that sixteenth-century English world that begins with Lord Berners translating Froissart's *Chronicles* (more this, I think, than Malory) and ends with the Euphuistic doublets and triplets of John Lyly, following the more sober doublets and triplets of Thomas Cranmer. And of course there is the Biblical or Enochian echo in "High King over all Kings" ("King above all Kings, Lord above all Lords"). (And we know Lewis read *The Book of [the Secrets of] Enoch*, because that is where there are bubble-trees in the Third Heaven, though when I asked him about it, he said the proximate cause of the bubble-trees in *Perelandra* was a child's mispronunciation of laboratory as bubble-tree.) My point here is that the very language of the "royal" parts of Prince Caspian is the language of the Past—Narnian Past and English Past.

I will not quote here the description of Peter's combat with Miraz (very like boys' fights in Henty, but in fancy dress), nor the treachery of the Lords Sopespian and Glozelle who stab Miraz when he has tripped and fallen, then blame Peter and so begin the battle he has sought to avoid, nor the apocalypse at the end, turning the space-time envelope inside out, sending the Telmarines who do not wish to stay in the reborn Old Narnia back to the now-uninhabited isle in the South Pacific from which they originally dropped into Telmar, returning the children to the railway junction from which they were drawn into Narnia. But I will quote the passage describing the victory of Old Narnia in the battle (pp. 190–91):

> But almost before the Old Narnians were really warmed to their work they found the enemy giving way. Tough-looking warriors turned white, gazed in terror not on the Old Narnians but on something behind them, and then flung down their weapons, shrieking, "The Wood! The Wood! The end of the World." But soon neither their cries nor the sound of weapons could be heard any more, for both were drowned in the ocean-like roar of the

Awakened Trees as they plunged through the ranks of Peter's army, and then on, in pursuit of the Telmarines. Have you ever stood at the edge of a great wood on a high ridge when a wild south-wester broke over it in full fury on an autumn evening? Imagine that sound. And then imagine that the wood, instead of being fixed to one place, was rushing at you; and was no longer trees but huge people, yet still like trees because their huge arms waved like branches and their heads tossed and leaves fell around them in showers . . . In a few minutes all Miraz's followers were running down to the Great River in the hope of crossing the bridge to the town of Beruna and there defending themselves behind ramparts and closed gates. They reached the river but there was no bridge. . . . Then utter panic and horror fell upon them and they all surrendered. [The bridge had been destroyed by great strong trunks of ivy summoned by Bacchus, and the river-god thus loosed from his chains].

When I first read this, I had just heard in Chapel the passage where Jesus opens the scroll of Isaiah and finds the place where it was written [Luke 4:18–19, RSV] "The Spirit of the Lord is upon me, because he has anointed me . . . to preach deliverance to the captives and recovery of sight to the blind, to set at liberty them that are oppressed, to proclaim the acceptable Year of the Lord"—and I thought of the wine of Holy Communion and Bacchus as the God of Wine, here and in the following pages delivering the captive and setting the oppressed at liberty. And I thought of the wildness of Bacchus and of Aslan ("He's not a tame lion") and my imagination was stirred.

As it was, indeed, by Lewis's question about standing at the edge of a great wood and a high ridge—but not, as it happens, when he ventured on further description of the huge people who were like trees, tossing their heads and the leaves falling around them. I thought first of Lewis's comment on Milton's fault in overmuch description of the indescribable in *Paradise Lost*, until I realized that my principal problem with the description was in the falling leaves, because that phrase conveyed an autumn picture to me, while what the picture meant was a great storm in which still-green leaves are torn from the trees in the wind. But by making the trees in a sense responsible for the wind, moving their arms, much of the force of the image was lost. A false step I thought, and still think—but implicit in the anthropomorphic tree-people. He should have left them more as trees.

This is, I think, a problem in the form of the children's story, that would have been obviated if he had stuck to the form of the fairy-tale or *Marchen*, which does not explain (recall Coleridge's remark to Mrs. Barbauld)—but then we would not have had the great simile of the south-wester, or much of the rest of the book. The fact is, Lewis's *forte* is description, and if he sometimes goes too far to make the picture clear, to explain as well as to paint, that is simply the defect of his virtue—and it isn't common. Part of the problem comes from the same process he noted in Tolkien's *The Hobbit*—it is as if the Battle of Toad Hall had become a serious *heimsökn* and Badger had begun to talk like Njal—with the result that we have the fairy-tale or children's-book trappings, and the great Story at the center. (But then, Lewis would argue that the Great Story is in fact a *Marchen*.)

In the "Note" setting out future (Narnian) books (*Past Watchful Dragons*, p. 46), Lewis lists first "Ship. Two children somehow got on board a ship of ancient build. Discover presently that they are sailing in time (backwards) . . . Various islands (of Odysssey and St-Brendan) can be thrown in. To be a v[ery] green and pearly story." Now this is pretty clearly a reference to an early stage of the story in *The Voyage of the "Dawn Treader"* but the important things to note here are 1. that this was to be a past-and-present story (a time-travel story), and 2. that Lewis had a visual image ("a very green and pearly story") of the story as a whole. *Prince Caspian* is not a very green and pearly story (though the title character bears the name of a sea): it is rather a wilderness and wild-nature story, one could even say a story of the pagan sort (of the *pagani*, the fields, and the woods).

That being the case, its objective correlatives will come, at least some of them, from the pagan past—Bacchus and Silenus and the Maenads, the River-God, Dryads, Naiads, Fauns—and those from the Christian past will be from the amalgam of Christian belief and Pagan practice that made up the Middle Ages (trial by combat, for example, as with Peter and Miraz). But here it is time to look more fully at the second point—that Lewis had in mind a visual image of the whole story when he began to write it. I think we might reasonably look at the first fully memorable image of the Past in the Present, which is the ruined castle of Cair Paravel in the woods, the golden chess knight with one ruby eye lost in the overgrown orchard, the long-forgotten treasure chamber. And here I have two suggestions, one dealing with the ruined castle, one more generally with the Past in the Present.

First, the ruined castle is a commonplace of late-eighteenth-century and early-nineteenth-century Romanticism, Alison on the Sublime, the whole cult of the Gothick, Beckford's Folly, all those stories and poems with the castle or great house mostly in ruins—and one wonders if the golden knight is not likewise a sign of the great past in ruins, and how the mighty are fallen by time. But there is a difference. The apple trees are still bearing, miraculously, thirteen hundred years after Pomona planted them. They are indeed fully alive in the present. They are in fact fulfilling their ancient promise. And second, on this matter of the Past alive in the Present, that is, as has been elsewhere noted, a characteristic of the Edwardian adventure story.

Let me list the various characteristics of the Edwardian adventure story here (from *The Rise of Tolkienian Fantasy*, p. 167). First, the story is framed in familiarity. In this, it is like a fairy-tale, but unlike the fairy-tale, its action is time-specific. Second, the characters are types, though they may rise to the dignity of archetypes. Third, and connected with the second characteristic, it is the character of nature, not the characters of the actors, that is "realized" (in the French sense of the word). Fourth, the adventurers are not solitary, but they are frequently (in fact, almost universally) a happy few. Fifth, the adventures are generally narrated (frequently in the first person) by the most ordinary of the happy few. Sixth, there is a recurring motif (perhaps the recurring motif) of the Past alive in the Present. And seventh, the world of the adventurers is essentially an aristocratic world. It might also be argued that there are fewer shades of grey in the actions of the characters than we are accustomed to seeing in our present-day world.

Except for the avuncular omniscient narration (by "Uncle" or "Godfather" C.S. Lewis), *Prince Caspian* fits the bill perfectly. Its action is time-specific both in our time and Narnian time. There is no characterization beyond archetypical identification with Trumpkin and Cornelius and Miraz—not even as of Eustace in *The Voyage of the "Dawn Treader,"* or the four children in *The Lion, the Witch, and the Wardrobe*. We see extensive characterization of Nature. The adventurers are the Band of Brothers (and Sisters). We have the motif of the Past alive in the Present, beginning with Cair Paravel. We have an aristocratic world and few shades of grey. All of these are true in part for all the Chronicles, but they seem true in fuller part for this one.

I said that *Prince Caspian* had less in the way of characterization—and less importance to characterization—than, for example, *The Voyage of the "Dawn Treader."* After all, the opening line of the *Voyage* is "There was a boy called Eustace Clarence Scrubb, and he almost deserved it" (p. 1), and the story is, in fact, what we used to call a *Bildungsroman*—a "growing-up" novel. So the first of the series, *The Lion, the Witch, and the Wardrobe*, was designed as a kind of fairy-tale children's story after the "manner of E. Nesbit," and the second, *Prince Caspian*, was a children's version of an Edwardian adventure story. This one, *The Voyage of the "Dawn Treader,"* is a *Bildungsroman* which is also a children's story. The fact is, they are the Chronicles of Narnia;

they are all part of the same story, involving the same set of characters (though serially); they are all children's books; but they are not all the same kind of book. So let's look now in more detail at *The Voyage of the "Dawn Treader."* And we'll begin by quoting a preface to one of G.A. Henty's books for boys. In *The Young Buglers*, he writes in his preface (addressed to "My dear lads"),

> I remember that, as a boy, I regarded any attempt to mix instruction with amusement as being as objectionable a practice as the administration of powder in jam; but I think that this feeling arose from the fact that in those days books contained a very small share of amusement and a very large share of instruction. I have endeavoured to avoid this, and I hope that the accounts of battles and sieges . . . will be found as interesting as the lighter parts of the story.

Not too much powder in the jam, not too much "grown-up" stuff woven with the purer fabric of childhood (or young-adulthood), or else Olympus will be rearing its head in Arcady. But can there be a *Bildungsroman*, a "growing up" novel, that does not permit Olympus to rear its ugly (or even a snow-capped) head? Well, yes. The trick is to maintain the atmosphere of the children's story, or at least the fairy-tale. How? Well, a dragon or two wouldn't be a bad thing, at least not in this context. But there is also—and this is what Lewis does, and I think does well—the possibility of writing in a way the child (or very young adult, or "teenager") will most appreciate. Let me begin by quoting the scene with the picture on the wall at Uncle Harold and Aunt Alberta's house.

> "It's a rotten picture," said Eustace. "You won't see it if you step outside," said Edmund. "Why do you like it?" said Eustace to Lucy. "Well, for one thing," said Lucy, "I like it because the ship looks as if it was really moving. And the water looks as if it was really wet. And the waves look as if they were really going up and down." Of course Eustace knew lots of answers to this, but he didn't say anything. The reason was that at that very moment he looked at the waves and saw that they did look very much indeed as if they were going up and down. He had only once been on a ship (and then only to the Isle of Wight) and had been horribly seasick. The look of the waves in the picture made him feel sick again. (p. 6) (A ship to the Isle of Wight would be something like a ship from Cape Cod to Martha's Vineyard, or perhaps Nantucket—not a long voyage, and to a summer resort.)

The waves are going up and down, the ship's prow down into the waves and up again, the wind is blowing out of the picture, the seawater splashes out of the picture, and soon Lucy and Edmund and Eustace are drawn into the picture and find themselves in the sea alongside the "Dawn Treader," from which they are rescued by Caspian, now three years older than when we left him at the end of *Prince Caspian*. But notice the interplay between and among Edmund and Lucy and Eustace, and the humor (at least the intended humor) in it. In fact, what Lewis has done to appeal to his readers is to tell the story humorously, as was done by Ruskin and Thackeray and Lang and E. Nesbit. And throughout the story, he keeps the tone very much at this level. And yet this is a story of Eustace's growing up—real growing up, real change, really ceasing to be "that record stinker, Eustace." Dragons have a way, it would appear, of concentrating the process of change (like the Remora and the Firedrake in *Prince Prigio*), and at the same time, it seems that, if you can manage dragons and humor together, you can keep your reader's attention on that process.

When they are hauled aboard, Caspian calls out, "Hey! Rynelf, bring spiced wine for their majesties" (*Voyage*, p. 10), which—by using the word "majesties"—leads to an auctorial aside to the effect that when the Pevensies had returned to Narnia (in *Prince Caspian*), it was "as if King Arthur came back to Britain as some people say he will. And I say the sooner the better" (p. 10)—which says something—quite a bit—about what was in Lewis's mind when he was writing the books. King Arthur leads us into the distinction, later on, between History and Chronicle, and what in Lewis's writing, has helped make the whole set of "Nanioa" books successful.

The spiced wine also leads Eustace, on swallowing the wine, to make faces, and spit it out, and get sick again, and ask for Plumptree's Vitaminised Nerve Food, made with distilled water—"and anyway he insisted on being put ashore at the next station" (p. 10). Hot spiced wine is, of course, associated with winter festivities—including Christmas—while Plumptree's Vitaminised Nerve Food (with or without distilled water) is an object of fun, or at least here it is. Eustace, on seeing the valiant Reepicheep, Chief Mouse, Knight of the Order of the Lion, calls him a horrid thing and says he can't stand performing animals. Reepicheep is about to challenge him to a duel, when Lucy sneezes, and Caspian gets the three children below to dry off and put on dry clothes. Now Reepicheep may have his origins in the long-ago days of Boxen, but Eustace is a Thackeray caricature. In fact, he sent me at one point to the *Book of Snobs*, but I cannot report any great exploratory success.

We find out that Caspian is going voyaging to seek out the seven Lords of Narnia, the last loyalists to Caspian's father (and thus to the child Caspian), whom Miraz sent off to explore the unknown Eastern Seas beyond the Lone Islands. These are the Lords Revilian, Bern, Argoz, Mavramorn, Octesian, Restimar, and Rhoop. It may be remembered from *Prince Caspian* that Miraz had gotten rid of other loyalists in other ways—Belisar and Uvilas were shot with arrows on a hunting party; the great house of the Passarids died all in fighting giants on the Northern frontiers; Arlian and Erlimon and a dozen others were executed on trumped-up charges of treason; the two brothers of Beaversdam he shut up as madmen—though they never apparently reappear after Miraz's death.

The names are a remarkable mix: Belisar (Belisarius) and Uvilas (Ulfilas) come from the Later Roman Empire; the Passarids sound like they are from late Graeco-Persian days; Mavramorn is Greek (I believe), Rhoop could be pseudo-Welsh; Octesian is Roman or pseudo-Roman; Bern is Anglo-Saxon (or something like it); Revilian and Restimar and Arlian and Erlimon have a French Medieval sound to them (and go with Caspian and Drinian and Rilian and Turian). The one thing they have in common is that they seem to come from the border time between (someone's) Classical culture and (someone's) Middle Ages. They all suggest a time like our past, even though these are in the year twenty-three hundred in Narnia. They also suggest countries south and east of England (or Narnia).

Lucy uses her cordial to cure Eustace's seasickness, and after finally being convinced he cannot be instantaneously returned to his parents' house in Cambridge, he puts on Narnian clothes, and becomes a most reluctant participant in the voyage of the *Dawn Treader*. And he keeps a diary (which, of course, is appropriate to a *Bildungsroman,* though unusual for a children's story, at least in those days). It begins August 7th and its point is, as we would expect, that the way Eustace sees things is not the way we are to see things. And it introduces his "trouble with Reepicheep" in which he picks Reepicheep up by the tail and swings him around, only to have Reepicheep draw his sword and jab Eustace in his hand, then pick himself up off the deck and chase Eustace into the presence of Caspian and Edmund and Lucy sitting at table. When Eustace finally realizes that the others take Reepicheep's challenging him to a duel very seriously indeed, he apologizes with bad grace, and there begins the first of the island visits that make up the voyaging part of *The Voyage of the "Dawn Treader."* This is the visit to Felimath (an Island of Sheep where the three children and Reepicheep are kidnapped by Pug, the slave trader) and Doorn and Avra (where Lord Bern has settled at Bernstead).

These are North Sea or Scottish islands, and the Isle of Sheep may come from John Buchan. After Bern buys Caspian from Pug, he recognizes him, does homage to him, and helps him land on Doorn as the King and remove the governor Gumpas from office. (Which gives us the scene in which one of Gumpas's secretaries says "'suppose all you gentlemen stop play-acting and we do a little business. The question before us really is—" 'The question is,' said the Duke, 'whether you and the rest of the rabble will leave without a flogging or with one'" (p. 48). And then, when all this has been pleasantly settled, and after feasting and High Holiday, the *Dawn Treader* is towed out of Narrowhaven harbor and is out to sea again. But after a short time there is a great storm.

> There came an evening when Lucy, gazing idly astern at the long furrow or wake they were leaving behind them, saw a great rack of clouds building itself up in the west with amazing speed. Then a gap was torn in it and a yellow sunset poured through the gap. All the waves behind them seemed to take on unusual shapes and the sea was a drab or yellowish color like dirty canvas. The air grew cold. The ship seemed to move uneasily as if she felt danger behind her. The sail would be flat and limp one minute and wildly full the next . . . The hatches were battened down, the galley fire was put out, men went aloft to reef the sail. Before they had finished the storm struck them. It seemed to Lucy that a great valley in the sea opened just before their bows, and they rushed down into it, deeper down than she would have believed possible . . . (p. 56).

The storm goes on so long—eighteen days—they cannot turn back and expect to make it with their supplies left on board: what happens next is introduced by passages from Eustace's diary for September 3rd through September 11th. The entry for September 11th is the last in Eustace's diary, for reasons we learn as we go on. The entry (in full) reads (p. 62):

> Caught some fish and had them for dinner. Dropped anchor at about 7 P.M. in three fathoms of water in a bay of this mountainous island. That idiot Caspian wouldn't let us go ashore because it was getting dark and he was afraid of savages and wild beasts. Extra water ration tonight.

After which Eustace forgot about keeping a diary for a long time. After they landed on the island, he slipped away from the others, climbed a high ridge (showing his time in Narnia had improved him physically) so that he could look down, was caught in a thick fog, tried to find his way back, and slipped and slid into an entirely unknown valley. And not unlike like Lewis's Elwin Ransom in the caves under Perelandra, he has found his way into a place by sheer luck, and cannot see his way clear to getting out (or like Buchan's Davie in *Prester John*). But that turns out to be not the greatest of his worries.

> At the bottom of the cliff, a little on his left hand was a low dark hole—the entrance to a cave, perhaps. And out of this two thin wisps of smoke were coming. And the loose stones just beneath the dark hollow were moving (that was the noise he had heard) just as if something were crawling in the dark behind them. Something was crawling. Worse still, something was coming out. Edmund or Lucy or you would have recognized it at once, but Eustace had read none of the right books. (p. 69)

It is, of course, a dragon, and as it turns out, it is just about to die. The dragon dies, Eustace crawls down to the dragon's pool to drink, the rain falls ("such rain as one never sees in Europe"), Eustace crawls into the dragon's cave, puts a diamond arm ring on his arm, and falls asleep on the dragon's horde. Meanwhile, back at the landing place the others are searching for him, but before they get very far, it is morning, Eustace has awakened to find himself a dragon (sleeping on the dragon's hoard with dragonish thoughts in his mind—the scene in which he recognizes this fact is well done, I think), and eventually, that night, he flies over the ridge and comes down near the landing place. "'We must all show great constancy,' Caspian was saying. 'A dragon has just flown over the tree-tops and lighted on the beach. Yes, I am afraid it is between us and the ship. . . .' 'With your Majesty's leave—' began Reepicheep.' 'No, Reepicheep,' said the King very firmly, 'you are not going to attempt a single combat with it.'"

As you will recall, they determine the dragon is friendly, and Lucy notices the arm ring cutting into its foreleg, applies her cordial (which doesn't apparently work perfectly for dragons), then Caspian sees it is the Lord Octesian's arm ring, and they ask the dragon (who cannot speak but can nod) whether he is the Lord Octesian, then whether he is someone else enchanted, then whether he is Eustace. And, of course, he is. He tries to write his story on the sand for them, but dragon-claws aren't made for writing, and in any case, Eustace had "never read the right books" and had no idea how to tell his story. He had read books full of pictures of grain elevators and fat foreign children doing exercises (books common enough at the time—I recall a contemporary of mine who had visions of millions and millions of Communist Chinese children doing calisthenics in blue uniforms, or was it blue snowsuits—in any case there were in those days lots of very dull schoolbooks of precisely that kind, but not books useful for telling about being a dragon).

Eventually, Aslan rips and peels off Eustace's dragon skin and he bathes in the Sacred Pool and is un-dragoned. He begins to be "a different boy" (which he is, of course, in his new and different skin), and when he is un-dragoned, and no one wants the Lord Octesian's arm ring, they toss it up, flashing in the sun's light, and it catches and hangs "as neatly as a well-thrown quoit," on a projection in the rock, and "there, for all I know, it is hanging still and may hang till that world ends" (p. 93). It may seem far-fetched, but I hear an echo.

In Buchan's *Prester John* (which is echoed in *Perelandra* and in Eustace in the valley of the dragon), after Laputa has put Prester John's collar around his neck and plunged into the Labongo, Davie Craufurd muses (p. 224), "Far from human quest, he sleeps his last sleep and perchance on a fragment of bone washed into a crevice of rock there may hang the jewels that once gleamed in Sheba's hair." The jewels hanging on the rock till the world's end—and I believe Lewis had that vision at the back of his mind, to be called forth here. And after that vision, the story changes, as in *Prester John.*

Up to this point it has essentially been Eustace's growing up, but now the corner is turned, and we go back to the Odyssey and Saint Brendan. To be sure, these navigations are pilgrimages: certainly the *Odyssey* and the *Navigatio Sancti Brendani* can be taken in that way. Indeed, the word "pilgrim" in Elizabethan times has a general sense of traveler or even wayfarer. In Ralegh's *Passionate Pilgrim* it has its old sense as in Lydgate—the travel (or travail) through life. Ralegh would not have described his voyages, traffiques [traffickings?], explorations, or discoveries as pilgrimages, nor would Richard Hakluyt, who chronicled *The Principall Voyages, Traffiques, Explorations, and Discoveries of the British Nation.* But in the next generation, when Samuel Purchas published the follow-up, *Hakluytus Posthumus,* he subtitled it *Purchas His Pilgrims.* (And who had been reading and writing about Ralegh and Hakluyt and Purchas about the time of *The Voyage of the "Dawn Treader"*?—Lewis, of course, for his *English Literature in the Sixteenth Century, Excluding Drama.*)

On this question of pilgrimage, we may recall that Professor W.P. Ker once remarked that *The Pilgrim's Progress* (most famous of English pilgrimages) "has the same plan which saves even some of the dull romances from total failure, and is found in some of the best. It is the simplest thing in the world; scarcely to be called a plot—merely a journey with adventures. Yet what more is wanted to give the romancer his opportunity? It is one of the things that never grow old, from Theseus and Jason to Sir Percival, and so on to the *Pilgrim's Progress* and so to modern examples" (Ker, *Romance*, English Association Pamphlet, 1909).

Let us look a little further toward this matter of the pilgrimage in English literature. It has perhaps three principal incarnations before the English Renaissance, by which incarnations I believe it entered into the English common mind. The three incarnations are the framework (though not the tales) of Chaucer's *Canterbury Tales*, Lydgate's *Pilgrimage of the Lyfe of Man* (which is partly or mostly Deguileville's *Pélèrinage de la Vie Humaine*), and Langland's *Piers Plowman*. These are, of course, three very different poems, with three very different uses of the pilgrimage. Chaucer takes advantage of the fourteenth-century longing "to go on on pilgrimages" as a *motif* and linkage for his *Canterbury Tales*. But the pilgrimage is prologue and framework. Lydgate's pilgrimage is an allegory of the human soul or life of the soul: it descends from the ancient tradition of the *psychomachia*, and it is peopled with abstractions. In Bunyan, the *pélèrinage de la vie humaine* is the engine (so to speak) driving Christian's adventures, but it is the characters of the fellow pilgrims (as with Chaucer) and of those in the fair field full of folk (as with Langland) that give them life.

And there is a ferly "of faery" (in Langland's words) there in Bunyan also. Remember the Enchanted Ground (in Book II of *Pilgrim's Progress*). Remember the opening: "As I walked through the wilderness of this world, I lighted on a certain place, where was a den, and I laid me down in that place to sleep, and as I slept I dreamed a dream." And we recall that Lewis avidly read Chaucer, and Langland (so did Rudyard Kipling), and Bunyan. So we could reasonably expect to find that the rest of the story is a pilgrimage (journeying, navigation) that is also a *psychomachia*, where the principal difference between the growing-up of Eustace (up to p. 94) and the rest of the story is that, now Eustace is sufficiently changed to be part of the band of pilgrims, we have all of them involved in the story—beginning with the discovery of the coracle (which recalls Saint Brendan), and then going on to the narrow escape from the sea-serpent (when Eustace breaks Caspian's second-best sword), and then onto the island where they find the pool that turns all things to gold (including, as it happens, the Lord Restimar).

In all of these, Eustace plays a full (if not always distinguished) part. Next comes the Island of the Voices, which is the island of the Monopods (who may be found, of all places, I have been told, in St. Augustine) or "Dufflepuds." These are one of Lewis's better comic creations, though we should not allow their comicality to blind us to the pattern here, where the Chief Voice demands that the "little girl" (Lucy) go upstairs in the big house to find the Magician's book and read aloud the spell to make the "Voices" visible, because it can only be done by a little girl. (And Ransom must make his space-voyage because the Oyarsa of Malacandra has demanded that a human be brought to him, and the original scheme for *The Voyage of the "Dawn Treader"* had in it a child to be brought into the past because a king in the past needs blood from a boy in the far future—first any human, then only a child.)

So we have the child as ransom, and we have the big house. And then, when Lucy goes upstairs, and reads the spell (after eavesdropping by magic on two of her schoolmates—by magic, but it's still eavesdropping), not only the Monopods but also Aslan become visible—though Aslan has been prefigured by the Chief Voice's words about the Magician, who "always did go about with his bare feet on, making no more noise than a great big cat" (p. 119).

In looking through the Magician's book, Lucy finds a wonderful story (but the pages go blank as soon as she turns them over)—a story so good that "ever since that day what Lucy means by a good story is a story which reminds her of the forgotten story in the Magician's Book" (p. 133). And she asks Aslan (p. 136), "'Shall I ever be able to read that story again, the one I couldn't remember? Will you tell it to me, Aslan? Oh do, do, do.' 'Indeed, yes, I will tell it to you for years and years. But now, come. We must meet the master of this house.'"

So, having restored the "Dufflepuds" to visibility, they meet Coriakin, the Magician (sent to govern the Dufflepuds, as we later find out, as a punishment for a star's faults); after a meal he creates a map from Drinian's story of their voyage (two copies, one for the voyagers); he mends the "Dawn Treader" where damaged by the sea serpent; and thereafter they set sail from the Magician's island, twelve days east with a gentle wind, and then into smooth solid blackness. They sail into the Darkness, the Blackness of Darkness (Jude 13), and therein rescue the Lord Rhoop, tattered and torn, from the island where dreams come true—"This is where dreams—dreams, do you understand—come to life, come real. Not daydreams; dreams" (p. 156). (We recall that Lewis, earlier in his life, was haunted by nightmares.) And as they try to sail out of the Darkness, Lucy breathes a prayer to Aslan, and there comes a light.

"At first it looked like a cross, then it looked like an aeroplane, then it looked like a kite, and at last with a whirring of wings it was right overhead and was an albatross" (p. 159)—I suppose that same albatross that came to Coleridge's Ancient Mariner: "At length did cross an

Albatross, / Thorough the fog it came; / As if it had been a Christian soul, / We hailed it in God's name. / . . . / In mist or cloud, on mast or shroud, / It perched for vespers nine; / Whiles all the night, through fog-smoke white, / Glimmered the white Moon-shine."

There may be other places where the albatross is a type or representation of Christ, but this is the best known, from a voyage very famous in literature (and perhaps Lewis's readers in Britain might catch the reference, though fewer American readers would). Then, when they succeed in leaving the Dark Island, promising Rhoop never to ask him what happened there, the voyagers come in sight of land on their starboard bow, sail along its coast to a wide and shallow bay, anchoring a good way from the beach (like Buenos Ayres?—only they land by boat, not cart), and coming ashore find great towers ("'It might be giants,' said Edmund in a lower voice" p. 165), and in the great oblong space surrounded by them find a long table on which is set out such a banquet as they had never seen, and at the table three sleepers, who turn out to be the Lords Revilian, Argoz, and Mavramorn. The voyagers take places at the table, not eating, until a "tall girl dressed in a single long garment of clear blue" (p. 171) tells them the enchanted sleepers never ate the food—they are enchanted (because one caught up the Knife of Stone brought there after the Witch used it to kill Aslan), but the food is not enchanted.

The girl is Ramandu's daughter; Ramandu is a retired star made younger each day by the fire-berries brought each day from the sun by the sun-birds (this comes out of Andrew Lang, I think); and the enchantment of the three lords will be broken when a ship sails to the World's End and there leaves one of the crew—which, of course, is what Reepicheep wants, seeking the Utter East. So they plan to start off for the World's End, but the crew are reluctant. Rynelf reminds them that when they left, "'there were some standing on the quay who would have given all they had to come with us. It was thought a finer thing then to have a cabin-boy's berth on the "Dawn Treader" than to wear a knight's belt'" (p. 183). And then Caspian gives a speech reminiscent of Crispin Crispian.

We will choose those who may come with us, he says. "'Why, every man that comes with us shall bequeath the title of Dawn Treader to all his descendants and when we land at Cair Paravel on the homeward voyage he shall have either gold or land enough to make him rich all his life. . . .'" (p. 185) And I hear a voice saying, "'He that shall live this day and comes safe home, / Will stand a-tiptoe when this day is named, / And rouse him at the name of Crispian" (*Henry V*, Act IV, scene iii, ll. 42–44)

. . . "And Crispin Crispian shall ne'er go by / From this day to the ending of the earth / But we in it shall be rememberéd /—We few, we happy
few, we band of brothers. . . ." (ll. 58–61). So they go on to the Utter
East, where Reepicheep tastes the sweet water, they see the Mer-people,
Edmund and Eustace and Lucy land at the edge of Aslan's Country,
Caspian wants to go with them and with Reepicheep seeking the World's
End, until Edmund threatens to put him under arrest (as with Odysseus
and the Sirens) and then Aslan appears to him, and he gives up his will
to Aslan. Reepicheep goes off in the coracle, and Edmund and Lucy and
Eustace enter Aslan's Country, and there is the Milk-White Lamb . . .
and then they are back in the bedroom in Cambridge where the picture
of the "Dawn Treader" was on the wall in the beginning, and Eustace is
a changed boy.

Which brings us to *The Silver Chair*, which is dedicated to Nicholas
Hardie, son of fellow-Inkling Colin Hardie (1906–1998), and, among
the questions originally proposed at the beginning, brings us to the question, *What exactly is the real world?* Before we get to that question, we
can enjoy the way Lewis sets the scene at Experiment House, the
embodiment, I should say, of all the things that in Lewis's view, could be
wrong with modern education. And that, recalling his strictures in *The
Abolition of Man*, and at least in "Screwtape Proposes a Toast"—not to
mention other clues along the way—is saying quite a bit. True, he has
brought the description of the Headmistress (including what happens to
her in the end) back out of the discarded Lefay fragment (where it
described Aunt Gertrude)—but then, some dishes are better on the second day, warmed over. In any case, the description of Experiment House
is simply the introduction to the gate in the wall into Narnia.

Eustace falls off the great cliff they come to (Jill might just as well
have pushed him, since he fell trying to pull her back when she was
showing off), and is blown away on the Lion's breath. Jill finds a stream
of running water—and there is the Lion (pp. 15–16):

> "Will you promise not to—do anything to me, if I do come?" said Jill. "I
> make no promise," said the Lion. Jill was so thirsty now that, without notic-
> ing it, she had come a step nearer. "Do you eat girls?" she said. "I have swal-
> lowed up girls and boys, women and men, kings and emperors, cities and
> realms," said the Lion. It didn't say this as if it were boasting, nor as if it
> were sorry, nor as if it were angry. It just said it. (p. 17)

There is something Roman here in the simple declarative, as in (for
example) the obituary lines of the Emperor Diocletian, "Pastor arator

eques pavi colui superavi / Capras rus hostes . . ." ("As shepherd, farmer, knight, I've pastured, tilled, subdued, herds, farms and enemies . . ."—I owe the reference to my friend, the late Russell Kirk). Or, again, the simple declarative of the Roman epitaph, "Saltavit. Placuit. Mortuus est" (which Benét translated as "He danced with me. He could dance rather well. He is dead"). No excess words, and, in this way, a very Classical lion. Finally Jill drinks, and after she tells Aslan that Eustace fell off the cliff because she was showing off, he tells her that he has blown Eustace into Narnia, but her own task is the harder for what she did.

He gives her a task, "'that you seek this lost Prince until either you have found him and brought him to his father's house, or else died in the attempt, or else gone back into your own world'" (p. 19), and he gives her four Signs to guide her in her—their—quest. Eustace will see an old friend and must greet him; she must go north to the city of the ancient giants; she must do what the writing tells her; and, fourth, the lost Prince will be the first person she meets in her travels who will ask her to do something in Aslan's name.

Aslan warns her that "'the Signs which you have learned here will not look at all as you expect them to look, when you meet them there'" (p. 21). As we know, when Jill and Eustace saw the splendid ship departing Cair Paravel, Eustace did not recognize the ancient and doddering King as Caspian, his friend, and Caspian set sail without Eustace having spoken to him. One Sign muffed.

But after a Parliament of Owls (shades of Chaucer!), Eustace and Jill set off into Ettinsmoor to find the ruined city of the giants, guided first by Glimfeather the Owl (and Jill sees without realizing the cause that Eustace is already growing strong in the Narnian air, a carryover from his long-ago adventures with Caspian) to find Puddleglum the Marsh-wiggle to guide them and go with them. In the night they arrive at the wigwam of a marsh-wiggle. ("Wigwam" I suppose because "Marsh-wiggle.")

Puddleglum the Marsh-wiggle is the only character in any of Lewis's fiction recognizably based on a real person, specifically Fred Paxford, Lewis's gardener. The name Puddleglum almost certainly comes from a line in John Studley's 1570s translation of the Senecan *Hippolytus*, where the phrase Tacitae Stygis is translated as "Stygian puddle glum" (*English Literature in the Sixteenth Century, Excluding Drama*, p. 256). The creature with its conical hat and froglike skin and marsh-weedy hair comes from Lewis's imagination, but the voice is Paxford's: "'Good morning, Guests,' it said. 'Though when I say good I don't mean it won't probably turn to rain or it might be snow, or fog, or thunder. You didn't get any sleep, I dare say'" (p. 58). But he goes with Jill and Eustace, across the River Shribble, to the Ettinsmoor—where they see the Silent Knight and his Green Lady, and the Lady directs them to the castle of the gentle Giants at Harfang, where they are to say they have been sent for the Autumn Feast; snow comes and they fall into what seem to be some trenches, and then they glimpse the lights of Harfang.

Of course, afterwards, when they look down on the trenches from above, they see they were in the letters of "Under Me" and they have muffed the next two signs, leaving only one. They are brought into the castle and Puddleglum takes several drafts from the Giants' bottle to warm up, and is then quite drunk. "A very respectable Marsh-wiggle. Respectowiggle . . . Nothing wrong with me . . . Not a frog. Nothing frog with me. I'm a respectabiggle" (p. 93). They are carried into the King and Queen, then put to bed, and in the night Jill dreams (if it was a dream) that Aslan has brought her to the window and shown her that the rocks through which they were struggling the night before and the trenches the letters "Under Me"—and in the morning she looks down and there are the second and third Signs, the ruined city and the directions.

Somehow (Jill doing splendidly here) they get through the day and find in the kitchen the Giant's cookbook opened to the page telling how to prepare "Man" and "Marsh-wiggle."—and make a bolt to leave the castle, which they do, but to avoid the Giants out on a hunting party they dive into a crack and slide down in the cave below, where they are discovered and seized by the Warden of the Marches of Underland. "'Many fall down, and few return to the sunlit lands,' said the voice. 'Make ready now to come with me to the Queen of the Deep Realm.' 'What does she want with us?' asked Scrubb cautiously. 'I do not know,' said the voice. 'Her will is not to be questioned but obeyed'" (*The Silver Chair*, p. 122).

The creatures of the Underworld are revealed in a cold grey-blue light. of all sizes, tailed and tail-less, with noses long and short and blobby, heads horned or with no horn, faces bearded or smooth, but all pale, still, and sad. The Warden with his Underworlders padding along takes them past sleeping beasts (mostly dragon-ish) who have found their way down under ("Many come down, and few return to the sunlit lands," p. 126). They see an enormous man, asleep, white-bearded, with a pure silver light resting on him: "'That is old Father Time, who was once a king in Overland.' said the Warden, 'And now he has sunk down into the Deep Realm and lies dreaming of all the things that are done in the Upper World. Many sink down, and few return to the sunlit lands. They say he will wake at the end of the world'" (p. 127).

Then into a cave where a strip of pale sand runs down to still water, and there is a jetty, and beside it a many-oared ship. Puddleglum asks if anyone from Overland has ever made this trip before. "'Many have taken ship at the pale beaches,' replied the Warden, 'and few . . .'"—at which point Puddleglum finishes for him, "'And few return to the sunlit land'" (p. 127). (The Tacitae Stygis, I think—the River Styx, the "Puddle Glum" in old John Studley's country speech translating Seneca.)

They are brought to the Green Castle of the Queen of the Deep Realm and are to be kept imprisoned there till the Queen returns, but from above they hear the voice of a young man, a Prince, who turns out to have been the Knight in Black accompanying the Green Lady who directed them to Harfang. He tells them of the Queen's plans to set him on the throne of the Overworld, breaking out from below with a thousand Earthmen: before long they are heartily tired of his conversation, but when he tells them it is the hour when fits come upon him and he must be bound in his chair by the Earthmen, they choose to remain rather than be imprisoned to await the Queen's return They hide in the next room while he is bound, then return to keep him company, vowing that nothing he says can make them release him—until, as we half expect (p. 145), "'Once and for all,' said the prisoner, 'I adjure you to set me free. By all fears and all loves, by the bright skies of Overland, by the great Lion, by Aslan himself, I charge you'"

It is the fourth Sign, and after hesitation, and fearing death, they cut him loose, he seizes his sword and destroys the silver chair in which he has been bound He is, of course, Prince Rilian, and then, as they are planning their escape, the Green Lady returns and seeks to re-enchant them with incense and incantations. Puddleglum to the rescue! As they are succumbing to the incense and enchantment, he stamps his foot in the fire, changing the incense to the smell of burnt marsh-wiggle, their minds clear, and at the end, the Witch (for the Green Lady is indeed a Witch) turns into the serpent which had slain Prince Rilian's mother (that would be Ramandu's daughter) years before. Let me give you a description of such a change:

> But now the very color of her skin was changing; it became blotched and blurred with black and yellow and green; not only that, but it seemed distended about her. The face rounded out till it was perfectly smooth, with no hollows or depressions, and from her nostrils and her mouth, something was thrusting out. In and out of her neck and hands another skin was forming, over or under her own. . . . Another and an inhuman tongue was flickering out over a human face, and the legs were twisted and thrown from side to

> side as if something prisoned in them were attempting to escape. . . . Her arms were interlocked in front of her, the extreme ends of her fingers touched the ground between her thighs. But they too were drawn inwards; the stuff of her dress was rending in places; and wherever it rent and hung aside he could see that other curiously-toned skin shining behind it. . . . No longer a woman. but a serpent indeed surged before him in the darkening room, bursting and breaking from the woman's shape behind it.

No, as you will recognize, that is not the description of the Green Witch as she is taking her serpent's shape in *The Silver Chair*. It is instead Dora Wilmot taking her true serpent's shape in Charles Williams's *The Place of the Lion* (Eerdmans ed., pp. 151–52), and it reminds us that the Beasts in Narnia are, in a way, Platonic Forms or perhaps elementals—and that *The Place of the Lion* made a huge impression on Lewis when he first read it back in 1936.

So the Prince slays the Green Witch in her serpent's form, and they go out from the castle—to find a riot of sound and the roof lit by fires from the lands still further under. The enchantment that held the Earthmen silent in what they think of as the Shallow Lands is broken by the Witch's death, and they are returning to the Land of Bism (Abysm) still further under. For those interested in Lewis's sources and analogues, we can say we have moved from Charles Williams and the Platonic elementals to George MacDonald and Curdie and the gnomes in the caverns of the mines, and even back to Novalis and the foundations of German Romanticism with the Bergmann, the miner, and an acknowledgment that the true Spirit of the mountains inhabits not their heights but the deeps under them. I recall that the number (or absence) of fingers and toes on the goblins in the Curdie books was a matter of interest to the miners, and indeed the Earthmen in the Underlands are not at all unlike the goblins in the Curdie books—except, of course, that the gnomes turn out to be friendly, once released from their enchantment, while the goblins are not.

It is in Novalis we first find the idea to which Lewis gives allegiance here—that the true spirit of the earth lies way down. Here is the gnome Golg speaking to Jill (*The Silver Chair*, p. 182). "'Yes,' said Golg, 'I have heard of those little scratches in the crust that you Top-dwellers call mines. But that's where you get dead gold, dead silver, dead gems, Down in Bism we have them alive and growing. There I'll pick you bunches of rubies that you can eat and squeeze you a cup full of diamond-juice. You won't care much about fingering the cold dead treasures of your shallow mines after you have tasted the live ones of Bism.'"

Shortly thereafter he dives through the narrowing crack into Bism below, and then (p. 184), "with a shock like a thousand goods [= freight] trains crashing into a thousand pairs of buffers, the lips of rock closed." And Rilian and Puddleglum and Jill and Eustace go on past the dying lamps, with the water rising, up toward the Overworld, reaching earth rather than rock with a cold light above: Jill gets up on Puddleglum's shoulders, reaches through the hole into the Overworld—and disappears.

Her first glimpse through the whole shows fauns and dryads dancing on the moonlit snow—that's the cold light—and just as she's crying out for help, a snowball thrown by a Dwarf gets her fair and square on the mouth. But she makes herself heard, and the revelers (for it is the Great Snow Dance of Narnia) dig away the hillside, and first Eustace (striking about with his sword), then Puddleglum, asnd then Rilian come out into Narnia. All the noise dies away into silence "as the noise dies away in a rowdy dormitory if the Headmaster opens the door" (p. 199) when they see the Prince.

Even those who do not know him, even those who do not remember his father in his youth, recognize in him the look that is "in the face of all true kings of Narnia, who rule by will of Aslan and sit at Cair Paravel in the throne of Peter the High King" (p. 199). And then there is a great tying-up of loose ends, and they all return to Cair Paravel, to which Caspian's ship is also returning, Jill and Eustace riding centaur-back. Rilian awaits his father, who is carried off the ship in a litter, raises his hand to bless his son, and dies, and there begins a keening funeral music—and then, behind Eustace and Jill, there is a deep voice:

> "I have come" . . . They turned and saw the Lion himself, so bright and real and strong that everything else began at once to look pale and shadowy compared with him. And . . . he opened his mouth wide and blew. But this time they had no sense of flying through the air: instead, it seemed that they remained still, and the wild breath of Aslan blew away the ship and the dead King and the castle and the snow and the winter sky. For all these things floated off into the air like wreathes of smoke, and suddenly they were standing in a great brightness of mid-summer sunshine, on smooth turf, among mighty trees. (pp. 210–11)

The funeral music for King Caspian goes on, and "there, on the golden gravel of the bed of the stream, lay King Caspian dead" (p. 211), but Aslan weeps three great tears and tells Eustace to drive a foot-long thorn into his paw, and there came a great drop of blood, "redder than all redness you have ever seen or imagined" (p. 212), and by the tears and the blood, Caspian rises from the stream-bed no longer white-bearded and frail, but a young man in joy, who turns to Eustace and says (p. 213) "Eustace! So you did reach the end of the world after all! What about my second best sword that you broke on the sea serpent?" And there is the comic line again, the *buffo* amid the *serio* as Mikhail Bakhtin would have it in his study of carnival. I think we might take this opportunity to say a little more than we have said on this subject of carnival in children's literature.

The comic and the fantastic are both types of carnival, in the Bakhtinian sense. Fantasy and humor need not be, and humor (in the English "sense of humor" sense) is in fact unlikely to be. It should be emphasized that these distinctions and definitions are here drawn and made very much in an English context, though the distinction between carnival and order is worldwide, and the distinction between the release of the fantastic and the release of the comic arguably applies as widely. This distinction between carnival and order has some affinities with Kenneth Grahame's distinction between the Arcadians (who are frequently children) and the Olympians (who are frequently adults). In the early Victorian period in England (1837–1861), the point of linkage between the two frequently occurs at Christmas, in the so-called Christmas books of such authors as Dickens and Thackeray.

It is far from accidental that Thackeray's *The Rose and The Ring* was published as a Christmas Book, and indeed the Victorian institution of Christmas is one of the few examples of Victorian carnival. In his story of Scrooge, as certainly in his earliest work, Dickens enters that realm of carnival, of *bouleversement*, of suspension of normal rules: the very name of Scrooge has the sound of carnival, and while the story is comedic (in Northrop Frye's sense), it is told very much in the comic vein. Of course, it too is a Christmas book. (I pass over here the possibility of considering *A Christmas Carol* as an apology for Old England against the descendants of Puritans bearing such given names as Jacob and Ebenezer.)

Dickens and (especially) Thackeray took advantage of the lingering aspects of carnival in the early Victorian Christmas, finding a way in which to present to the Victorian audience a work both comic and fantastic, but with the comic taking precedence. Forty years later, with that route apparently closed, Andrew Lang sidesteps into comedy (in Frye's sense) and humor, both creatures of order; and he treats the fantastic as though it were merely the fantastical. This is perhaps the inverse of the humor of exaggeration, and not unlike what Dunsany did later (as perhaps also in Kipling's *Just-So Stories*, which have an influence on Dunsany). It requires some realism of technique and involves the humor of observation applied to the unreal—as with Prigio's alternately cheering on the Firedrake and the Remora (in *Prince Prigio*), or the townee/schoolboy slanging of Ricardo by the Yellow Dwarf (in *Ricardo of Pantouflia*)—which we might call trash-talking. Also, as Bakhtin has pointed out, carnival is linked to the past.

A precise statement occurs in his discussion of the "privatization" of the comic (*Rabelais and His World*, p. 101): "Limited to the area of the private, the eighteenth-century comic is deprived of its historical color." The first implication of this statement of importance for our purposes (there are at least two others also of importance) is that carnival builds its positive strength on the consciousness of past carnival, and preferably on its continuity with past carnival. In our day, for example, the Herod of *Jesus Christ Superstar* echoes the Herod of the morality plays. To be sure, the Bakhtinian distinction between the culture of order and the culture of carnival, though basic and highly useful (and true), seems to leave out any consideration of what might be called the culture of the numinous.

But Lewis's achievement in the Narnian stories suggests that the numen can dwell in either order or carnival. For we are now, after Caspian's resurrection, suddenly in the culture of carnival. Aslan and Caspian and Eustace in his Narnian armor and with his Narnian sword and Jill in her Narnian clothes, come to the wall of Experiment House. Aslan roars, and thirty foot of wall falls down; he turns his back toward Experiment House, but Jill plies her riding crop and Eustace and Caspian the flats of their swords on the students who were pursuing Jill and Eustace in our world, who flee in terror. The Headmistress sees the fallen wall and the Lion and three glittering figures with weapons, and of course calls the police to find none of what she has reported (for Aslan and Caspian have returned to Aslan's Country and Jill and Eustace have slipped off)—and so she is removed from Experiment House to become first an Inspector of Education and then into Parliament (like Aunt Gertrude in the Lefay fragment) where (Lewis assures us) "she lived happily ever after" (p. 216). It is scarcely accidental that Jill later wears her Narnian finery to a fancy-dress ball (which is also, in our world, a place where order and carnival meet). It is likewise scarcely accidental that we find this carnival in what is essentially a children's pastoral.

The Silver Chair begins with Experiment House and then Aslan's breath (what the Psalms would call God's *ruach*), and ends with Aslan's breath (God's *ruach*) and then Experiment House. The greatest of

Lewis's achievements here, in this fourth book of the "Chronicles" of Narnia, is the blending of carnival and the numinous—but we should see that the book also has roots in the Classical world (thus in Fable, I think), including the Platonic—or, rather, neo-Platonic—world, in German Romanticism and the Fairy-tale (of grim—or Grimm—sorts), in the classic fairy-tale mode (of progression from the familiar to the enchanted), in the Arcadia of Victorian children's stories, and, as we have mentioned, the comicality of the Christmas-book (think, for Thackeray, *Mrs. Perkins's Ball, Our Street, Dr. Birch and His Young Friends, The Kickleburys on the Rhine*, and then finally *The Rose and the Ring*).

And it has origins also in the medieval Quest narrative (as that narrative becomes a type of the later *Märchen*). In fact, though *The Silver Chair*—even to the Giants at Harfang—is the closest thing to pure fairy-tale in all the Narnian stories, there is still a great intermixing. And in a way, it is (in the order of publication) a bridge between the narratives including Lucy (one might call them the "Pevensie" narratives), the first three in the series, and the narratives of the Creation and the Last Things in *The Magician's Nephew* and *The Last Battle*. Of course, there is another link, the reverse *Thousand Nights and a Night* tale of *The Horse and His Boy*, to which we shall shortly turn. But before we make that turn, there is something else to be said here, keeping in mind the importance of mythic patterns.

We are accustomed to think of fairy-tales as those sorts of tales collected by the Brothers Grimm and published in that collection we know as *Grimm's Fairy Tales*—in other words, what John Buchan and others over the years (including Lewis and Tolkien) have called *Märchen*. These are pattern-stories, and it is to Buchan we owe our understanding that the great Victorian novels repeat the *Märchen* patterns. *The Silver Chair* is close to this. But when Lewis was growing up, there was Andrew Lang (1844–1912) and his *Blue Fairy Book* and *Red Fairy Book* and *Green Fairy Book* and *Violet Fairy Book*—and I have forgotten how many others. And these included as "fairy-tales" not only *Märchen* but *contes* and stories out of the *Thousand Nights and a Night* and out of Classical authors and other sources as well. Lang's definition of fairy (many would now say faerie) was wide and in some ways undiscriminating (though I think with an agenda, as we might say). In that sense there are fairy-tale elements throughout the Narnian books. It's just that this is the purest case.

The major study on this point—of what is or is not a fairy-tale—is of course Ronald Tolkien's "On Fairy-Stories" (the Andrew Lang

Eight Children in Narnia

The Making of a Children's Story

Jared Lobdell

LITERATURE / FANTASY / C.S. LEWIS STUDIES

Already a prolific writer and literary scholar with a formidable reputation, C.S. Lewis decided quite late in life to write something completely new to him: a story for children; he drew upon his own childhood memories as well as his literary and philosophical theories to write his *Chronicles of Narnia*, which eventually totaled seven books.

In this path-breaking study of the Narnia books, Jared Lobdell provides fascinating information about the origins of these works and identifies their key influences, motifs, and themes. The result is a new and surprising perspective on Lewis's many-sided creative genius.

"What Jared Lobdell has to say is always worth reading: his writing is personal, reflective, and conversational, but deeply informed and wide-ranging. Here Lobdell delves into the sources of Narnia in C.S. Lewis's bookish childhood, adult appreciation of the fairy tale, and 'essential schoolboyishness', and discovers the mythic truth in the unique Narnian blending of the numinous and the carnival."

—JANET BRENNAN CROFT, Editor of *Mythlore*

JARED LOBDELL is the author of The Rise of Tolkienian Fantasy (2005), The Scientifiction Novels of C.S. Lewis (2004), and The World of the Rings (2004).

Eight Children in Narnia:
The Making of a Children's Story
ISBN 978-0-8126-9901-2
paperbound, vii + 232 pages; trim: 6" x 9"
Index. References.
List Price $49.95
October 2016

Please send two tear sheets of any review or mention to:
Open Court Publishing Company
Attn: Marketing Department
70 East Lake Street, Suite 800, Chicago IL 60601
For additional information on this book, please call
(312) 701-1720 x329, fax (312) 701-1728,
or email dsteele@cricketmedia.com.

Publication Date: 1st O...

Distributed by Perseus/Publishers Group West

www.opencourtbooks.c...

Lecture for 1938). Tolkien rules out travelers' tales, the beast-fable, stories with dream-frames and in the dream tradition, many of the *contes*, retellings of folklore, indeed all stories that do not have at their heart the primal desire for the realization of imagined wonder (in *The Monsters and the Critics and Other Essays,* p. 116). And he goes on to make another point we should note here. Fairy-stories contain old elements that have now by their very age speak to that primal desire—but then, they have probably retained those elements through the ages because they speak to that desire (p. 129).

One does not get a fairy-tale simply by mixing together old elements. But age and the appeal to the past is important in this as in carnival. One further point: The title of the book you are reading (in case you've forgotten amidst all the other that have come into our reflections) is *Eight Children in Narnia*—only of the eight from our world, not (for example) the boy Caspian. Childhood, in Grahame's term, goes with Arcady, but a child's Arcady is likely to be peopled with a child's creatures, and they are likely to have the forms of faerie. And *The Silver Chair* is no less Arcadian, no less pastoral, for being a fairy-tale, or for its carnival—and I remind you, English pastoral (like other comedic forms) ends in judgment and sorting-out. Now we can make the turn to *The Horse and His Boy* and its cry, "For Narnia and the North!" (Note that the Pevensie children here are not immediately from Earth, and though they are there from Earth, it is not as children; they are adults in their Narnian life.)

If *The Silver Chair* is fairy-tale (though not quite like *That Hideous Strength*, a fairy-tale for adults), then *The Horse and His Boy* is—what? And another question—admitting that a book on the Narnia stories ought to cover all the Narnia stories—how can we include *The Horse and His Boy* under the general title *Eight Children in Narnia* when none of the eight is a child in Narnia in *The Horse and His Boy*? But Peter and Edmund and Susan and Lucy are still children in our world when the story takes place and they are in Narnia: the story takes place during the first time in Narnia for all four (Narnian years 1000–1015).

One affirmation of the story of Aravis and Shasta (Cor) in *The Horse and His Boy* is that Narnia is the land of the children's story even when the Pevensies are grown-up in Narnia, just as one lesson of *The Magician's Nephew* is that Narnia is the land of the children's story even before the Pevensies are born in our world. In a sense, *The Horse and His Boy* is a story from Narnian history, one might say a story from *A Child's History of Narnia* (but written, of course, for children in our world). It may also be a story that suggests another book (or perhaps series of books) of the "Chronicles of Archenland."

Here's the problem. We know that the Kings of Archenland descended from Col, younger son of King Frank V of Narnia (*Past Watchful Dragons*, p. 41) who leads his followers into Archenland, then (180 A.N.) uninhabited. The Archenlanders (including the Kings of Archenland) have names like Lune, Col and Colin, Dar and Darrin, Cor and Corin, Olvin, and there is no indication that the line of descent has ever been broken. Why then are the four thrones at Cair Paravel empty—indeed why are there four thrones—inasmuch as the descendants of the first King of Narnia (King Frank I as we learn from *The Magician's Nephew*) are still alive in Archenland? Lewis, whose foster-sister Maureen Moore Blake acceded to the lands and title of (Lady) Dunbar of Hempriggs, was surely aware of the theme of the heir in the wilderness. For a rationalizer and systematizer of history, he seems curiously to be a trifle unsystematic here.

Yes, I know her accession to Dunbar of Hempriggs was after the book was published, but so was his outline of Narnian history printed in *Past Watchful Dragons*.) Well, let that pass. (The outline's derivation of the Calormenes from Archenland outlaws less than a quarter-century after the settlement of Archenland raises other historical questions as well, which we'll also let pass here.) The story we have in *The Horse and His Boy* is probably the closest Narnian approximation to a Boxen story, with a land of Talking Beasts (Animal-Land?) linked to a land of men (India?). It is a good story, I think, taking pretty full advantage of the Arabian Nights world of Calormen and the "barbarian" world to the North. We have already spoken, in an earlier chapter, about the huge impact of the idea of the North on Lewis, and it is worth noting that this is the only one of the Narnian books in which Narnia is specifically linked with the North.

It is also worth noting that this is the book in which the old British idea of "the East" plays a part (though here it's called the South). We should remember that as Britain is northwest of Europe (in our world), so Turkey and Araby and Persia—the lands of the East—are in fact southeast. Whether the carpets of Calormen are Turkish carpets or Persian carpets I cannot say, though my bet would be for Persia. (After all, Jadis and Aslan have Turkish antecedents and they are both northerners to Calormen.) In any case, the diction in Aravis's story-telling is clearly from the *Thousand Nights and a Night* (or the *Arabian Nights*, if you will). And Lewis takes pains to point this out (*The Horse and His Boy*, p. 35, "She's telling it in the grand Calormene manner and no story-teller in a Tisroc's court could do it better"). I think it may be a good idea here to look at this matter of the "eastern" tale at the time Lewis would first have come in touch with it (remembering that Lewis was born in 1898).

As a kind of background here, we may look at a comment by G.K. Chesterton and a story by Saki (H.H. Munro). In a story called "The Wrong Shape" (in *The Innocence of Father Brown*, 1911, reprinted in *The Father Brown Omnibus*, p. 90.), Chesterton's murder victim is an author who has

> attempted . . . to compose . . . tales of tropical heavens . . . of burning gold or blood-red copper; of eastern heroes who rode with twelve-turbaned mitres upon elephants painted purple or peacock green; of gigantic jewels that a hundred Negroes could not carry, but which burned with ancient and strange-hued fires. In short . . . he dealt in eastern heavens, rather worse than most western hells; in eastern monarchs, whom we might possibly call maniacs; and in eastern jewels which a Bond Street jeweler (if the hundred staggering Negroes brought them into his shop) might possibly not regard as genuine.

And Saki wrote a story ("For the Duration of the War") in which his clerical hero, or perhaps antihero, the Reverend Wilfrid Gaspilton, creates Ghurab of Karmanshah, a hunter-poet of the past, and provides his poetry to the *Bi-Monthly Review*, where its "comfortable, slightly quizzical philosophy was certain to be welcome" and where its reception was enthusiastic.

"Elderly colonels, who had outlived the love of truth, wrote to the papers to say that they had been familiar with the works of Ghurab in Afghanistan and Aden, and other suitable localities a quarter of a century ago" (*Saki*, Modern Library ed., p. 602). The point is that in the years before the Great War, the oriental tale (whether far-eastern or near-eastern or in-between-eastern) had become a subject for humor, whether quizzical and ironic as with the Rev. Mr. Gaspilton and his creator, or savage and paradoxical as with Chesterton. In one sense, of course, the quizzicality and paradox were there from the days of *The Thousand Nights and A Night*, which may be taken as the origin of the (secular) oriental tale in English (unless it's Moirier's *Hajji Baba of Ispahan* or Beckford's *Vathek*).

To be sure, the English also liked their tales of the east "pure" or at least poetic. James Elroy Flecker and The Golden Journey to Samarkand received no gibes from Saki, indeed quite the contrary ("A Defensive Diamond" in *Saki*, Modern Library ed., pp. 396–401, where he quotes approvingly Flecker's "The dragon-green, the luminous, the dark, the serpent-haunted sea"). Children grew up with Andrew Lang's *The Arabian Nights Entertainment* (Lang 1898), though Lang felt he had to say that these were "only fairy tales of the east . . . not for children, but for grown-up people" (p. x), from which (p. xii) he has omitted "pieces only suitable for Arabs and old gentlemen." Then when E. Nesbit turned her humorous eye on magic, it was eastern magic (in *The Five Children and It, The Phoenix and the Carpet, The Story of the Amulet*). Even in the early days of the English oriental tale—not *Vathek*, admittedly, but in *The Shaving of Shagpat* (1856)—there is something of the blend of humor and the east, though that might perhaps be accidental. In any event, let us take it, at least *arguendo*, that the blend is well-established by the early years of the twentieth century.

This is important as background for *The Horse and His Boy*, but for the moment, let us look at the story, stripped of its "eastern-ness" or "Calormenity" (if we can), looking at the kind of story-pattern it presents. It begins, as you will recall, with "This is the story of an adventure that happened in Narnia and Calormen and the lands between, in the Golden Age when Peter was High King in Narnia and his brother and two sisters were King and Queens under him" (p. 1 in Chapter I, "How Shasta Set Out on His Travels"). Shasta, a boy in his very early teens (I think), is sold as a slave by his supposed father, Arsheesh, runs away, is helped by Bree, a Talking Horse from Narnia, who needs a rider to escape to "Narnia and the North"—and in their escape they are coerced by a lion to meet with Hwin, a Talking Horse from Narnia who is being ridden by the Tarkheena Aravis, escaping the marriage with the despicable (and ancient) Ahoshta Tarkaan into which she is being forced—in fact, a different version of slavery, from which Aravis, on Hwin, is likewise escaping to the North. So the four of them make it together as far as Tashbaan, Aravis and Bree talking most to each other, Aravis not to Shasta at all, and the shy mare Hwin not talking much.

And when they are in Tashbaan, and Shasta is trying to back Bree out of the way, suddenly they are at the front of a crowd making way for a small party of half a dozen fair-haired men, "in tunics of fine, bright, hardy colors" (p. 54), with steel or silver caps, "one with little wings on each side of it" (p. 55), who seize Shasta as a runaway from their party, and so "before they were half-way through Tashbaan, all their plans were ruined, and without even a chance to say good-bye to the others Shasta found himself being marched off among strangers and quite unable to guess what might be going to happen next" (p. 56). What happens, of course, is that the Narnians (for that is who they are) welcome him as a royal truant, the Faun Tumnus decides "His Highness" has a touch of the sun, and so Shasta lies down, but he listens to what is being said, hoping to find the way to Narnia over the desert.

The Narnians themselves need to escape from the trap they have entered in, by listening to the proposals of Prince Rabadash (of Calormen) for marriage with Queen Susan, and coming to Tashbaan. Thinking that Shasta is Prince Corin (of Archenland), they expect him to be going with them—but in the nick of time, the real Prince Corin turns up, crawling in through the window of the room where Shasta is to sleep. So (but not till the boys have suddenly found they were friends) Shasta escapes out the same window and rejoins Aravis and Bree and Win as planned. Well, not quite as planned—he needs to be frightened and comforted by a lion or a cat to spend the night and next day at the Tombs where they are to meet.

Aravis has met her friend Lasaraleen Tarkheena, who (after much pleading and cajoling) has helped her with her escape—in the course of which, she and Lasaraleen wind up hiding in the room where they hear the plotting of the Tisroc and Prince Rabadash and the Grand Vizier Ahoshta Tarkaan (to whom—age, humpback, obsequiousness and all—Aravis has been betrothed). The scene is done for comedy, and the Tisroc (old and very fat and "a mass of frills and pleats and bobbles and buttons and tassels and talismans"—p. 104) is made both a figure of fun and a figure of fear. "'If you were not my father, O ever-living Tisroc,' said the Prince, grinding his teeth, 'I should say that was the words of a coward.' 'And if you were not my son, O most inflammabe Rabadash,' replied his father, 'your life would be short and your death slow when you had said it.' (The cool placid voice in which he spoke these words made Aravis's blood run cold.)" (p. 107). But now Shasta knows the way across the desert and Aravis knows that Prince Rabadash with two hundred horse is riding to surprise Anvard, the Archenland castle that holds the pass into Narnia. The horses are forced to their last full measure of speed by the lion, and at the gate of the Hermit of the Southern March, Shasta turns back to help Hwin and Aravis, who have fallen behind, and the lion turns back.

They enter the Hermit's gate (a Hermit, by the way, who speaks like St. Francis of Assisi of his cousin horses), and the Hermit points Shasta to run straight to Anvard, but before he gets there, he comes across King Lune of Archenland and his court on a hunt. They put Shasta on a horse to go with them, but he lags behind (not knowing how to use his reins), is lost in the fog, hears Rabadash and his two hundred horse passing in the fog, knows the way to Anvard is cut off and is again comforted by the Lion—for it is Aslan, and it has been all along. "'I was the lion who forced you to join with Aravis. I was the cat who comforted you among the houses of the dead. I was the lion who drove the jackals from you while you slept. I was the lion who gave the Horses the new strength of fear for the last mile so that you could reach King Lune in time. And I was the lion you do not remember who pushed the boat in which you lay, a child near death, so that it came to shore where a man sat, wakeful at midnight, to receive you'" (p. 158).

After the night of the lion's comfort (and it is here that Aslan—"the Voice"—tells Shasta, p. 159, "'I am telling you your story, not hers. I tell no-one any story but his own.'"), Shasta tells his story to—among others—Chevy the Stag, who brings it to Cair Paravel, where Edmund and Susan are just docking (with Prince Corin). The High King Peter is away fighting Giants on the Northern frontier, but Edmund and Lucy the Valiant bring Narnia to aid King Lune at Anvard. Corin talks Shasta into putting on armor and following behind—and when the Narnians charge down on the Calormene two hundred assaulting Anvard, it is a mass of confusion for Shasta, and at this point Lewis takes us to the smooth pool beneath the spreading tree at the garden of the Hermit of the March, where the Hermit can see what is happening at Anvard and tell Aravis and Bree and Hwin—and so we are enabled to follow the battle more easily than Shasta could.

> "Five Calormenes have fallen, but not many will. They have their shields above their heads. Rabadash is giving his orders now. With him are his most trusted lords, fierce Tarkaans from the eastern provinces. I can see their faces. There is Corradin of Castle Tormunt [this sounds like a name out of the Chanson de Roland], and Azrooh, and Chlamash [sounds like something out of Lord Dunsany], and Ilgamuth of the twisted lip [more *Chanson de Roland*], and a tall Tarkaan with a crimson beard——" "By the Mane, my old master Anradin!" said Bree. (p. 181)

As the battle is ending, Rabadash, with a tear in the back of his hauberk, jumps up to a mounting block, back against the wall, then tries to jump down again— "The bolt of Tash falls from above!'" (p. 186)—and the tear in his hauberk is caught on a hook, and there he hangs. And then, in this polyphonic interlaced narrative, we go back to the Hermit's garden (a walled garden—Paradise?), with Aravis and Hwin and Bree—and then, suddenly, Aslan is there, and Hwin and (in a scene reminiscent of Doubting Thomas) Bree believe, and Aravis asks what is happening with the slave girl she drugged to make her escape, to be told (ungrammatically this time?), "'No-one is told any story but their own'" (p. 194). But now come a herald and a trumpeter, with two soldiers, and "His Royal Highness Prince Cor of Archenland desires an audience of the Lady Aravis" (p. 195).

It is, of course, Shasta, who has turned out to be Prince Corin's elder twin. He tells Aravis that he was kidnapped by a Lord Bar, who had been guilty of embezzlement and, being allowed to remain in Archenland, had been in the pay of Calormen, and hearing that Cor would someday save Archenland from a deadly danger, took it personally and kidnapped him. Bar was defeated in a great battle at sea, but he had sent the boy off with one of his knights before the battle, in the boat that (and we can surely see this coming) Aslan blew to the Calormene shore after the knight died, starving himself so Cor might eat and survive. Cor tells Aravis "Father's an absolute brick. I'd be just as pleased—or very nearly—at finding he's my father even if he wasn't a king. Even though Education and all sorts of horrible things are going to happen to me" (p. 197).

Four points come to mind here: first, I was surprised to find that in Boxen the "hock-brown" little bear James Bar, Purser, is a sympathetic though possibly not entirely trustworthy character (this being a rare case of a name carried over from Boxen to Narnia—was it accidental?); second, the slang "Father's an absolute brick" comes down from the nineteenth century; third, "Education and all sorts of horrible things are going to happen to me" certainly does not reflect Lewis's own feelings as a child or a schoolboy (except perhaps about his own "education" at "Wyvern"); fourth, and much the most important, this is a classic "Lost Heir" story, popular throughout the Victorian age, and indeed a *motif* of a number of Henty's books (including *The Lost Heir*). This is, as John Buchan has told us ("The Novel and the Fairy-Tale" *English Association Pamphlet no. 79*, July 1931, p. 9), the "Recognition" (*Anagnorisis*) form of "Reversal of Fortune" (*Peripeteia*). In other words, this is a classic Aristotelian form—often embedded in *Märchen*. Which helps explain why we have the nineteenth-century slang and the departure from the author's own experience, and (I suspect) why it is not a story about his this-world children as children. Here Lewis is certainly acting as a conscious *makar*, a creator of a particular kind of literature.

But we have not finished the story. Rabadash must still be dealt with. He threatens; he blasphemes; he shrieks; he wiggles his ears; and when Aslan comes among them he spurns him—and then his fate overtakes him. He turns into a donkey—an ass. "'You have appealed to Tash,' said Aslan, 'and in the temple of Tash you shall be healed. You must stand before the altar of Tash in Tashbaan at the great Autumn Feast this year and there, in the sight of all Tashbaan, your ass's shape will fall from you for Prince Rabadash'" (p. 211). But if he goes more than ten miles from Tashbaan he will change back again, and "from that second change there will be no coming back." So he (it?) is sent back to Tashbaan, and there ensues the great sorting-out that comes at the end of Comedy or Romance, and we are told Cor will be king, and Corin always a prince (and it is princes who have all the fun), and the boys fight like any brothers (Was this part of the book actually completed by 1952, as we have been told it was? Or was it added when the book was dedicated to David and Douglas Gresham?).

And Cor and Aravis keep fighting and making up, so eventually they get married so as to do it more easily. (This seems to be along the same line as the "Education and all sorts of horrible things"—said for humorous or even comic effect.) As to the matter of Lord Bar the embezzler and James Bar the purser, someone more learned in Boxoniana than I may be able to come up with an answer here, but though Lt. James Bar, R.N., Paymaster, is portrayed with some degree of sympathy in the Boxen stories, and seems to reform (more or less) in the end, he is certainly desperate and might be considered a villain—and thus a desperate villain, and even (for a while) a deserter. In any case, there is more ambiguity of character in James Bar in Boxen than in Lord Bar in Archenland.

The second part of the title of this chapter is "Realizing the World of Dragons"—that is, making the World of Dragons real. This may seem odd. After all, it is only in *The Voyage of the "Dawn Treader"* that there is a dragon, though, to be sure, there are dragon-like beasts who have come down into the Underworld and are asleep there in *The Silver Chair*. And of course *Prince Caspian* is about the same world in the same age as *The Voyage of the "Dawn Treader,"* and while there are no dragons (or even dragon-like beasts) in *The Horse and His Boy* (any more than in *The Lion, the Witch, and the Wardrobe*), their absence there points something out, or at least suggests it. The dragons come in the more Medieval and more "Old Western" parts of the Chronicles of Narnia—they are, so to speak, where (in our own history and mythology) they belong. As Boxen went from contemporary times to the medieval, so, in a way, did Narnia (complicated by the fact that the more contemporary Narnia is in A.N.—Anno Narniæ—1000–1015 and the more medieval in and after A.N. 2300). Lewis's answer to the problem of making his invented world real, dragons and all, lies in part in adopting the mode of narrative appropriate to the time and the world.

This is not what he did in *The Lion, the Witch, and the Wardrobe*, or not so much. There he went by the pictures, pretty much allowing them to form the story. But the other books (perhaps *Prince Caspian* the least) are constructs, made stories. We have seen how often we have voices (or Voices) and references to story and the right kind of books (thus far) in the "Chronicles of Narnia"—in *Voyage* and *The Silver Chair* and *The Horse and His Boy*, Lewis chose voice and story-pattern appropriate to his material.

The Voyage of the "Dawn Treader" is Edwardian adventure story; *The Silver Chair* is nineteenth-century invented fairy-tale; *The Horse and His Boy* is *Marchen*. All are humorous or even comic in nature. All use techniques appropriate to their type—which, of course, is a very different matter from whether the techniques are used well. It is unfortunate that Ronald Tolkien did not read some of the later books in the series, when the jostling pictures were no longer creating the jostling story (or stories), when it was Lewis acting as *makar* of the Chronicles. (The word *makar* is the Middle English and especially Middle Scots for poet, literary creator. It is our word maker, but given a special meaning.)

Tolkien could have told us whether Lewis was successful—in Tolkien's informed view—in making the world of dragons, the world of Faerie, come alive—and if so, was it because he was conforming to time-tested techniques and time-tested types. One thing, of course, is sure: when Lewis was speaking of the very limited amount of description in fairy-tales, he was not speaking of his own Narnian books.

In the end, as we will see even more in the next chapter, these books may be filled with greater wonder than the Boxen stories, but much of it comes from references to (or objective correlatives from) the Greatest Story Ever Told, and the corpus of "Old Western" literature. Lewis echoes his sources and analogues, has passages of brilliant—and of simply good—description, has built a structure of mostly traditional story and a world that many have admired. It is time now to look at the beginning and the end, *The Magician's Nephew* and *The Last Battle*.

[5]
First Things, Last Things: The Second Larger Life

"In my end is my beginning"—those were the words Mary, Queen of Scots, embroidered during her captivity in England, "En ma Fin git mon Commencement." In my death begins my new life. And she took the salamander, dying in fire to be born in fire, as her symbol. We might also say, looking at the two "book-end" volumes of the Chronicles of Narnia, that "In my beginning is my end." We might also give another twist to Mary's words, which could be taken here to mean that those present at the end will at least include those present at the beginning— in that sense, in my end is my beginning. Indeed, we could put it all together—and we will—to see how *The Last Battle* is implicit in *The Magician's Nephew*, the whole series implicit in *The Magician's Nephew*, and *The Last Battle* implicit in the whole series. After all, so far as we know, they were all written by the end of 1952 (note in Lyle W. Dorsett and Marjorie Lamp Mead, eds., *C.S. Lewis: Letters to Children*, New York 1985, p. 31). It is not as though any of the last five to be written really preceded any others of the last five. But let us look a little more in detail at these two "book-end" volumes.

Beginning at the beginning—or at least at the page after the title-page of *The Magician's Nephew*—we find that this creation story of the world of Narnia is dedicated to the Kilmer Family. I didn't particularly notice this when I first read the book, and if I noticed it at all I thought (in a teen-age sort of way) that the Kilmer Family must be this family that are friends of C.S. Lewis. But the story is more complex—and now to me more interesting—than that. The Kilmer family of Washington D.C. and suburban Northern Virginia were Kenton Sinclair Kilmer (1909–1995), his wife Frances Frieseke Kilmer (1914–1991), and their eight children, Hugh, Anne, Noelie, Nicholas, Martin, Rosamund, Matthew, and Miriam, and they were introduced to Lewis when his correspondent Mary Willis Shelburne sent him a bundle of letters and pictures (in 1954, I think) "from the eight children of Mr. and Mrs. Kilmer."

At least that is when the children were introduced to him, or he to them. But there is some indication that Mr. and Mrs. Kilmer had in fact suggested to Mary Willis Shelburne that she write Lewis back in 1950. How Kenton and Frances Kilmer came to know or know of Lewis in the first place I do not know. One thing that is evident, however, is that the Kilmers were an altogether extraordinary family.

Kenton Sinclair Kilmer (I believe the "Sinclair" was for the author) was the eldest child and eldest son of the poets (Alfred) Joyce Kilmer (1886–1918) and Aline Murray Kilmer (1888–1941): he was himself a poet, editor, and translator. Frances Frieseke was the daughter of (and model for) the American Impressionist painter Frederick Frieseke (1872–1939), born in Flint, Michigan, but resident first in Paris and later in Normandy for most of the last forty-five years of his life. Kenton and Frances Kilmer were the founders (in 1942) of the Green Hedges School (a K–8 independent school begun in their house in Arlington with ten students). All the Kilmer children attended Green Hedges, and here is what their parents, the founders, had to say about the goals of a Green Hedges education (quoting from a Green Hedges brochure).

Kenton Kilmer remarked that "education should open the doors of a child's mind to the delight of the unknown, the strange, the antique, the foreign, the new—it should open the doors of the soul." Frances Kilmer added that "the children graduating from Green Hedges would meet adulthood with the excitement of a worthy challenge, fully enlightened idealism, the innocence of childhood, and the courage of real wisdom." I cannot say how well their educational doctrine worked for others, but I have read and enjoyed some of Nicholas Kilmer's novels (the ones I have read are detective novels), and Martin Kilmer's study of the diet of the Norsemen at Anse-aux-Meadows (Newfoundland), though not any of his work on Greek art. I have looked at Hugh Kilmer's book on his grandfather Frieseke. (Hugh was some months younger than I: he died last year.) So far as I know every one of the eight has done well in writing or music or sculpture or painting, and I have seen an entire website dedicated to the works of the various members of the family.

It is unlikely that Green Hedges had any connection with the Waldorf or Steiner school movement with which Lewis's friends Cecil Harwood (directly) and Owen Barfield (less directly) were involved (the Kilmers were Roman Catholic, which would make this unlikely). But I have read those of Lewis's *Letters to Children* (1985) that were written to the Kilmer children, beginning with the letter of March 19th 1954, to all eight (pp. 40–41). Possibly the letter to Hugh (April 28th 1954, p. 43) is to Hugh Kilmer, since it comments on his drawing of Eustace as a dragon.

There is a letter to all eight on May 26th 1954 (p. 44), and another mentioning the birth of their sister Deborah on June 9th 1954 (p. 47), a letter to Martin on January 15th 1955, to Hugh on July 20th 1955 (on the dedication of *The Magician's Nephew*, p. 55), another to Martin on March 26th 1956 (p. 60), and others to Martin on May 14th 1956 (p. 62), and on July 23rd 1956 (p. 65), and January 22nd 1957 (p. 67), and July 10th 1957 (pp. 70–71), to Anne and Martin August 7th 1957 (pp. 73–74), to Martin on April 24th 1958 (pp. 78–79), July 21st 1958 (p. 79), September 29th 1958 (pp. 82–83), November 23rd 1958 (pp. 83–84), January 3rd 1959 (pp. 84–85), March 27th 1959 (pp. 85–86), August 18th 1959 (pp. 89–90), then five theological letters to Hugh, November 18th 1959 (p. 91), February 15th 1961 (pp. 96–97), February 17th 1961 (pp. 97–98), March 13th 1961 (pp. 98–99), April 5th 1961 (p. 100), and another letter to Hugh on March 26th 1963 (pp. 106–07). More than one-third of the letters in *Letters to Children* are to the Kilmers, and Hugh must have been in his twenties at the time the last one was written. But they make it quite certain that, if the "Kilmer Family" were not friends of C.S. Lewis when the correspondence began, some of them at least surely were by the time it ended with Lewis's death—and still are. They were also, as I said, an altogether extraordinary family.

We may look a little at some of these letters as we go along, but it's time we got beyond the dedication to *The Magician's Nephew*, at least to the first line of the first page of the story (p. 1): "This is a story about something that happened long ago when your grandfather was a child. It is a very important story because it shows how all the comings and goings between our own world and the land of Narnia first began." In the first of these two sentences, Lewis has told us that this is not a traditional "once upon a time" fairy-tale, nor is it a look through the door of the timeless, as in George MacDonald's *Phantastes*. In the second sentence, Lewis has told us that this is an explanatory book, the work of Lewis the systematizer as much as of Lewis the poet.

Let us begin with this matter of taking us back to a specific time, "when your grandfather was a child." I doubt if Lewis knew much about the grandfathers of the children to whom the book was dedicated, so it is probably (but not certainly) accidental that Joyce Kilmer was a child in the 1890s (Frederick Frieseke was a child in the late 1870s and early 1880s, which is too early, but the dates of Joyce Kilmer's childhood would be just about right).

We will get more into that specific time as we go on into the book and into this chapter. For the moment, we can compare it in this respect with some other books we have already talked about, specifically Thackeray's *The Rose and the Ring* (1854), Andrew Lang's *Prince Prigio* (1889) and *Ricardo of Pantouflia* (1893), and the three E. Nesbit books, *Five Children and It* (1902), *The Phoenix and the Carpet* (1904), *The Story of the Amulet* (1906). I have pointed out elsewhere (*The Rise of Tolkienian Fantasy*, p. 84, and above in Chapter 1) that we should remember, in reading *The Rose and the Ring*, that King Bomba of the Two Sicilies (Ferdinand II, 1810–1859) had been headline and break-fast-table news in England for a dozen years in 1854, and would be for nearly half a dozen more.

Thackeray's Christmas-book is by way of being a topical satire. (We will speak more of satire later on.) Note that the edge of the edged weapon, and the recognition of the satire, comes from a knowledge of what was going on in 1854: it does not inhere in the book itself. The book, in that sense, is time-specific with a vengeance, but it does not set the time because the time is the present. It is not so with Lang's two books (at least not so far as the vengeance is concerned), though we know from the date of the check for ten thousand purses that King Grognio wrote to Prince Prigio, in Falkenstein, in Pantouflia (in *Prince Prigio*), that this adventure took place in July 1718, a year pretty much supported by the appearance of a young Prince Charles Edward Stuart ("Hero" of the 1745 Jacobite uprising in Scotland and England) in *Ricardo of Pantouflia*, a generation later. In one way, this is a move apart from the contemporaneity of *The Rose and The Ring* (or, for that matter, of *Five Children and It*): it is not, however, a move into the once-upon-a-time mode of the fairy-tale, but into a distancing by history. The date may be noted to suggest a connection, as I remarked before, with *Gulliver's Travels*.

Edith Nesbit Bland (E. Nesbit 1858–1924) and Andrew Lang (1844–1912) were in fact contemporaries and acquaintances—and though it would be possible to take her three books mentioned here as the beginnings of a reaction against Lang, to do so would be at best extreme oversimplification.. In fact, as I also pointed out, the Flying Carpet got a very short rest after its use by Lang in 1889 and 1893, till its use in *The Phoenix and The Carpet* in 1904. The Fairy of the Desert was transmogrified from her (or its) unpleasant appearance and activity in *Ricardo of Pantouflia* to become—or perhaps to give birth to—the Sand-Fairy, the "It" of *Five Children and It* (1902). The carpet, of course, is the eponymous *machina* of *The Phoenix and The Carpet* (1904). E. Nesbit follows Lang in bringing these machines of the time-less fairy-story into a time specific—whether 1718 (his case) or 1902 (her case). It may be noted also that Thackeray, though contemporaneous with his story, is not time-specific in quite the same way as E. Nesbit, or for that matter, Lewis in *The Magician's Nephew*—and, of course, he engages in a distancing by space, even if ironic, that she does not, and Lewis does not in *The Magician's Nephew* (at least not till the children get to the Wood Between the Worlds). Our principal point here is that Lewis does distance by time but to a time (more or less) specific—which he makes more specific as time goes on. After all, he is writing almost about the times of his own youth. And this brings us to a question. Does this fact—that Lewis is writing about the decade in which he was born—help give some additional degree of reality or realism to the book?

To put it another way, are Digory and Polly friends of Jacks? Is the framework, at least, for their adventures really out of his youth? I do not mean, are their adventures taken from the books of his youth, though, as we will see, some of them are—but then, some of the Pevensies' adventures are too. No, what I am looking for here is some evidence as to whether there is a real-world (in C.S. Lewis's childhood) basis to at least some of the scenes in *The Magician's Nephew*. The first evidence is strongly positive.

After setting the scene (including the time) of the story in literary terms—"In those days Mr. Sherlock Holmes was still living in Baker Street and the Bastables were looking for treasure in the Lewisham Road"—we go on to this passage (pp. 1–2): "In those days, if you were a boy, you had to wear a stiff Eton collar every day, and schools were usually nastier than now, But meals were nicer; and as for sweets, I won't tell you how cheap and good they were, because it would only make your mouth water in vain." We know C.S. Lewis hated Eton collars, as he hated restrictive clothes most of his life. We know he considered his school experience pretty nasty (as indeed some of it was); and we know he considered "nasty" as a word particularly suitable to early childhood—as also the word "nice" (see *That Hideous Strength*, where the "nursery" distinction between *nice* and *nasty* is given prominence). Here at least is the voice of his childhood and boyhood.

And as we go on, the two voices mix—the literary and the personal. Digory is living with his aunt and uncle in one of a long row of houses, where Polly lives next door, which is how they meet, and, in a wet summer, go exploring along the attic "tunnel" running from one house to another. Now some of this exploring, with the cistern and the box-room attic, is reminiscent of Albert Lewis's "great house in the country," Little Lea, but some also brings to my mind the explorations of Stalky and

M'Turk and Beetle in Kipling's *Stalky & Co.* (1899), along the connecting attics of the dormitories at Westward Ho! I would call this, as I would much of the scene-setting, a mixture, as we would expect of the child grown man whose chief child's pleasures were in books. (It is possible that the semi-detached double house where the Lewises lived at Dundela Villas—now destroyed—before they lived at Little Lea, could have provided a long attic linking two houses, but I would still plump for Stalky.)

In any case, Digory and Polly come down from the attic tunnel not into the vacant house next door but into Uncle Andrew's forbidden study, and he entices Polly into picking up one of the rings made with dust from another world—"I don't mean another planet, you know; they're part of our world and you could get to them if you went far enough—but a really other world—another Nature—another universe" (p. 21). The dust was from Atlantis but what was in it was Atlantean magic, not simply a memento from Atlantis. Polly vanishes right out of this world, of course, and we'll come back to that by the next but one paragraph.

Here we should point out that the Amulet in *The Story of the Amulet* is likewise Atlantean. So, for that matter, is the magic in *That Hideous Strength*. So (syncretistically) is Tolkien's Númenor, but it is the origin of Lewis's interest in Atlantis that we are looking at here (whatever may be the origins of Númenor), and that seems to be from *The Story of the Amulet*. Of course, that part of the scene-setting has to be from books, unless we make some kind of strange assumption that Lewis had direct experience of Atlantean magic.

In any case, when Polly vanishes out of Uncle Andrew's study, Uncle Andrew tells Digory he must take a Green Ring (for return) to Polly, and one for himself, and follow her (using a Yellow Ring of the kind she had touched). And so Digory follows Polly from our world into the Wood Between the Worlds. And here, in our commentary, we shift gears a little, away from the history and background of children's literature to the origins of fantasy and particularly the origins of what I have called the stream of fantasy and feigned (or invented) history. "The Wood between the Worlds" has something of the sound of "The Well at the World's End" and the sound is the sound of William Morris (1834–1896).

I have elsewhere (*The Rise of Tolkienian Fantasy*, pp. 35ff) chosen William Morris as the author with whom fantasy enters the genre of feigned history. Morris appears to qualify on three counts. He presents us with the quality of fantasy (perhaps especially in his titles). He possesses some of the fair elusive beauty of which Tolkien spoke when he talked about creating a mythology for England—the fair elusive beauty for which modern fantasy seeks. And he is an inventor of tradition, a seeker for a usable past, and in a way a creator of feigned history. It is true that he is not always and everywhere doing all of these things, and his creation is far from being limited to writing. But the presence of the fantastic in his writing is evident and it comes from his using the Romanticized past, indeed from his soaking himself in it. You see, the wood (whatever wood), as Lewis observed in his essay in the collection of essays presented to Ronald Tolkien, was enchanted after all, and this *Wood between the Worlds* is part of it, with all the enchantment of the past there at least potentially (though some of that enchantment can be very disagreeable indeed).

What I tried to do in *The Rise of Tolkienian Fantasy* was to tie the concerns of literary history and *genre* studies with the concerns of social history, because social history is what tells us about the atmosphere in which Tolkien's—and here Lewis's—generation grew up. Morris and his archaizing are part of Victorian social history, and thus part of Lewis's family background and childhood milieu. We see Morris's conscious medievalizing or archaizing of the *sögur*, or the Four Branches of the *Mabinogion*, or the Cattle Raid of Cooley. We see Morris's search from the early days of the first Earthly Paradise, through Jason, through the Sagas, into the late romances, for a Paradisal vision through feigned history. The highly romanticized (and "blended"?) version of Ragnarók, Ogier's being borne to Avallon by Morgan le Fay, are merely two examples of the feigning of a new history.

You see why I think the suggestiveness of "The Wood Between the Worlds" important. Lewis knew perfectly well what he was doing, and what he was doing was tying the whole story of Narnia into Morris's creation that linked fantasy—not, or certainly not necessarily, for children—and feigned or invented history (say, for example, the history of Narnia). And Morris was one of Lewis's favorite authors. That being said, we can go back into *The Wood between the Worlds*, a dreamy in-between-sleeping-and-waking world pretty much without time and almost without memory.

The simile Digory uses in telling Polly how he thinks things work is very interesting—"No, do listen. Think of our tunnel under the slates at home. It isn't a room in any of the houses. In a way, it isn't really part of any of the houses. But once you're in the tunnel you can go along it and come out into any of the houses in the row. Mightn't this wood be the same?—a place that isn't in any of the worlds, but once you've found that place you can get into them all?"

"'And of course that explains everything,' he said. 'That's why it is so quiet and sleepy here. Nothing ever happens here. Like at home. It's in the houses that people talk, and do things, and have meals. Nothing goes on in the in-between places, behind the walls and above the ceilings and under the floor, or in our own tunnel. But when you come out of our tunnel you may find yourself in any house. I think we can get out of this place into jolly well Anywhere! . . .'" (*The Magician's Nephew*, pp. 34–35)

"Jolly well Anywhere" turns out, as we know, to be the dying world (or Empire) of Charn, and it may be a good thing to look for the origins of the name. I do not myself think it is the same kind of echoic borrowing that Tolkien found in Lewis's Tor and Tinidril in *Perelandra* from Tolkien's Tuor and Idril. I have heard it suggested that the origins lie in charnel, as in charnel house, the place of dead bodies. It could be, of course, but charnel is a form of carnal, of the body, and this seems to me a misdirection.

Although the name might of course be from the Judaco-Slavic *charn-* root, meaning *dark*, my own suggestion goes back to Lewis's Arthurian studies, or at least his Arthurian interest: the stony wasteland now called Charnwood, in Leicester (near Loughborough), by the Charnwood Hills. Since current thinking accepts *Rate Corioneltavori* as the place name and origin of the present Charnwood, and *Corieltauvi* as the tribal name, it is unlikely that we can go any further—beyond noting the oddity that Charnwood is not really the name of a wood but of what used to be a wood and is now a stony waste. Obviously this is highly conjectural. But my own inclination is to look in Arthur's direction (more on this in Chapter 7).

In Charn they come to the throne room of the dead (reminiscent of Rider Haggard, as the last Queen or Empress of Charn is perhaps reminiscent of Ayesha in Kôr—and of course there is some linguistic similarity between Charn and Kôr). There is no need to repeat at length here what happened next—suffice it to say that Digory and Polly and Jadis, the last Queen of Charn, wind up first back in the Wood between the Worlds, and then in London, where the scene is strongly reminiscent of the Queen of Babylon in *The Story of the Amulet*—but much more written for its comic and humorous aspects even than E. Nesbit.

"Peace! You talk far too much." [This is said to Uncle Andrew.] "Listen to your first task. I see we are in a large city. Procure for me at once a chariot or a flying carpet or a well-trained dragon, or whatever is usual for royal and noble persons in your land. Then bring me to places where I can get clothes and jewels and slaves fit for my rank. To-morrow I will begin the conquest of the world" (p. 71). "'I'll go and order a cab at once,' gasped Uncle Andrew." (p. 71)

They return, with the spoils of a jewelers' on Jadis, in a hansom cab, or rather Jadis driving the cab from the roof, Uncle Andrew inside, and Polly and Digory manage to grab hold of each other and the rings and Jadis, Queen and Witch, holding the part of a lamp-post she has wrenched off as a weapon—and Uncle Andrew and the horse and the cabby—first into the Wood Between the Worlds, then into another pool, into a warm darkness, and the cabby, to keep up their spirits, begins to sing a hymn. Here are the words of the hymn sung before the creation of the world in Narnia.

> Come, ye thankful people, come, / Raise the song of harvest-home: / All is safely gathered in, / Ere the winter storms begin; / God, our Maker, doth provide / For our wants to be supplied; / Come to God's own temple, come, / Raise the song of harvest-home. // All the world is God's own field, / Fruit unto his praise to yield; / Wheat and tares together sown, / Unto joy or sorrow grown: / First the blade and then the ear, / Then the full-corn shall appear; / Grant, O harvest Lord, that we / Wholesome grain and pure may be. // For the Lord our God shall come, / And shall take his harvest home; / From his field shall in that day / All offences purge away; / Give his angels charge at last / In the fire the tares to cast, / But the fruitful ears to store / In his garner evermore. // Even so, Lord, quickly come / To thy final harvest home; / Gather thou thy people in, / Free from sorrow, free from sin; / There, for ever purified, / In thy presence to abide; / Come, with all thine angels, come, / Raise the glorious harvest-home.

The tune, by the way (at least in the Hymnal I grew up with, the Episcopal *Hymnal* of 1940), is St. George's Windsor.

Talk about the ending in the beginning. Before Aslan begins to sing the world of Narnia into existence (in a scene strongly reminiscent of Tolkien's creation scenes in *The Silmarillion*), the prayer has been entered for God's swift judgment, the acknowledgment has been made that "All the world is God's own field," and it is almost as though the creation of the world of Narnia has been begun by the cabby's singing the hymn of Thanksgiving and Judgment—no wonder then that the cabby becomes the first King of Narnia. Lewis comments that the hymn "was not very suitable to a place which felt as if nothing had ever grown there since the beginning of time" (p. 97)—though it was very cheering—but I believe it becomes appropriate as Aslan sings his first song that calls up the stars and the sun, and then his new song singing up the trees (which is when Jadis, the Witch, throws the lamp-post bar at Aslan), then another song singing up the animals—and then (p. 116) "the deepest wildest voice they had ever heard was saying: 'Narnia, Narnia, Narnia, awake. Love. Think. Speak. Be walking trees. Be talking beasts. Be divine waters'."

And they are—but of course Uncle Andrew cannot see what is happening, having deliberately made himself stupid, so that he does not hear the songs but only the lion's roar, does not hear the words of the talking beasts but only barkings and growlings such as you might hear from the dumb beasts of this world. So as Digory (with the cabby's horse, Strawberry) and Polly and the cabby go off to talk to Aslan and the beasts he has chosen as councillors, the other beasts debate whether Uncle Andrew is a plant or an animal, decide he is to be planted (but at least they put him legs down after having him wrong end up so that the change falls out of his pockets), and plant and water him.

He is, of course, terrified—but this is all a *buffo* interlude in the carnival. The real *serio* business going on is with Aslan and Digory. For Aslan asks Digory how Jadis (now "the Witch") got into Narnia, and he confesses his fault. Aslan sends him off—on Strawberry, now grown wings and become Fledge—beyond the Western border of Narnia, into the Western Wild, through the great mountains to a green valley with a blue lake in it, walled around by mountains of ice (but this is the Western border—not the Northern), to a green hill at the end of the lake, where there is a garden (walled with green turf), and in the center of the garden is a tree.

Digory is to pluck an apple from the tree and bring it back to Aslan, where it will grow into a tree that will protect Narnia from the Witch for many years. So Fledge flies off with Digory and Polly on his back, to the walled garden, where Digory, going alone on his errand into the garden, finds on the golden gates "Come in by the gold gates or not at all, / Take of my fruit for others or forvear, / For those who steal or those who climb my wall / Shall find their hearts desire and find despair" (p. 157).

Digory touches the gates and they swing open, and he goes into the solemn (indeed *solempne*) place—"a happy place but very serious" (p. 158) and picks one of the great silver apples on the tree—and then is tempted to keep it for his mother, but there "on a branch above his head, a wonderful bird was roosting . . . The tiniest slit of one eye was open. It was larger than an eagle, its breast saffron, its head crested with scarlet, and its tail purple" (p. 159), and Digory rejects the temptation. Then the Witch, who has come over the wall and stolen an apple for herself, tempts Digory again, and he rejects that temptation, and brings the apple back to Aslan—perhaps in part because children were better brought up in those days?

"All day Fledge flew steadily with untiring wings, eastward with the river to guide him, through the mountains and over the wild wooded hills, and then over the great waterfall and down, and down, to where the woods of Narnia were darkened by the shadow of the mighty cliff, till at last, when the sky was growing red with sunset behind them, he saw a place where many creatures were gathered together by the riverside. And soon he could see Aslan himself in the midst of them. Fledge guided down, spread out his four legs, closed his wings, and landed cantering. Then he pulled up" (pp. 164–65)—and Digory has brought the apple to Aslan.

So after Digory tosses the apple to the soft earth, and Aslan breathes on the wretched Uncle Andrew and gives him sleep, and crowns have been fashioned from the gold and silver of the trees that grew from the coins dropped from Uncle Andrew's pockets (for coins were real gold and silver in the days of Lewis's youth), and King Frank (the cabby) and Queen Helen (his wife) are crowned, and lo! a new apple tree has grown up to guard Narnia, Aslan tells Digory to pluck an apple from that tree to take back to his mother. "For a second Digory could hardly understand. It was as if the whole world had turned inside out and upside down. And then, like someone in a dream, he was walking across to the Tree, and the King and Queen were cheering him and all the creatures were cheering too. He plucked the apple and put it in his pocket. Then he came back to Aslan. 'Please,' he said, 'may we go home now?' (p. 176). And then comes Chapter XV, "The End of This Story and the Beginning of All the Others"—in my end is my beginning. (And here at the end of Chapter XIV, I might add, there is a reminiscence of Lewis's own *Perelandra*, with the King and the Queen, and the Eldila and the creatures, and Ransom the Man from Thulcandra—and Digory is Ransom, and thus *the* Ransom, in a sense the Anointed One, and the scene is Paradise (in the West the walled garden) in the Third Heaven. Or at least the Hesperides, or the Country of the Blest.)

Then Digory and Polly are back in the Wood between the Worlds, with Uncle Andrew still asleep, and then in the street in London, with Uncle Andrew awake, and they sneak him into the house. Digory cuts up the apple and gives it to his mother, and she recovers (but Lewis's mother, in this world, did not recover). He plants the core in the garden and a tree begins to grow up there overnight. Digory and Polly bury the rings around the tree. As Digory's mother is recovering, they hear from Digory's father in India, that Great Uncle Kirke has died and the great house in the country "would now be their home: the big house with the suits of armor, the stables, the kennels, the river, the park, the hot-houses, the vineries, the woods, and the mountains behind it" (p. 183). It sounds to me a little like Dorincourt Castle in *Little Lord Fauntleroy*, but I daresay there's a closer source, a more proximate cause.

The tree that sprang from the Apple in Uncle Andrew and Aunt Letty's back yard grew to be a fine tree, but it blew down in "a great storm all over the south of England" and Digory (by then Professor Kirke, a famous learned man and great traveler) had wood from the tree made into a wardrobe which he brought down to the great and grand house in the country. And, of course, it was through that wardrobe that Lucy and then Lucy and Edmund and all four of the Pevensie children found their way to Narnia. In that sense, of course, the beginning of the rest of the story is indeed in the end of *The Magician's Nephew*. But there is more to it than this, I think. There is the full story of Digory Kirke, the little boy who can bring life to his dying mother, who hears not doom but hope in the whispered words of the adults downstairs. And in Narnia, there is the Witch whose theft of an apple for herself begins her life of despair. One can see this beginning implicit in the ending of Charn. She is not a salamander (nor a phoenix, like the bird watching Digory in the garden): she is a snake. And where else have we heard about a serpent in a garden?

And the story of Digory Kirke? He struck the gong that awakened Jadis in the throne room of Charn, and repented, and went to that World's End to the walled garden and plucked the apple for others, resisted the temptation to keep it, and was permitted by Aslan's grace to bring it back to his mother. At this point, for Digory, *incipit vita nuova*—here begins the new life. He who traveled to that world's end becomes a great trav-eler in this world. He who learned lessons from Aslan in that world becomes a great and learned man in this world.

He is not, I think, as some would have it, principally a picture—even an idealized picture—of C.S. Lewis. As Professor Kirke, he is another picture, if you like, of Elwin Ransom, who also is bearded. As young Digory, he may be a picture of what C.S. Lewis wished he could have been, but in any case, it is a picture from real-life memory mixed with literary memory. More will become clear when we look at Digory's next appearance in *The Last Battle*. Meanwhile, there is something more to be said about *The Magician's Nephew*. For it ends in a kind of humor-ous *penseroso* mode (pp. 185–86):

When Digory and his people (that is a Victorian way of putting it) went to live in the big country house, they took Uncle Andrew to live with them; for

Digory's Father said, "We must try to keep the old fellow out of mischief, and it isn't fair that poor Letty should have him always on her hands." Uncle Andrew never tried any Magic again as long as he lived. He had learned his lesson, and in his old age he became a nicer and less selfish old man than he had ever been before. But he always liked to get visitors alone in the billiard room and tell them stories about a mysterious lady, a foreign royalty, with whom he had driven about London. "A devilish temper she had," he would say, "But she was a dem fine woman, sir, a dem fine woman."

I used the words "the *penseroso* mode" to draw attention to the possibility of looking at this book particularly in terms of Northrop Frye's *Anatomy of Criticism* (1957). Northrop Frye has pointed out (*Anatomy*, pp. 158–239, passim) the congruence between and among seasons, cityscapes, and the four great patterns or *mythoi* of literature: spring, village, and Comedy; summer, country-town, and Romance; autumn, baroque city, and Tragedy; winter, megalopolis, and Satire. A pastoral can move its idealized figures across the landscape in any season, and what I have elsewhere (*Extrapolation* 37 [1996], pp. 341–356) called a stone pastoral can move its idealized figures across the cityscape in any season. The cityscape I looked at then was London, in three books Lewis read, Chesterton's *The Napoleon of Notting Hill*, Orwell's *Nineteen Eighty-Four*, and Anthony Burgess's *A Clockwork Orange*. I am curious to see where this can lead us: after all, Lewis was not a Londoner.

Chesterton's *The Napoleon of Notting Hill* is a *psychomachia* which begins with a satire and ends with a romance: indeed, using Frye's terms, begins with Satire and ends with Romance. Orwell's satire of Stalin and Trotsky and their ilk in *Nineteen Eighty-Four* becomes Tragedy: he created in Big Brother and Newspeak ideas of mythic proportions, and in both O'Brien's character and the ending in which Winston Smith is truly brainwashed (as we now call it), he followed his invention to its Euclidean conclusions. But then, striking the deepest chord of response in his readers, he dared introduce sex and love and pathos and the fall of a good man into a satire, and created what was not in the end Satire (Frye's capitalization here), but Tragedy. (And note this passage— "'What are the stars?' said O'Brien indifferently. 'They are bits of fire a few kilometers away. We could reach them if we wanted to. Or we could blot them out. The earth is the center of the universe. The sun and the stars go round it'" (p. 219). Is that Orwell's O'Brien or Lewis's Green Witch in *The Silver Chair*?) And in Burgess's *Clockwork Orange*, what started as satire has become (at least in the English version) comedy—

or rather what started out as Satire has become Comedy, ending, like Romance, with a *penseroso* phase. In the English version, the final chapter of *A Clockwork Orange* is the twenty-first chapter. For as Burgess says (Introduction, 1987 ed., p. vi): "Twenty-one is the symbol of human maturity, or used to be, since at twenty-one you . . . assumed adult responsibility. . . . Novelists of my stamp are interested in what is called arithmology, meaning that number has to mean something in human terms when they handle it." *The Napoleon of Notting Hill* is a *psychomachia*, and when Auberon and Adam go off together on the twenty-first birthday, it is an end to the Romance of growing up, or perhaps of the Romance of Youth. But with *A Clockwork Orange* the twenty-first chapter is an end to the Comedy of Youth.

Why bring this up here? After all, Lewis is writing children's books, which are generally not looked at as an appropriate subject for this kind of analysis. (We shall look further at this particular book in what some may consider an even less likely way a little later on, by way of Edmund Spenser.) But these are all books about children growing up (though not all quite so obviously as *The Voyage of the "Dawn Treader"*), and even about salvation (or damnation), and they are thus not unlike at least two of these three transmuted London satires. Lewis, who never lived in London, starts there, in the megalopolitan cityscape of Sherlock Holmes and the Bastables.

But the evidence of these books is that his story could not remain in London unless it was satire (for which Uncle Andrew is certainly a candidate), or unless Lewis could transmute London into village or town or Baroque city (which would probably have required his knowing it better). So, by a cumbersome machine of yellow and green rings with humming sounds, made of Atlantean dust, he takes us out of London by taking us out of this world First, by the Wood between the Worlds, to the ultimate cityscape and ruined wasteland of megalopolitan and imperial Charn. Then, by the same Wood between the Worlds, into the new world and countryside of Narnia, called into being by Aslan's song, itself apparently called into being by the cabby's hymn of harvest home. (I can hear C.S. Lewis protesting, "But I didn't mean that," and I can hear the Charles Williams reply—by whomever given—"It is the courtesy of Deep Heaven that when you mean well, he takes you to mean better than you knew.") So let us follow Northrop Frye this little while.

We begin with the four great *mythoi*, Spring and the village for Comedy, Summer and the country-town for Romance, Fall and the Baroque city for Tragedy, Winter and the megalopolis for Satire. In megalopolitan London, Chesterton found country-town boroughs, little city-states at war with each other. Orwell found parks and pawnshops and the remnants of Baroque London. And Burgess's Alex goes from the Municipal Flatblocks and Stajas (State Jails) of the megalopolis to the tea-and-coffee mesto where he meets his former droog Pete and his wife, and thus to a Comedic end in a London of neighborhoods ("villages") in the future.

But in *The Magician's Nephew*, we go (when Strawberry drinks from the pool in the Wood Between the Worlds) from London city into the Creation of Narnia, to Eden (or the Garden of Nevvid Nav Neivion) in the High West, the "fair elusive beauty that some call Celtic," and true Spenserian Pastoral. And we recall that it was to London that Spenser came home again from time to time from the pastoral of his Ireland (see his *Colin Clout's Come Home Again*, 1595). We have, if there were such a thing, a stage before the first of Professor Frye's four great *mythoi*—the story-patterns of Comedy, Romance, Tragedy, and Satire. Or it is simply Comedy after all—*Divina Commedia*—with, for village, the *koinonia*, the community, where many creatures were gathered together by the riverside, and Aslan in the midst of them. (And we remember that "wherever two or three are gathered together in Thy Name, Thou art in the midst of them"—from Isaiah.)

The gathering by the riverside echoes some nineteenth-century hymns, but I cannot tell whether this particular echoing is merely accidental. I am not sure where Lewis—known for his dislike of hymns—would have come across such an exotic as "Shall We Gather at the River?"—though there is a possibility that this wildly popular American Baptist hymn (1864) made its way to the Primitive Methodist gatherings where Lewis's grandfather Richard Lewis preached—"Yes. we'll gather at the river, / The beautiful, the beautiful river, / Gather with the saints at the river / That flows by the throne of God." But we cannot be anything like as sure of this as we are of St George's Windsor and the harvest home, which I believe to have been sung at Lewis's other grandfather's church, St. Mark's Dundela.

Let us look a little bit more at Edmund Spenser. After all, he is in Lewis's *Allegory of Love* (1936) and in his *English Literature in the Sixteenth Century, Excluding Drama* (1954), and in his *Spenser's Images of Life* (1967), to say nothing of fifty pages on Spenser in his *Studies in Medieval and Renaissance Literature* (1966), including one essay ("Edmund Spenser 1552–1599") written as he was writing the Narnia books. Let me quote from Lewis's remarks on Spenser and Ireland (*Studies*, p. 126):

Spenser's visit to England had been a disappointment. He was not made for the fashionable world. The contrast between the "vain shows" of court and the simplicities of rustic life recurs increasingly in the later parts of *The Faerie Queene*. Shepherds, hermits, satyrs, even the Savage, become types to which he turns with love. . . . He was coming to need that Irish life: the freedom, the informality, the old clothes, the hunting, farming, and fishing (he was proud of the super-excellent trout in his own river at Kilcolman). He may, as a poet, have needed the very country. There is a real affinity between his *Faerie Queene*, a poem of quests and wanderings and inextinguishable desires, and Ireland itself—the soft wet air, the loneliness, the muffled shapes of the hills, the heart-rending sunsets. It was of course a different Ireland from ours, an Ireland without potatoes, whitewashed cottages, or bottled stout: but it must already have been "the land of longing." The *Faerie Queene* should perhaps be regarded as the work of one who is turning into an Irishman. . . . It is true he hated the Irish and they him: but as an Irishman myself, I take leave to doubt whether that is a very un-Irish trait.

As an Irishman myself—that's the key. We know, especially from the C.S. Lewis Centenary, just how much the Narnian scenery draws from that about Belfast and the Holywood Hills, and here is the evidence that all this is in his mind as he is writing the Narnia books and especially this one. (The essay, published in an introductory collection of Spenser's writing in 1954, was apparently completed well in advance of publication, about the time—1952—when the bulk of *The Magician's Nephew* was being written.)

In my end is my beginning—in my beginning is my ending. *The Last Battle* is implicit in the harvest home song in Narnia even before Aslan's song in *The Magician's Nephew*. I am reminded of the matter of "degrees of freedom" in statistical analysis. When we know the average of, say, seven amounts, we can pick six of them freely ("six degrees of freedom"), but the seventh must be what it is to go with the other six to make the average. Lewis had, as it were, six degrees of freedom in writing the seven Narnian books, but his freedom in the seventh was severely circumscribed, because the full pattern of the story had already been established. As *The Magician's Nephew* was the beginning, something very like *The Last Battle* must be the end—and the new beginning. As Digory had ridden Fledge to the Uttermost West in The Magician's Nephew, he must be there again with Fledge in *The Last Battle*. But only children can visit the world of Narnia. So it must not be merely a visit. What is particularly interesting to me is that *The Magician's Nephew* is a very Irish book, but the cast of *The Last Battle* is more Norse or Icelandic. "The Giants and the Trolls will win—Let us die with Father Odin!"

In fact, if *The Lion, the Witch, and the Wardrobe* is a helter-skelter children's book after the manner of E. Nesbit, and *Prince Caspian* is Edwardian adventure story, and *The Voyage of the "Dawn Treader"* is *Bildungsroman* and pilgrimage, and *The Silver Chair* is quest narrative, and *The Horse and His Boy* is *Marchen*, then *The Magician's Nephew* and *The Last Battle* are cosmogony. All are children's books, to be sure, but mostly not fairy-tale (despite what Lewis may have said) and certainly very different from each other in *genre* or at least in *sub-genre*.

One thing they have in common is that—once he is working from the implications of the original pictures more than from the pictures themselves—these are books giving Lewis pretty full rein for his abilities in description. Another (less observed, I think) is that Lewis is making references in these books to a variety of sources and analogues and even worlds (almost in the way T.S. Eliot described as using the objective correlative), choosing them to support his stories, to round them out, to "realize" them.

Thus, for example, in *The Last Battle*, when Puzzle brings the lion-skin out of the Caldron Pool for Shift, and is shivering from his time in the pool, Shift sends him off on a brisk trot to Chippingford to warm up, and besides, "it's market day at Chippingford to-day." Chippingford? There is a Chippingford in Surrey (GU8 4QW) and one in Oxfordshire (OX21 9AA), and may be others: the point here is that the "Chip" of "Chippingford" is the "-chepe" of "Eastchepe" (in London), and indeed at the root of our "cheap"—it comes from Old English *ceap* for market. Of course a market-day would be at the ford where there is a market— Chippingford. But that would be in England. In fact, of course, Lewis is writing for an English audience and his points of reference or objective correlatives will be English.

Puzzle brings the lion-skin from the pool to the Ape Shift, who tells him to put it on and act as though he's Aslan, and the great deception begins. "About three weeks later, the last of the Kings of Narnia sat under the great oak which grew beside the little door of his hunting lodge" (p. 11), with his best friend, Jewel the Unicorn, talking about the tidings that Aslan has come again, when there comes the great golden-bearded centaur, Roonwit, to tell them (p. 15) that "The stars say nothing of the coming of Aslan, nor of peace, nor of joy. I know by my art that there have not been such disastrous conjunctions of the planets for five hundred years [say since A.N. 1998, when the Telmarines conquered Narnia]. It was already in my mind to come and warn your majesty that some great evil hangs over Narnia. But last night the rumor reached me that Aslan is abroad in Narnia. Sir, do not believe this tale. It cannot be.

The stars never lie, but Men and Beasts do. If Aslan were really coming to Narnia, the sky would have foretold it. If he were really come, all the most gracious stars would be assembled in his honor. It is all a lie" (p. 15). (Well, after all, a star foretold the coming of Christ here on earth, or so the stories have it—"a star brighter than all the sky shone").

Then come the calls of the dryads that men are felling the holy trees, and Tirian Last-King goes to bid the evil cease. Of course he is caught, with Jewel, by the Calormenes whom Shift has invited in to fell the trees and enslave the Talking Beasts. And Tirian in his agony calls out (p. 42), "'Children! Children! Friends of Narnia! Quick. Come to me. Across the worlds I call you; I Tirian, King of Narnia, Lord of Cair Paravel, and Emperor of the Lone Islands!' And immediately he was plunged into a dream (if it was a dream) more vivid than any he had had in his life." In the dream he is in a lighted room with seven people sitting around a table—two of them "very old" and the others young, wearing "the oddest kind of clothes." They are, of course, the seven friends of Narnia (Susan is not there); the High King Peter charges Tirian to speak; he cannot and fades away—and immediately after Tirian fades back into Narnia, Jill and Eustace appear there, rescue Tirian from his captivity, and Jewel from his—and Puzzle from his.

And then some Dwarfs, who, far from joining Tirian and Jill and Eustace, fight both them and the Calormenes: "The Dwarfs are for the Dwarfs." (We will see what happens to them in the end.) All except for the Dwarf Poggin, who escapes from the others and joins Tirian and Jewel and Eustace and Jill and Puzzle. Tirian and the others return to the deserted guard tower in the Lantern Waste where they have their headquarters.

> It was at the coldest hour of the night, just before dawn, that they got back to the Tower. . . . They drank from a stream, splashed their faces with water, and tumbled into their bunks, except for Puzzle and Jewel who said they'd be more comfortable outside. This perhaps was just as well, for a Unicorn and a fat full-grown donkey indoors always make a room feel rather crowded. (p. 75)

The passage here rather turns Lewis's dictum on Tolkien on its head: It is as though a serious *heimsökn* had changed into the Battle of Toad Hall, and Njal had begun to talk like Badger. Or, if we are looking to Victorian antecedents, it is rather clerical than avuncular and more like Charles Kingsley in *The Water-Babies* than any of the authors we have talked about before. Certainly there is a bit of carnival—the *serio* and the *buffo*, and indeed the very quick passage from the one to the other. It isn't a Christmas book, of course—or is it? Listen to Lucy a little later on (pp. 140–41): "'Yes,' said Queen Lucy, 'In our world too, a Stable once had something inside it than was bigger than our whole world.'" But before we get there, we have to get into the Stable.

And before that, here are the words of Jewel the Unicorn to Jill (pp. 88–89):

> He said that the Sons and Daughters of Adam and Eve were brought out of their own strange world into Narnia only at times when Narnia was stirred and upset, but she mustn't think it was always like that. In between their visits there were hundreds and thousands of years when peaceful King followed peaceful King till you could hardly remember their names or count their numbers . . . He talked of whole centuries in which all Narnia was so happy that notable dances and feasts, or at most tournaments, were the only things that could be remembered, and every day and week had been better than the last . . .

Jewel mentions King Gale, ninth in the line from the first King Frank, who delivered the Lone Islands from a dragon. But if peaceful King followed peaceful King, in the line of King Frank, what happened to the line before the Pevensies came, and (as we asked before) why were there four thrones at Cair Paravel? (And why didn't Frank's descendants in Archenland take the throne of Narnia?)

But that must be outside our present concerns. Jill says she would like to get back to those good ordinary times—"'Oh Jewel—wouldn't it be lovely if Narnia just went on and on—like what you said it has been.' 'Nay, sister,' answered Jewel, 'all worlds draw to an end; except Aslan's own country'" (p. 89). Then comes Farsight the Eagle, to tell Tirian he was with Roonwit in his last hour, slain by a Calormene arrow, and that Roonwit told him to tell the King, "to remember that all worlds draw to an end and that noble death is a treasure which no one is too poor to buy" (p. 91). And they know they are going to their death, and it is evident that their world is drawing to an end, with living Calormenes and dead Narnians in Cair Paravel. They go back to the stable, to hear Shift tell the Beasts that a wicked ass has dressed up in a lion-skin and "Tashlan" is very angry. The Beasts may go into the Stable to see Tashlan, but he's not coming out, and they go in one at a time— "'Dilly, dilly, come and be killed'" (p. 106).

The cat Ginger, Shift's lieutenant, goes in—and comes out stricken of speech, turned back to a dumb beast. Then comes the Calormene

Emeth. "'My Father,' he said to the Captain, I also desire to go in'" (p. 110). After argument the Calormene commander, Rishda Tarkaan, allows him to go in, saying "'Bear witness all that I am guiltless of this young fool's blood. Get thee in, rash boy, and make haste'" (pp. 111–12).

By now it is pretty well known that *emeth* is the Hebrew word for truth—or, to be more accurate, trueness as in the plummet dropping true or the level showing true. And Rishda Tarkaan is beginning to sound a little like Pontius Pilate, "I am innocent of the blood of this just person: see ye to it" (*Matthew* 27:24, KJV). Just as Tolkien in *The Return of the King* used Hebrew psalmody as the referent, or the objective correlative, for the song of triumph for the West, so Lewis in *The Last Battle* uses Gospel referents (or references or correlatives). In a way, as we suggested in mentioning the statistician's degrees of freedom, this is by way of being (for Lewis) a forced choice. He has established the almost-identity between Aslan and Christ, and the ending of the story must be with Aslan and Narnia as it is to be with Christ and our world.

To be sure, Lewis did remark (in a letter 8th June 1960, *Letters to Children*, p. 92) that he was not representing Christ by Aslan, but "more saying 'Suppose there were a world like Narnia and it needed rescuing and the Son of God (or [of] the 'Great Emperor oversea') went to redeem it, as He came to redeem ours, what might it, in that world, all have been like?" It all hinges on what is meant by "a world like Narnia" and why Narnia needed redemption. But if Narnia needs a Son of Adam on the throne, then Narnia is in some sense—theologically if not "literarily"—a derivative world, and its story must be derived from ours. As, of course, it is. In fact, I have heard it questioned whether Lewis's distinction between representing Christ by Aslan and asking how a world like Narnia might be redeemed by the Son is in fact a distinction without a difference, and of course the world most clearly derivative is one where the derivation is through allegory.

But in this case I do not think Lewis was really being disingenuous— which an allegory denied would be. We should go back to the fact that the furniture of Lewis's mind is obviously furnished by things of this world and particularly, in his case, by his reading in this world. A system of referents and correlatives is not at all the same thing as allegory. Here is Tirian issuing his challenge in a great voice (p. 113): "Here stand I, Tirian of Narnia, in Aslan's name, to prove by my body that Tash is a foul fiend, the Ape, a manifold traitor, and these Calormenes, worthy of death. To my side, all true Narnians. Would you wait till your new masters have killed you all, one by one?" That is out of our Middle Ages (and particularly from Froissart's *Chronicles*, through Berners, or from Malory's *Morte D'Arthur*). And then there is Lewis's richly humorous description of the coming of the Talking Dogs to Tirian's side (p. 114):

> Their coming was like the breaking of a great wave on the seabeach: it nearly knocked you down. For though they were Talking Dogs they were just as doggy as they could be: and they all stood up and put their front paws on the shoulders of the humans and licked their faces, all saying at once: "Welcome! Welcome! We'll help, we'll help, help, help. Show us how to help, show us how, how. How-how-how?"

Remember that Lewis's contemporary, the historian of the English sense of humor, Stephen Potter (1900–1969), has traced his own sense of that sense of humor (Potter, *Sense of Humour*, 1954, pp. 27–28) to a particular education out of school hours:

> I knew every page of my father's ten-volume edition of *Punch* selections . . . When I read about Germany, the picture, and the only picture, which came to my mind was a cartoon of the Kaiser playing with toy battleships on the end of a string. 'Wealth'—and I saw a Du Maurier drawing of Sir Gorgius Midas. 'Drunkenness'—there was the John Leach drawing of the man lying in the gutter who had 'dined well but not too wisely' . . . The caricatures and the pictures were life, it seemed, as I turned from them to the shadowy world of real people. Later on, in my teens, *Punch* was at its English-sense-of-humor peak, all light touch and mild smile . . . Our childhood books were humorous, filled with humorously funny animals . . . There are certainly worse places to grow up in than a world in eyes were supposed to twinkle and the mouths to have deep corners. The mid-nineteenth-century clergymen tended to be grim over nothing. Our own parsons were jolly about nothing, which was certainly an improvement, even though it seemed equally far away from religion . . .

All this is in Potter's introductory essay, which ends—p. 43—with the Coleridgean definition of humor as "'bringing forward into distinct consciousness those minutiae of thought and feeling [I would add, of action] which appear trifles, [seem to] have an importance only for the moment, and yet almost every man feels in one way or another.'"

Here, in Narnia, and especially here, in *The Last Battle*, it might be said that Lewis, though not a clergyman, yet writing almost as one, has found the missing connection between good humor and religion. But it may be well to explore what Potter says about his own reaction to those bound volumes from *Punch* on his father's shelves. He notes in the course of his essay that humor requires a kind of standing-aside from the author, even in the days of the "founding" of English humor (Chaucer) or the beginnings of the age of humor (Addison and Steele, Dr. Johnson, Sterne), and the beginnings of its maturity (Dickens, and I would add Surtees and Thackeray). That is at the root of the avuncular or Godfatherly pose. But he notes especially his youthful reaction that what was in *Punch* was the reality, and "real life" not so.

Note here that at least one figure in one of Lewis's Boxonian illustrations ("another customer entered" in *Boxen,* p. 68) is evidently copied from a book illustration, and the figure of Viscount Puddiphat (p. 58 and back of dust-jacket) is evidently based on one. I cannot be sure of my own experience here, but it seems to me that I recognized the world of books as in some way the ideal world, and the world of my daily life was real—but if I wrote, I immediately entered the "ideal" world—in fact, reading and reciting poetry and writing were my ways into that world, so the net effect of my perception on my writing was the same as the effect of what may have been his different perception was on Lewis's. Only I didn't have the bound volumes of *Punch* until I was in my late teens. And I was in no way talented in drawing, unlike my father and sister. So my imitations were verse imitations—light verse, mostly. Perhaps I did not have the patience to write stories; I certainly did not have the talent to illustrate them.

So as the Last Battle for Narnia is ending—and it is "The Giants and the Trolls will win; let us die with Father Odin" combined with the Christian *eschaton*—and combined with other echoes from long-ago reading? When I hear Poggin cry "'Ware arrows,'" I hear the cry "'Ware Saintlache arrows'" in Kipling's *Rewards and Fairies*. And then there is the door with sunlight on both sides of it but the dark visible through it—a door not unlike the door through which the Children and the Telmarines are sent at the end of *Prince Caspian*, Lewis reusing a vision. The Dwarfs in the Stable still bound by their own self-set walls ("The Dwarfs are for the Dwarfs!") are, like Uncle Andrew in *The Magician's Nephew*, impervious to any help from outside. But soon all of this is swallowed up. Aslan calls "Time!" and the Door flies open, and they look out on the Blackness of Darkness.

The Giant Jill and Eustace saw under the moors in *The Silver Chair* has awakened—and (p. 150), "'Yes,' said Aslan, though they had not spoken. 'While he was dreaming his name was Time. Now that he is awake he will have a new one.' Then the great giant raised a horn to his mouth. . . . After that—quite a bit later, because sound travels so slowly—they heard the sound of the horn: high and terrible, yet of a strange deadly beauty . . ." The stars are being called home. And there is a description here of the growing blackness of the sky that parallels the description of the ascent from Malacandra in *Out of the Silent Planet*. Then with the stars called home, and casting their light from behind Aslan and the children, they see enormous animals crawling and sliding into Narnia, dragons and their like (the Dragon and all his   , and then the sounds of creatures (including men and strange unearthly things from the unknown lands to the West) "racing up the hill for dear life" (p. 152).

And as in a dream, they see the creatures look Aslan in the face, and go either left into his shadow or right into the sunshine. Then the dragons and their like tear Narnia down to the bare rock and shrivel up and die and skeletons lie there on the dead rock, and the sea rises, and when the sun comes up twenty times as big as it should be, and very dark red, so that in its reflection the shoreless sea is blood-red. The moon comes up, and the flames of the sun reach out and engulf the moon—and great lumps of fire fall into the shoreless sea. The giant reaches forth his hand and squeezes the sun like an orange and all is dark. Peter pulls the door to, over the ice, takes out a golden key and locks it. And then begins the final part of this story—or perhaps I should say, the final part of this part of the story. For now they are—where?

Aslan cries out "'Come further in! Come further up!'" Night has fallen on Narnia, and Lucy mourns, as they follow Aslan further in and further up. They meet the Calormene Emeth, who tells them his encounter with Aslan (pp. 164–65):

> He answered, "Child, all the service thou hast done to Tash, I account as service done to me . . . Not because he and I are one but because we are opposites, I take to me the services thou hast done to him, for I and he are of such different kinds that no service which is vile can be done to me, and none which is not vile can be done to him. Therefore if any man swear by Tash and keep his oath for the oath's sake, it is by me he has truly sworn. . . ." But I said also . . . "Yet I have been seeking Tash all my days." "Beloved," said the Glorious One, "unless thy desire had been for me thou wouldst not have sought so long and so truly. For all find what they truly seek."

This disposes neatly of those who have served Tash or his equivalent, but what about the virtuous Pagans who have confused lesser gods with God, or Buddhists, or Zoroastrians or Gnostics or Manichaeans or Muslims who have served God in different understandings. Perhaps they too have their reward according to what they truly seek—and I think of the "between the paws of Aslan" in Narnia, and "between the paws of Zurvan" as spoke Zarathustra.

As they go on, their surroundings seem more and more to remind them of something (or somewhere). Was it somewhere the Pevensies went on vacation? And eventually they realize the mountains to the south are very like the mountains on the southern border of Narnia, but, as Digory says (he's now the Lord Digory and Polly the Lady Polly), they're "more like the real thing" (p. 169). And then he tells us what is happening, and where we are.

> "Listen, Peter. When Aslan said you could never go back to Narnia, he meant the Narnia you were thinking of. But that was not the real Narnia. That had a beginning and an end. It was only a shadow or copy of the real Narnia, which has always been here and always will be here [but where is here?]: just as our own world, England and all, is only a shadow or copy of something in Aslan's real world' . . . You may have been in a room [this is Lewis speaking directly to us] in which there was a window that looked out on a lovely bay of the sea or a green valley that wound away among mountains. . . . And as you turned away from the window you suddenly caught sight of that sea or that valley, all over again, in the looking glass. And the sea in the mirror, or the valley in the mirror, were in one sense just the same as the real ones: yet at the same time they were somehow different—deeper, more wonderful, more like places in a story: in a story you have never heard but very much want to know . . ." (p. 170)

Now, notice what Lewis has done here. The real Narnia is like a mysterious Narnia glimpsed in the looking glass—deeper and more wonderful than the old Narnia ("Now we see in a glass darkly, but then face to face" or—better—that passage in James where he speaks of looking into the perfect law of liberty as a glass), more like a place in a story ("In the beginning was the Word"), a story you have never heard but want to hear. And, of course, the word *myth* designates (among other things) a pattern story. We will say more on Lewis on voice and story shortly, but our point here is that by this transposition between the real and the less real, with the real being in the mirror and in the story, he is bringing us more and more into a theological world, and the theology is Christian.

As we see more and more as they come to the garden where Digory and Polly came the day that world was born—and there is Fledge, and through the golden gates comes Reepicheep—and there is Tirian's father as he remembers him from his early youth (and "the very smell of the bread-and-milk he used to have for supper came back to him"—p. 177), and Glimfeather the Owl and Puddleglum and Rilian the Disenchanted, and Caspian and Trumpkin, and Cor of Archenland and Queen Aravis, and then from further in the past the two good Beavers and Tumnus the

Faun—and they gather before the Throne of King Frank and Queen Helen. Lucy stands with Tumnus and looks down at Narnia far below them, and at Narnia within the garden: "'I see now. This garden is like the Stable. It is far bigger inside than it was outside.' 'Of course, Daughter of Eve ... the further up and further in you go, the bigger everything gets. The inside is larger than the outside'" (p. 180). There is Narnia within Narnia, "'like an onion: except that as you continue to go in and in, each circle is larger than the last'"—a larger and larger life.

Then they look out over one of the deep valleys, and see their own father and mother waving at them, and we hear a simile from Lewis's own Belfast youth (p. 182): "It was like when you see people waving at you from the deck of a big ship when you are waiting on the quay to meet them.'" And then comes the great news, the final transposition. Lucy says (p. 183):

> "We're so afraid of being sent away, Aslan. And you have sent us back into our own world so often." "No fear of that," said Aslan. "Have you not guessed?" Their hearts leaped and a wild hope rose within them. "There was a real railway accident," said Aslan. "Your father and mother and all of you are—as you used to call it in the Shadow-Lands—dead. The term is over: the holidays have begun. The dream is ended: this is the morning." And ... the things that began to happen after that were so great and beautiful that I cannot write them ... All their life in this world and all their adventures in Narnia had been only the cover and title page: now at last they were beginning Chapter One of the Great Story ... (pp. 183–84)

Aslan had promised to be telling Lucy the story she had read back in *The Voyage of the "Dawn Treader"*—and now is all the Story being told, "which goes on forever; in which every chapter is better than the one before" (p. 184). You will see, by the way, that it is life in this world and adventures in Narnia that have served as cover and title page. We suggested earlier (following Owen Barfield) that the adventures in imagination (and perhaps especially dream or dreamlike adventures) were the first larger life: now (as the Prayer for the Faithful Departed that began this chapter tells us) death is the second larger life. But let us look a little more closely at the last stages of the travel to the garden.

When Lucy is standing with Tumnus in the garden, and she looks down over the wall, she finds that hill where the garden was far higher than she had thought: "it sank down with shining cliffs, thousands of feet below them" (p. 180). They had reached the top of that hill, swimming up the great waterfall, running faster than flight over hill and dale and then finally up that green hill—and after the garden, they walk in a great procession "up towards mountains higher than you could see in this world even if they were there to be seen" (p. 182). And then "a great series of many-colored cliffs led up in front of them like a giant's staircase' (p. 182). We have reached the mountains on which the eternal sunrise hung at the end of Lewis's dream in *The Great Divorce*. But I think we have met these mountains before that.

Are these not the Delectable Mountains?

> They went, then, till they came to the "Delectable Mountains," which mountains belong to the Lord of that hill of whom we have spoken before. So they went up to the mountains, to behold the gardens and orchards, the vineyards and fountains of water; where also they drank, and washed themselves, and did freely eat of the vineyards. Now there were on the tops of these mountains shepherds feeding their flocks; and they stood by the highway side. The pilgrims therefore went to them; and, leaning upon their staves (as is common with weary pilgrims when they stand to talk with any by the way), they asked, "Whose delectable mountains are these? and whose be the sheep that feed upon them?" And the Shepherds answered: "These mountains are Immanuel's Land, and they are within sight of his City; and the sheep also are his, and he laid down his life for them."

Note that the very high mountains of Aslan's Land have no snow, but "there were forests and green slopes and sweet orchards and flashing waterfalls, one above the other, going up forever" (p. 182). The Delectable Mountains are, of course, in Bunyan's *The Pilgrim's Progress*, and if we wondered what manner of book *The Last Battle* was, we know now; it is the pilgrims' progress, pilgrimage, if you like, as well as *Eschaton*, the Last Things.

And lest we think the military references (or referents or correlatives) of our title here are without earlier parallel, let us remember that great passage where Mr. Valiant-for-Truth crosses over: "Then said he: 'I am going to my Father's: and though with great difficulty I am got hither, yet now I do not repent me of all the trouble I have been at to arrive where I am. My sword I give to him that shall succeed me in my pilgrimage, and my courage and skill to him that can get it. My marks and scars I carry with me, to be a witness for me that I have fought His battles who now will be my rewarder.' So he passed over, and all the trumpets sounded for him on the other side." The military note is clear—clearer if we can get away from our recollections of class wills in school graduation ceremonies, and we see in Bunyan the same linking of pilgrimage and battle that Lewis makes in *The Last Battle*. And was not Lucy called Queen Lucy the Valiant (and Valiant precisely for Truth)?

I find myself misquoting "Further up and further in" as "Higher up and further in"—the descriptions of the Delectable Mountains, of the uprush of the running and flying up the great height, of the great waterfall and of the ascent of the great waterfall, have all led to that. Of course, Lewis was conscious of the difference of highland and lowland from the beginnings of his life, and it plays out in the *harandra* and *handramit* on Malacandra in *Out of the Silent Planet,* of the ascent of the mountain in *Perelandra*, of the everlasting mountains in *The Great Divorce*, and throughout the Narnian stories (or Story). But this is more than the difference between highland and lowland. This is something more akin to the popular understanding of Psalm 121, "I will lift up mine eyes unto the hills, from whence cometh my help," the Presence on the Hills (and His are the animals—the cattle—on a thousand hills), and the mountains of Immanuel's Land in Bunyan.

Speaking of the "popular understanding" of Psalm 121, I wish Lewis had said something on this psalm in his *Reflections on the Psalms*, but he did not—and in fact, the *Reflections* do not tell us nearly enough about Lewis's experiences with the Psalms. As I understand it, the original intent of Psalm 121 was to distinguish between help from the Canaanite gods of the hills and help from the Lord (and also, in passing, between the power of the Sun and the Moon, a god and a goddess, and the power of the Lord), but because the popular mind links the heights of earth with the heights of heaven, the psalm has a new—and for many a better—meaning, placing the Lord Himself in the hills. As He is in Bunyan, and as he is in *The Last Battle*.

One thing that does come through in the *Reflections* is the joyfulness—sometimes, thinking of Aslan, even the "friskiness" and certainly the "animality"—of worship and divinity in the Psalms, David dancing before the Lord (a favorite passage of Charles Williams), and in *The Last Battle* Aslan Himself "leaping down from cliff to cliff like a living cataract of power and beauty" (p. 183). (Compare the description of Tor and Tinidril in *Perelandra*, though here the word used is torrent—a "living torrent of perfect animality" p. 207—rather than cataract.)

When the Time-Giant reached out and squeezed the red sun like an orange, we seem to be in something like a Norse world, but the strange unearthly beauty of the horn that calls the stars home is neither Norse nor Hebrew, though it may have elements of both. The shofar blown on the heights of Zion (note, again, the heights) may have something of that, and the stars play a role in Hebrew life specifically and Mediterranean and Near Eastern life generally greater than in other places and other mythologies.

But we must always beware of straying too far from Ireland in our discussion, and we must also remember Lewis's view of the truth of myth across cultures, so that we should expect some kind of blending of cultures and myths—in fact, a blending in some ways demanded by the mixed origins of the pictures from which Narnia came, and the mixed furniture of Lewis's mind. We will speak more of that in the next chapter, but for the time being we will turn back to looking at the two "book-end" volumes, *The Magician's Nephew* and *The Last Battle*, as they begin and end the Story of Narnia (though not, of course, the story of Lewis's creation of Narnia).

The traditional framework of the Edwardian adventure story is "There and Back Again"—which, you will recall, is the subtitle of *The Hobbit*. The traditional framework of the fairy-tale is "Once upon a time" and then "They lived happily ever after." The traditional framework of the pastoral (particularly the English pastoral) is adventure and then judgment. The traditional framework of the pilgrimage depends on the type of the pilgrimage—Chaucer's *Canterbury Tales* are told on a "there and back again" pilgrimage, but those pilgrimages that descend from Deguileville (*Pélèrinage de la Vie Humaine*) through Lydgate (*Pylgrymage of the Lyfe of Man*) and from *Piers Plowman* and through *The Pilgrim's Progress* are what we might call "one-way" pilgrimages, which need either a dream-framework (as in *Piers Plowman* or even Bunyan) or have introduction but no end, one might say, in their beginning is their ending.

And we note that the form of pastoral, adventures followed by judgment, and the form of the one-way pilgrimage are similar and similarly expansive. What I mean by that is the expansion of the particular into the general by judgment, matching the expansionary nature of pilgrimage (which, wherever it is to, models our pilgrimage of the human life). Though the separate volumes of the Story of Narnia may be *Marchen*, fairy-tale, or adventure story or pilgrimage, the seven volumes together are—I believe—pastoral, and we might say a little more about that ancient and obscure form here, looking at the book-ends. We looked at this matter of (Arcadian) pastoral earlier, but I think we might look at it a little more fully now.

In an earlier study on Lewis (*The Scientifiction Novels of C.S. Lewis*, Jefferson NC, 2004), I had a section entitled "Prologue, Arcadia, and the Pattern of Pageant," and I would like to apply some of the procedures suggested there for the Ransom stories at least to the book-end volumes of the Narnian Story. We begin with the matter of Prologue, which in some senses *The Magician's Nephew* certainly is. Now we are not used to the Prologue as an integral part of a literary—or dramatic—work, though perhaps more used to it in drama than in prose fiction. The classic case—where the Prologue (as Chorus) appears in the *dramatis personae*—is Shakespeare's *King Henry the Fifth*. "O! for a Muse of fire that would ascend / The brightest heaven of invention, /—A kingdom for a stage, princes to act, / And monarchs to behold the swelling scene . . . O! pardon, since a crooked figure may / Attest in little place a million; / And let us, ciphers to this great accompt, / On your imaginary forces work. / Suppose within the girdle of these walls / Are now confined two mighty monarchies, / Whose high unreared and abutting fronts / The perilous narrow ocean parts asunder: / Piece-out our imperfections with your thoughts; / Into a thousand parts divide one man / And make imaginary puissance; / Think, when we talk of horses, that you see them / Printing their proud hooves i' th' receiving earth—" That from the opening Prologue, and then again a Prologue for each act of the play.

Now, it is arguably true that this prologue is required because these things cannot be seen on stage, but for our purposes here what is important is that this is a pageant play, and the prologue is what links our flat quotidian world, even with its playhouses, to the imagined world of the pageant, making possible the "realizing" of the (apparently) unreal. For Arcady is apparently unreal. Of course, as a realm of the spirit, it claims a different kind of reality. Like Shakespeare's France. Like Lewis's Narnia. Or any myth.

In Olivier's *Henry the Fifth*, there is a dissolve from the Chorus in the Wooden O to the vasty fields of France: in a film, that is easily done. Of course, we take those vasty fields as historical: within our history they are, and designedly within Shakespeare's. But they are still the author's imagining. And as each act in the play begins with Chorus setting the scene, standing within our world and guiding us to the dissolve and the round world's imagined corners, so each book in Lewis's series (except one) begins in our world and guides us to the dissolve. But why do I say that our fields are Arcadian? The guide here is Sidney's (or the Countess of Pembroke's) *Arcadia*. And for the guidance, we turn to Lewis himself, in the OHEL volume (*English Literature in the Sixteenth Century, Excluding Drama*, Oxford 1954, pp. 333–342). From this we learn what we might not have guessed, that the model for the book that effectively introduces Arcadia into English letters is in fact a Menippean satire.

The two great influences on Sidney's romance are the *Arcadia* (1501) of Sannazaro and the *Ethiopian History* (fourth century A.D.) of Heliodorus. There are of course others; Malory possibly, Amadis probably, and

Montemayor's Diana. But Montemayor is himself largely a disciple of Sannazaro: it is from Sannazaro and Heliodorus that the two kinds of fiction which Sidney is fusing really descend. (p. 333)

Sannazaro's work belongs formally to an extinct species, the Varronian Satura Menippea in alternating proses and metres . . . The thread of narrative in the proses, though enriched with epic material . . . and romantic . . . is indeed very slight. But it has a momentous effect. It creates for the singing shepherds a landscape, a social structure, a whole world; a new image, only hinted by previous pastoralists, has come into existence—the image of Arcadia itself. That is why Sannazaro's work, though in one sense highly derivative—it is claimed that almost every phrase has a classical origin—is, in another, so new and so important . . . (pp. 333–34)

Heliodorus, translated by Thomas Underdowne in 1569 . . . had in Sidney's time an importance which the successive narrowings of our classical tradition have since obscured. In order to see that importance we must once more remind ourselves that the word 'poesie' could cover prose fiction. We must remember the taste for interlocked and endlessly varied narrative to which the medieval romances and Italian epics equally bear witness. These facts, taken together, explain why Scaliger cites the *Aithiopica* as a model of epic construction; why Sidney and Tasso both mention it among heroic poems. . . .

   From Sannazaro Sidney took over the Menippean form (though he made his proses so long that we hardly notice it) and the idea of Arcadia itself. From Heliodorus he took over the conception of the prose epic, filling his story with shipwreck, disguise, battle, and intrigue . . . The first thing we need to know about the Arcadia is that it is a heroic poesy; not Arcadian idyll, not even Arcadian romance, but Arcadian epic. To call it a pastoral is misleading. The title seems to promise that, and the first few pages keep the promise. But almost at once Sidney leads us away from the 'shepherdish complaynts of Strephon' to a shipwreck, to the house of a country gentleman, to affairs of state, and to the royal family. (pp. 334–335)

The implication here is that the complaints of Strephon are in fact prologue, but almost accidentally so. Perhaps. But in the Arcadian epic we are discussing here, the prologue is designedly Arcadian in the ordinary sense. Also, of course, it could be called a prologue in something like (though not the same as) the fairy-tale mode: we might say that it is not itself Arcadian, and that it is followed by the shift to Arcady. Or is it in fact Arcadian? At the very least, in some sense it introduces and foreshadows what is to come (as perhaps it did for Sidney), in much the way that Chorus (Prologue) in *Henry the Fifth* introduces and foreshadows what is to come.

It may well be argued that in its very beginning, *The Magician's Nephew* is not Arcadian: there is obviously not much countryside here. The participants are in fact in London (though cityscapes can be pastoral and thus Arcadian, as we have noted). But here (at the risk of the personal heresy) we may note that, in many respects, Lewis's own Arcady was in his great and grand house. It was from here his companions in Arcady came. And yet, Digory and Polly are outside when they meet, and there is no question that when they (and the guinea pig) reach the Wood between the Worlds, that is countryside indeed. Let us take a little side excursion here, thinking for a moment of these books as pageant through the countryside.

Lewis found Gavin Douglas's Prologues in his *XIII Bukes of the Eneados* saved from the flatness of mere description by the presence of the author. Lewis is no less directly and obviously present here than Douglas in his great book. We think of pageant as having its Medieval origins in the pageant plays—sometimes called the morality plays or miracle plays. Except for conscious reconstruction (as in *Jesus Christ Superstar*) and in the lingering attenuated form represented by circus parades, these in their original form of dramatic pageant are pretty much gone from the English-speaking world. The point to be emphasized here is that these plays represent a progress from the quotidian to the more-and-more miraculous, the more-and-more exciting, the more-and-more gilded and heraldic and wonderful (full of wonder), with comic relief along the way (Herod in the Miracle Plays, the clowns in the circus parade)—and, of course, a moral at the end. This fits well with the Arcadian pattern, as Sidney built it from Sannazaro's *Arcadia* and the *Aithiopica* of Heliodorus. Of course, the creaking carts of the Morality Play (or the circus parade) leave much to the imagination: the dissolve, the shift to the real Arcady (or in *Henry the Fifth* to the real vasty fields of France), is much easier for the writer of fiction. But the progress is the same. And the real is, in both cases, a realm of the spirit. And in written fiction, there must be a kind of machine to bring about the shift— unless, as here, the shift is part of the form.

Historically, in English literature, the shift—especially the Arcadian shift—has often been involved with dream. The *textus receptus* here is Kenneth Grahame's *Dream Days*—and also his *Golden Age*. Looking at the function of dream in the shift to Arcady leads also to the dream-time-lessness of Novalis and George MacDonald (those who are curious about this may look in my study of *The Rise of Tolkienian Fantasy*). An idyllic life is part of traditional Arcady, regardless of whether we are in Arcadian epic, rather than Arcadian idyll (or even, I believe, Arcadian romance). It might be suggested that we have still not fully justified the word Arcadian. Why not, for example (it is not an irrelevant question), Olympian?

After all, Olympus has to do with heights and Arcady with fields below them. Remember, as we said before, that "We can paint Arcadia all 'humble vallies comforted with refreshing of silver rivers,' all trees that 'Maintaine their flourishing olde age with the onely happinesse of their seat, being clothed with continual spring because no beautie here should euer fade.' . . . Such is the Arcadia we know from popular tradition before we open the book. And all this is really there. But it is not there alone. Against these passages we can quote almost as many of a sterner and graver kind. 'Judgment,' says Euarchus (as if he had been reading Burke), 'must undoubtedly bee done, not by a free discourse of reason and skill of philosophy, but must be tyed to the laws of Greece and the municipall statutes of this kingdome'." Judgment comes often from Olympus, true, or from the heights, but it is judgment in Arcady.

Has enough been said to suggest the applicability of the term Arcadian? There are, in fact, at least three reasons for using it. The first is the common meaning or significance of the word—what everyone knows about Arcady before reading about it: the pastoral, the country-side, the green and pleasant land with animals. The second is what one finds in Sidney's Arcadia: the Arcadian epic drawing from both Sannazaro's Menippean Satire and the epic adventure story of Heliodorus. The third is the particular irony of the eighteenth-century vision of Arcadia, most notable in Poussin but characteristic of the century. And, as we have said, the form—the *genre*—that goes with Arcadia is—whether epic or otherwise—a form of pastoral. I think the Victorian Age cherished the pastoral of old times, and (the life of the person reca-pitulating the life of the people) looked to childhood as pastoral, as the golden age for the person lost to the people as a whole.

Kenneth Grahame noted the loss of Arcady in adulthood (*The Penguin Kenneth Grahame,* 1983, p. 5):

Well! The Olympians are passed and gone. Somehow the sun does not shine so brightly as it used; the trackless meadows of old time have shrunk and dwindled away to a few poor acres. A saddening doubt, a dull suspicion, creeps over me. Et in Arcadia ego—I certainly did once inhabit Arcady. Can it be that I also have become an Olympian?

In this version of pastoral, the progress is, more or less, from the fields we know—the home fields, as it were, the daily life—through some kind of nexus where the physical and the spiritual touch, then the sense (perhaps the experience) of powers abroad in the land, spiritual powers as well as physical, and then, finally, climax and judgment. The fifth Book of the *Arcadia*, as we recall, performs the comedic function of sorting out the cross-identities and misadventures in the semblance of a trial and judgment.

We sometimes overlook the fact that this last book of *Arcadia* is indeed a legal trial—though the picture of Macedonia in Arcadia's seat, judging Pirocles and Musidorus, strains against our normal understanding of the phrase "legal trial." In any case, the judgment is in some sense the appropriate response to the amorality or highly mixed morality of the pastoral in progress. But that mixed morality or amorality is of the earth, earthly, and the adventures in Narnia are not. The judgment in Narnia is the Last Judgment. (But that too will be Earthly, will it not?) That *The Last Battle* is pageant is strongly suggested in the ceremony as the great figures of the Narnian past gather at the Throne.

The author is present; the shift is part of the form; judgment is part of pastoral; childhood, pastoral, and Arcady are linked; irony inheres in pastoral (and satire also); the real world is the world of the spirit ("It's all in Plato. Bless me! What do they teach them in these schools?"); the Story begins with Prologue, and goes on from there to Final Judgment—it is not the "There and Back Again" of many of Lewis's models, though it is a form both of pageant and pilgrimage (both, as I have argued elsewhere, appropriate to pastoral). The "book-ends" turn out to be book-beginning and book-end, and in the beginning is the end, and in the end is the beginning. It is now time to look more at voices and stories.

[6]
Child! I Tell No-One Any Story But His Own

It should be evident by now that our author is very conscious both of voice and story. There are, of course, various voices to tell stories to children—most particularly the parental voice (as with Tolkien, E. Nesbit, Kipling, possibly George MacDonald, some of G.A. Henty) or the avuncular voice (as with Edward Lear, Lewis Carroll, John Ruskin, some of G.A. Henty, and possibly Andrew Lang, possibly Beatrix Potter, though avuncular wouldn't be quite the right word for Miss Potter). We'll go into this more in a little while, but in the meantime we can take a look at a connected question. Are these real children? Which, of course, entails asking, "What do we mean by real?"

Of course, "real" need not mean "quirky" or "highly individual" or "odd"—we recall Lewis's dictum that he who sees strange sights should not himself be strange (*On Stories*, 1982, p. 60). Alice is a commonplace little girl. But she was a real little girl, Alice Liddell, the daughter of Lewis Carroll's (Charles Lutwidge Dodgson's) colleague, the Liddell of Liddell and Scott's *Lexicon*. And though Lewis Carroll was not in fact Alice Liddell's uncle, the avuncular (or godfatherly) tone of the beginning and end of *Alice's Adventures* is unmistakable. It is a tone perhaps earliest met (in children's books) in John Ruskin's anonymously published *The King of Golden River* (1841), and it is of course arguable—and may be true—that neither uncles nor godparents (or, for that matter, grandparents) see the real children as they are. But that does not mean the children are not real children. In fact, we might fairly conclude that pioneer children's photographer Carroll/Dodgson was almost ideally placed to see the real children (even if somewhat idealized by the slow drawn-out still-photographic process). And I have heard it suggested that he began to tell children's stories to keep the children still during photography. Real children, possibly even George MacDonald's children.

But the trouble with real children, even idealized, is that their reality must be handled carefully to fit in with the "unreal estates"—the fantasy or Faerie or mythological world. Fantasy or Faerie achieves universality by distancing, by pattern, but realism achieves universality by particularity. It's true that we can have realistic description of unreal estates, and in fact Lewis is very good at it (so is Swift in *Gulliver*—and so is Dante in the *Commedia*). But we come back to the point that having extraordinary adventures happening to extraordinary persons is one level of the extraordinary more than we can easily accommodate. Let us look at the Five Children in E. Nesbit's *Five Children and It* and *The Phoenix and the Carpet* and *The Story of the Amulet*. These children are real, with real nicknames (a "neke-name" is an "eke-name"—that is an "each-name"— that is, a personally identifying name). The five children, it will be recalled, are Robert, Anthea ("Panther"), Jane, Cyril ("Squirrel"), and "the lamb" (whose name when he is grown up will be Hilary St. Maur Devereux, but who is now "the lamb"). Robert is Robert and Jane is Jane, but Anthea is "Panther" and Cyril is "Squirrel" and baby Hilary is "the lamb." Now it is true Susan Pevensie is "Su" and Edmund is "Ed"— which are nicknames of a sort—but it is not the same thing.

And yet, E. Nesbit works it very well. Just as in the Bastable stories (*The Treasure Seekers*, *The Wouldbegoods*) or *The Railway Children*, one hears the mother's voice, and the children are real, and in the Five Children stories the stories are out of Faerie into Fantasy and with an admixture (or adumbration) of Myth. And by accepting the children as real, one can accept the events as real. Ronald Tolkien once made the observation that when a child, told a story about a dragon, asks, "Is it real?" he can be answered by saying "There are no dragons in England now" (or words to that effect). Long ago and in another country? That is a different matter. But Lewis (like E. Nesbit) has put the events into our current (or only very near-past) time. Are we then to look inside any wardrobe we see to try to find Narnia, or—less specifically—are we to keep ourselves open to the possibility that there could be (is?) A Wood between the Worlds? Maud Barfield worried that children would be drawn to go inside wardrobes and shut the door after reading *The Lion, the Witch, and the Wardrobe*, and Lewis thought enough of her concern that he repeated and repeated and repeated the warning not to shut the door.

This suggests that both Maud Barfield and Lewis himself saw it possible that children would take Narnia as a real, not a story-book, place. Maud (Douie) Barfield was born in 1884, and that may have been her experience of her childhood. (Certainly I have known children who could not easily distinguish between fantasy and reality—though it is only fair to add that some of them later could not distinguish between themselves and their characters in D&D). For Lewis (as our quotation last chapter from Stephen Potter suggests), books were real in a sense "real life" was not, which would mean that the real world of Narnia is in the books, not in (or through) the wardrobe. Even the "real" wardrobe (regardless of whether now in Illinois or California) was simply a machine to get to the invented world—even if Lewis did tell his cousins stories inside the wardrobe at Little Lea (and I hope he left the door open).

We might reasonably say that the Pevensie children are not "real" children—certainly not in the sense that Dan and Una are in Kipling's *Puck of Pook's Hill,* or even the four children in G.A. Henty's *Out on the Pampas*—and not even in the sense that they, though invented, are combinations of the real attributes of real children, as with the children in E. Nesbit's books. They are, as we see particularly in *The Magician's Nephew,* children out of books—but created by someone to whom books were the true "real" life. If you wonder why we are going into this, it is an approach to the underlying question of what Lewis was doing here, in these books. He is not telling John and Michael and Christopher Tolkien bedtime (or rainy-day) stories, and then going off to write them up after telling them. He is not telling Charlie and Hubert and Maud and Ethel Henty stories about Charlie and Hubert and Maud and Ethel Hardy *Out on the Pampas* and then going off to write them up after telling them.

He is, except for *The Lion, the Witch, and the Wardrobe,* which I think may actually have been written partly with Lucy Barfield in mind, simply writing children's stories and then dedicating them to children he knew (even if, with the Kilmers, only through letters—which is actually pretty much appropriate, if writing is as real as being). And, at least in any copy I have ever seen, he did not dedicate *The Last Battle* to anyone. In any case, though Lewis had no difficulty in creating (or, better, recording and reporting) adult characters, he never (I believe) in any of his books created a real child. But, of course, if what he was writing was pageant, we should not expect much more than stock figures, attitudes in fancy dress (and surely, in Narnia at least, they are mostly in fancy dress).

Were the "estates"—the conditions, the locations, the country—real? We know some of the origins of Narnia lie in the Ulster countryside, but more seem to lie in Bunyan and elsewhere in literature. I have recently had a fugitive impression (from long ago) revived and strengthened by rereading one of Major Lewis's (Warnie Lewis's) books. During the late 1940s and the 1950s the Major was mining his great collection of seventeenth-century French materials for a series of books published between

1953 and 1963. Part of the mining was translating the original French texts into English, and one of the longer texts was Labat's seven-volume 1735 edition of the *Mémoires du Chevalier d'Arvieux, Envoyé Extraordinaire du Roy, etc.*

Here is Major Lewis in his *Levantine Adventurer: The Travels and Missions of the Chevalier d'Arvieux 1653–1697* (1963, p. 86, on the Cedars of Mount Lebanon):

> The trees stand, he says, on a plain of perhaps three miles in circumference, on the top of the mountain, and all around are other mountains so high that they are always snow-clad; these form a crescent about the plain, except at one point where there is 'a frightful sheer precipice' from whose foot emerges a spring which becomes the River of the Saints and waters the valley of that name. Looking down on the valley "one gets the most agreeable and diversified prospect in the world; the valley is . . . enclosed by rocky heights on which trees have a foothold and fall numerous cascades . . . to rejoice the ear at the same time the eyes and nose are gratified by the beauty of the countryside and the sweet-smelling herbs."

This from a man of whom the Major says (p. 86) that "scenery usually interested him as little as it did Dr. Johnson"—an interesting comparison, given the frequency with which C.S. Lewis has been compared to Dr. Johnson (and the Major certainly knew it).

Of course, even if the Mountains of Narnia (or Beyond Narnia) are a continuation of Mount Lebanon (and they are—that is one of the spurs running down from the Great Mountains), Lewis's Mount Lebanon could still be taken as given reality by a book. After all, except for Ulster and the other three ancient Kingdoms (and France on childhood vacation and in World War I, and parts of England), C.S. Lewis did not travel, until he and Joy went with the Greens to Greece in 1960, after all the Narnian books had been published. (Major Lewis, on the other hand, had traveled pretty widely, including both the United States—at least on the east and west coast—and China and across the Pacific, in addition to service in both World Wars. When he was in New York, did he find himself on Warren Street in Lower Manhattan, named from the same Irish family that gave him his name?)

But what about C.S. Lewis and the Ulster landscape? Here we may look at an article by Mary Rogers, published in connection with the C.S. Lewis Centenary (an Ulster project). Mrs. Rogers divides the Ulster influence on Lewis into two parts, only one of which is relevant to us here. I'm quoting at length here from "Narnian Ulster" (from the *C.S.*

Lewis Centenary News, 1998) by Mary Rogers, lecturer on C.S. Lewis and author of three books on the Ulster countryside.

Back in the 1950s, my small daughter's first prize in the Girl's Collegiate School, Enniskillen, was *The Lion, the Witch, and the Wardrobe*. I looked at the book in some surprise. To me, the author, C.S. Lewis, was the distinguished and unique lecturer of my student days, his Prolegomena to Medieval Studies being the unforgettable series that opened our eyes and ears to the medieval world. I remembered with gratitude his war-time writings, such as *The Problem of Pain* and *The Screwtape Letters*, along with his *Broadcast Talks*; but the war was now over! What was he doing and why was he writing a children's fairy tale? An old friend of his (and mine), Janie McNeill, was equally perturbed. "He's done enough! He should be writing more books like the *Allegory of Love*. He's ruining his academic career," she moaned. I agreed. I had just given a paper on Lewis's literary criticism (which included his *Preface to Paradise Lost* and *The Abolition of Man*, as well as the *Allegory of Love*) to the only Belfast audience there was then for Lewis's works, the Drawing-Room Circle, founded by my mother in 1926. So together Janie and I sighed and wondered why.

But I'm glad to say that I now know the answer, since, in the early 1990s, I was asked to talk on Lewis to the English Benedictines at Elmore Abbey, Newbury. Father Basil, the Abbot, amazed me by telling me afterwards that when novices came to join the Order, the first books they were set to read were the Narnian Chronicles! So I have recently re-read them all in the correct order to see why. To begin with, I have found myself back in Ulster where I spent my childhood, and Lewis spent *his* (emphasis mine). Ulster for Lewis, of course, had the pre-Partition geography. His childhood and youth knew nine counties, including Donegal, beloved still of all children for seaside holidays at Inver, Rathmullan, and Portnoo. In addition, south of Carlingford, there is Co. Louth, once CuChullain's country, which stretched down south as far as modern Dundalk. This includes Annagassin, which later became familiar to Jack and Warnie through the Henrys. The Lewis brothers had a happy childhood, as long as their mother was alive. (She died of cancer in 1908, before Jack was ten, and Warnie three years older.) *Surprised by Joy* tells of those days, blest by good parents, good food, a large garden to play in, a good nurse, Lizzie Endicott from Co. Down, and kindly servants. We learn of his early paintings, drawings and stories, sometimes written down for him by his father. He writes of his first experiences of Joy, an unsatisfied desire which is more desirable than any other satisfaction. Their mother's death separated them from their father in his frantic grief. All settled happiness came to an end. No wonder Jack Lewis went back to those former sunlit days in his imagination when he wrote the Narnia books. Their Ewart cousins later took them on drives and picnics: perhaps to the places that were to become the essence of Narnia: we don't know when he first saw the Carlingford/Rostrevor area. . . .

Walter Hooper remembers that "if you want to plunge into . . . the very quiddity of some Narnian countyside, you must go to what Lewis considered the loveliest spot he had ever seen"— the Carlingford lough area, with its sea, woods and mountains. Jack would have known from *The Cattle Raid of Cooley* of these parts: Cooley point is on the eastern edge of the Carlingford peninsula. Jack and Warnie came to know the area well when they stayed with the Henrys at Golden Arrow cottage, Annagassin. Vera Henry, Mrs. Moore's goddaughter, had acted as maid at the Kilns for some time, and they were all very fond of her; she died suddenly in 1953, to their grief. When I went to see her brother, Major Frank Henry in the Abbeyfield Home near Rostrevor in 1994, he told me with such pleasure of the trips in his car, and Jack's typical Ulster punctiliousness in paying for all the petrol and expenses involved. . . .

I can think of many places in Narnia which may have an Ulster background: the shape of Aslan's How in Prince Caspian, for instance: like the round crown of a hilltop that marks a passage grave. The incised patterns on the stones have the same reference: see Knockmany, near Clougher, in Co. Tyrone. The stone structure inside the How suggests a dolmen (or portal tombs, as they're now called); most people have seen these—perhaps at Legananny in Co. Down, or in the Giant's Ring, south of Belfast. The caves in *The Silver Chair* may owe something to Belfast's Cave Hill. [But see my earlier discussion in this book of caves in the books Lewis read.] The ruined city the children had to find, and the steep climbs up stone steps, suddenly brought me back to the Giant's Causeway. When the children, under the land's surface, see chasms which lead down to even darker and worse places, a thought of St. Patrick's Purgatory in Co. Donegal flashed through my mind—and possibly had been in the back of Lewis's. He knew Donegal well.

Turning from the scenery to the stories themselves, we find his essay on the subject in *Of This and Other Worlds* interesting. He writes, "I put in what I would have liked to read when I was a child, and what I still like reading now that I am in my fifties." In other words, he is not writing down to children but from what is in himself.

Here Mrs. Rogers goes, quite well, into matters we have already discussed, and from thence into Lewis's "practicality" in story-construction—an Ulster practicality, of course—and thence into the "Ulsterness" not of scenery but of aura, so to speak. While this is interesting speculation, following this line further here would be to go amiss. But, as an example of a case where Ulster sees Ulster in Lewis, in other ways besides his scenery, I cannot forbear quoting this passage, even if it is off our track:

He uses memorable phrases that evoke Ulster echoes: as in the *Dawn Treader* where "everyman drew his sword and set his face to a joyful sternness." I at once see Orangemen on parade on the 12th of July, their banners held aloft, their bowlers straight, their white gloves gleaming—and with just that look on their faces. This solemn joy has something to do with the Ulsterman's love of ritual. The Ulsterman I knew best was, of course, my father. Regularly, every summer, he would take us on Saturdays by train to Bangor or Newcastle. We always had the same lunch at the same restaurant, too, the same walk along the beach to Ballyholme, Bangor, or the golf links in Newcastle. No-one thought of asking, "Can't we go somewhere else?" "May we try another café?" "May I have strawberries instead of ice-cream?" The Ulsterman likes to know what he is going to do next. I seem to remember his saying, "There's a right way and a wrong way of doing most things." Strawberries weren't wrong: but they weren't what we usually had.

The portrait of her father could be a portrait of Lewis's father, but here, of course, though like him, Lewis rebelled against his father (perhaps because he was so much like him), and Lewis was never good at ritual personally, though he had sufficient literary sources to describe it well. We owe Mrs. Rogers a real debt for this little paper, for though she may see Ulster in more Narnian places than it is, and though she is a generation younger than Lewis, she "speaks the language as a native" and can give us things we could easily have overlooked.

Lewis's father could not imagine taking a picture of the house without people in front of it; Lewis had house and scenery in his imagination, but if he did not report on actual people, he had trouble constructing them. Dick Devine in *Out of the Silent Planet* and *That Hideous Strength* is a portrait (mostly, if possibly unfairly, of Harry Weldon). But the only approach to a full portrait in the Narnian books is Digory Kirke, as child and as professor, and he is so much a composite that it's probably misleading to call him a portrait. Eustace Clarence Scrubb is satirical, as are his parents. But the scenery of Narnia is "real" in a way that the people are not. Far from "real children in unreal estates," what we have is more "unrealized children in realized estates." In fact, what we have, is pageant, taking place amid scenes that were the furniture of Lewis's mind. But what of the stories that guide the pageant? In fact, let us look a little more here at the connections between pageant, story, pilgrimage, and pastoral. And Arcadia—which, as Lewis said of David Lindsay's Tormance, is a realm of the spirit. Not solely an English realm of the spirit, to be sure, but in this case, pretty much that.

Let us remind ourselves here of 1. the Englishness of Lewis's art, then 2., principally for the first four Narnian books (in the order published) of the characteristic fairy-tale mode and movement from daily life through a connecting link or nexus into the perilous realms of the spirit, through 3. the climactic moment (which involves a threat within or to the realms of the spirit), and then 4. the journey homeward to habitual self, or the realms we know. (This is the process applied to the Ransom stories in my *Scientifiction Novels of C.S. Lewis*.) Perhaps it will be as well to begin with a brief discussion of Arcady as a realm of the spirit, and the pastoral belonging to it. And the pageant—and the pilgrimage, both of which are pastoral modes. We begin by looking at the matter of Arcadia (or Arcady) as a realm of the spirit.

A realm of the spirit? Perhaps the characteristic figure in the traditional Arcadia is the shepherd, the pastor of the pastoral, with his shepherd's crook. Now there was some kind of spiritual significance to Arcady and the signs of Arcady even in Greek times, though we cannot be entirely certain what exactly that spiritual significance was. In the Judaeo-Christian tradition, of course, there is no doubt of the spiritual significance of the sheep and the shepherd, the pastor who is also a priest, the shepherd's crook that is also the bishop's crozier. But when the revived Classical tradition mixes with the Judaeo-Christian in the Renaissance, there comes ambiguity, most especially in the famous Arcadian (or pastoral) paintings of Nicolas Poussin. These Narnian stories are pageant and pastoral and pilgrimage—in short, Arcadian fiction.

Moreover, the fairy-tale mode informs the Arcadian pattern of pageant and makes this Arcadian fiction a somewhat more complex thing than simple *Marchen*. What is going on is exploration of the realms of the spirit, even though the symbols used in that exploration may be taken from more than one religious tradition. In fact, in general, many of them come from the Classical tradition that was part and parcel of the eighteenth century—and the nineteenth. But though, with fauns and satyrs and all, we have been in a Classical world, Lewis's coign of vantage is set largely in the Middle Ages, which are the great ages of Faerie. (Of course, as Lewis remarked to Nevill Coghill, "The Renaissance never happened in England, or if it did, it was of no importance"—in Jocelyn Gibb, ed., *Light on C.S. Lewis*, London 1965).

One reminder here on the Englishness of English Art, and how this fits in with our inquiry. The point is that, in the English tradition, art exists to preach, and the best preaching is done by rehearsing the details of daily life, whether pictorially or verbally. If verbally, then there is of course a story, but the story, if not simply pilgrimage or travel, must be one of two things. Either it must be a story dictated by the symbols (in the Narnian case, the original pictures), or it must be an existing story or at least a commentary on an existing story. Most likely, as here, it will be both. It cannot be a story dictated by personalities—by the characters in the story. In short, in the twentieth-century dichotomy, it will be romance rather than novel. But it may not even be romance—perhaps we ought to look more at pageant as a form.

It does not much matter, I believe, whether our travel is time-travel or space-travel: so long as it is travel, it will have a pageant quality. That is, it will center on the pictures, the detail, the mysteries—in the sense Edgar Wind uses that word in his study on *The Pagan Mysteries of the Renaissance*, which Lewis admired. There is, perhaps, a small sub-section of these travel stories (apart from the humorous variety) where this is not the case. In these, what is important is the sense of travel. We do get something of that here. This pageant would participate in the Englishness of English art, the use of detail to point a moral as well as to adorn a tale, in an essentially didactic endeavor. But this does not mean that the pageant must be pastoral, nor that it must be in the fairy-tale mode. Nor does it mean—though the intersection of pastoral and fairy-tale may mean—that a prologue is a necessary part of the tale.

The classic English pastoral is *The Countess of Pembroke's Arcadia* (which is really Sir Philip Sidney's *Arcadia*), and the classic (albeit tendentious) study of the English pastoral tradition is William Empson's *Some Versions of Pastoral*. One of the things revealed by studying Sidney and Empson is that English pastoral demands judgment, making it, in essence, a version of redemptive comedy. And judgment-upon-pastoral, or the sorting-out of redemptive comedy, is in effect the same as Ronald Tolkien's eucatastrophe.

This is not merely another way of saying that romances have happy endings. It is a way of saying only that pilgrimage is adapted to pastoral only if the goal is salvation. It suggests that artistic "Englishness"—so well adapted to pageant—will be adapted to pilgrimage only when there is judgment, which is when types are raised to archetypes. This leaves open the question of the relationship of pilgrimage to pageant in the pastoral tradition. Now the figures in a pageant are usually stock figures—attitudes in fancy clothing, so to speak—as in *Alice in Wonderland* (which is a pastoral) or the medieval morality plays (which are pageant and at the very least lie behind the pageant and pastoral of *The Beggar's Opera*). As Lewis noted in his discussion of *Alice* (and we repeated it above), "who sees strange sights should not himself be strange." We should repeat that the individual characters who see the strange sights—or have the strange adventures—who are in the procession in the pageant—should not be individualized. That would be a distraction.

In a pageant, that is obvious, and it sets up no tensions: as we all know, the fineness of the pageant is in the costumes, in the gilding, which is part of this artistic Englishness. It is not in the individual delineation of character. And the *caveat* on distraction holds true for pilgrimage also, though the method may differ. Just as Everyman in the medieval play must be every man, so Christian in the *Pilgrim's Progress* must be every Christian, even though universalization by the particular is the hallmark of pilgrimage (as with Chaucer's pilgrims or—for example—Langland's Glotonyc), as it is of the modern novel.

Now parents' children are particular children, real children. Uncles' nieces and nephews may be a trifle less particular—if they have lots of them, or if otherwise they are not close to them. And the author posing as uncle or a godfather is still further removed from particularizing. We recall Lewis's remarks on the author being the child's equal, like the butcher or the dog next door—one might almost say, the Butcher, or the Dog Next Door—archetypes, we might say. Using the distinction we have set up, we can ask, are the Narnia stories avuncular stories or parental stories? The answer is *No*, but they are closer to the avuncular. But it is perhaps more useful to look not so much at the avuncularity (or "quasi-avuncularity") as at what may be its cause, the remove from reality that is imposed by pageant.

The use of prologue can be a characteristic of pageant (as in *Henry V*). It certainly is here, though neologists might want to call *The Magician's Nephew* a "prequel." And we might want to call the whole series of the Narnian stories—or, better, the whole Story of Narnia—redemptive comedy. Let us look a little more in that direction. Certain children's stories—it is also true of detective stories—can be spoken of as a kind of mythic comedy, a phrase used so as to catch at least an echo of Northrop Frye's mythos of comedy. Frye's four great *mythoi*, to repeat, are springtime's comedy, summer's romance, autumn's tragedy, winter's irony, with their contrapuntal motion. The point to which I am leading up, as those familiar with Professor Frye's *The Myth of Deliverance* may already have noted, is that quite a bit of Victorian fiction (including children's fiction) fulfills the same function and demands the same responses for and from the reading public in Victorian England that the popular comedic plays fulfilled and demanded in Shakespeare's day. Here is Professor Frye (*The Myth of Deliverance*, p. 4):

> In a famous chapter of the *Poetics* (xi), Aristotle speaks of reversal and recognition (peripeteia and anagnorisis) as characteristic of what he calls

complex plots . . . Sometimes the effect [of what Frye calls the "and hence" story, as opposed to the "and then" story] seems to reverse the direction of the action up to that point, and when it does we are normally very close to the end. Hence a reversal of the action often forms part of an *anagnorisis*, a "recognition," depending on how much of a surprise it is.

This *anagnorisis* is in fact a staple of Victorian popular fiction as well as of Shakespearean comedy: one need only think of the stolen or run-away child motif in—for example—G.A. Henty, or indeed the whole matter of *Lady Audley's Secret* (Wilkie Collins) or (in Edwardian times) the double *anagnorisis* of the first of G.K. Chesterton's Father Brown stories. It could even be said that the *anagnorisis* is the sensation of Victorian sensation fiction.

How does this tie in with Frye's myth of deliverance? By the *myth of deliverance*, Frye means the story-pattern whose essential drive is toward liberation, "whether of the central character, a pair of lovers, or the whole society" (p. 14). The comedy is a ritual enactment of this pattern of deliverance, highly conventionalized. The point is in the reader's participation in the dénouement, the anagnorisis. The taste was there, I think, in the popular mind before it was gratified in story. Dare we guess that the Romantic Revolution (of which children's stories are themselves a child) was in the hearts and minds of the crowd, as well as the poets? Poets may be the unacknowledged legislators of mankind, but their legislation may merely codify existing custom. One is reminded of Lewis's suggestion that the great mythic treatment of progress came before the machines and the Industrial Revolution (*De Descriptione Temporum*, p. 8).

One cannot argue—one can only affirm—the *ought* from the *is*. To affirm morality in the face of the Romantic Revolution (of the early Nineteenth Century) one must always see the triumph of the Good. Victorian fiction, it has been suggested, is only the traveling Morality stage writ slightly large: if we escape it, it is only into the slightly larger stage of Elizabethan Comedy (redemptive Comedy), or into some modern production where the King's Messenger arrives at the back of the theatre. (And that happens at the end of one of Empson's examples of pastoral, *The Beggar's Opera*.)

What I am getting at here is something like this: 1. Lewis was not so much telling children stories (though he was doing that) as he was creating a literary work, an *oeuvre*, if you like, a made thing (a *poiema*); 2. he chose a particular form (the children's story, though he seems to have claimed he was choosing the fairy-tale or *Marchen*); 3. if we look to the literary antecedents of the form he chose, particularly in light (a) of his own reading and (b) of the literary history leading up to his own reading, we find ourselves in a discussion of pastoral, pilgrimage, pageant, and prologue; 4. this leads us into Redemptive Comedy, Victorian formula fiction, and could lead us into further discussions of 5. Voice and *Mythos* (story-pattern), Northrop Frye, Aristotle, and the Bible—and correspondingly away from C.S. Lewis telling a story to children. All these, except possibly concentration on Lewis telling a story to children, are   I think   useful (obviously I think so, or otherwise we would not be discussing them).

But here particularly we should look at Lewis's continual reminder— "No-one is told any story but his own!"—"No-one is told any story but their own!" (oops?)—"Child! Do you really need to know that?" Over and over again the children in Narnia (even Narnian children like Shasta and Aravis) are reminded, and we with them, that Aslan (or Christ or God) tells us only our own stories, and to try to learn someone else's (whether by magic or not) is to go where angels will not tread. Yet and still, we are told Lucy's story, and Edmund's story, and Peter's, and some of Susan's, and Eustace's, and Jill's, and Digory's and Polly's (and even a story about Cor and Aravis).

Are we then to conclude that these stories are ours? Are we also to conclude that all the Narnian stories (including *The Last Battle*) belong not only to the children in each but to the children in all of them, and indeed to all of Narnia as to all of us? I think the answer must be *Yes*, and I think the reason that the answer is *Yes* is that what we have in Narnia is a version of what the American twentieth-century author and editor (Charles) Fulton Oursler (1893–1952) called *The Greatest Story Ever Told*.

So, what I want to ask here, is what we can learn about the connection between Narnia and the *Greatest Story Ever Told*—and we have already more than hinted at this when we talked about Dorothy L. Sayers and *The Man Born to be King*. You will recall that Miss Sayers created the radio plays broadcast as *The Man Born to be King*, to get us away from our "reassuring sensation that 'it can't happen here'" by striking through "the stately and ancient language of the *Authorized [King James] Version*, and by the general air of stained-glass-window decorum with which the tale is usually presented to us" (p. 6). This is akin to Lewis's presumed desire to give the Story in another guise, getting past the watchful dragons. And here is what Fulton Oursler said (*The Greatest Story Ever Told*, 1949, Doubleday Image Books ed., p. xv):

In writing anew the wonderful life of Jesus, the author has had but one thought in mind, and that was to induce readers to go to the Gospels and hear the story at firsthand. It was Rabbi Solomon B. Freehof, of a great Jewish temple in Pittsburgh, who said to me at dinner one evening that the unspoken scandal of our times was the hidden fact that Bible-reading had been largely given up in America. Later, as I traveled around the country and talked to many different kinds of men and women . . . I made casual allusions in conversation to biblical passages. I soon discovered that references which in my boyhood were clichés of front-porch talk had no meaning whatever for these later companions. Even such obvious phrases as "Thirty pieces of silver" or "The talent buried in a napkin" or "The angel that troubled the waters" left many listeners with blank stares. Yet when I explained the meaning, their interest was clear; a sample from the great history invariably roused the appetite for more.

Like *The Man Born to be King*, Oursler's *The Greatest Story Ever Told* was presented initially as a series of radio scripts (in this case on WABC). It may be worth noting that there are some other similarities between Miss Sayers and Mr. Oursler: both were born in 1893, both wrote popular detective fiction (Oursler as Anthony Abbot); both made their living from writing (Oursler also from editing *Liberty* magazine). And both wrote their series of radio broadcasts (or plays) in the 1940s to bring the listeners to thinking about what the stories meant, though Oursler was more interested in simply bringing knowledge of the Story to the listeners and then readers. (And by the way, Miss Sayers had a collaborator on the BBC Productions, Val Gielgud, who also wrote detective fiction—and by Northrop Frye's definitions, detective fiction is a version of redemptive comedy.)

What Lewis is doing, *per contra*, is showing the meaning by showing the pattern of the story—or, specifically, the pattern of the Story. The Greatest Story Ever Told. And note the emphasis throughout the Narnia books, on telling the story (and on the voice—or Voice—that one hears). "I tell no-one any story but his own." I tell no-one any story but his own. By showing the pattern, it is argued, Lewis is trying to bring his readers to perceive the pattern, the meaning, in the original Story, using Myth (story-pattern) to reacquaint them with Truth. And of course, Aslan creates the world of Narnia with his Voice—"In the Beginning was the Word."

The underlying assumptions of the three approaches—by Miss Sayers, by Fulton Oursler, by C.S. Lewis—are very different, and very interesting. Obviously Miss Sayers and Oursler are closer together in approach and assumption than either is to Lewis. It looks as though

Lewis would agree with John Buchan that there are only a certain number of plots, and *Märchen* and the great Victorian novels share basic plot structures, basic story patterns. It looks as though that was one of the things that came out of that long night walk and night talk with Ronald Tolkien and Hugo Dyson that played so great a part in Lewis's final reconversion to Christianity.

The story is well-known and often-told, how a long evening-into-night-into-morning conversation Lewis had with his friends Ronald Tolkien and Hugo Dyson on the Magdalen Walk had brought him to see that the pattern of the Christian Story fulfilled the promise of the Pagan stories—that is, the far from being simply one more dying god, one more sacrifice, one more story of a god walking on earth, one more story of choosing the good not because it would win but because it was the good, this story of the Anointed King coming to His own, with all the story-patterns combined and interlaced in it, was the whole Truth that confirmed the partial truths of Osiris and Zeus (and Castor and Pollux) and Odin They were all myths with some truth (and even some facts) in them, but this was Myth and Truth and Fact all together, God born as Man in a particular year in a particular place with a particular human name and dying in a particular year at a particular place under an undistinguished Roman proconsul.

We all know something about John Ronald Reuel Tolkien (1892–1973) and how he developed his understanding of Myth and Truth (and Fact) throughout the vast mythology he constructed for (or from) England, besides talking about it in his lecture "On Fairy-Stories" and in his work on *Beowulf* and in other scholarly works. We know far less about Henry Victor Dyson (1896–1975, called "Hugo"), a friend of Tolkien's from undergraduate days, recently (as of the great conversation in 1931) returned to Oxford from the provinces, a scholar of the late seventeenth, whole eighteenth and early nineteenth Century in English literature, a book collector (most of his collection is now in York), with some London and Bloomsbury connections in the 1920s, editor of the Clarendon *Pope: Poetry and Prose* (1933)—wherein his Introduction is a brilliant piece of work—and author of an essay or two on Shakespeare and a small book on English literature of the period of his expertise (with John Butt, *Augustans and Romantics 1689-1830*, London 1940).

Now the thing above others we should know about Hugo Dyson is that he was a brilliant conversationalist who ordinarily hid his own religious (and many of his other) views from public scrutiny, but his Introduction to the Clarendon *Pope* shows his ability to persuade, and I suspect that it was Dyson who persuaded Lewis of the truth of Tolkien's ideas. And here I think we should pause to look a little more at the matter of Myth (which we have briefly discussed quite a long way back, in Chapter 2, and *seriatim* since).

Perhaps we can get the matter in better focus by looking at one characteristic of Lewis's "mythopoeic" story: the story will retain its form and its essential genius even if told in other words. When Tolkien created a mythology for England, based (at whatever remove) on "Old English" language and literature, but also Welsh, and to some extent simply on Medieval England (as with Tom Bombadil), he used a traditional voice—the traditional words and word-patterns of a particular kind of English literature. Now Tolkien's books are stories, though *the Notion Club Papers*—and indeed a good amount of the History of Middle-Earth—suggest that the creation of story did not always come easily even to him. But it came.

Perhaps, as we have said, the rolling English road is not derived from the wonderment of the Angles and Saxons and Jutes, when Octa, called Hengest, came over from the world of Finn and Beowulf (on which see Tolkien's *Finn and Hengest*). But it is still a very English pattern story, and if stories of the road are particularly English, we should not be surprised to find the story growing from Tolkien's "mythology for England" to be a story of the road, high way and by-way. In a curious Pickwickian sense (as I have said elsewhere), *The Lord of the Rings* combines two mythic patterns, that of the English road, and that of the quest (or task) to destroy, which is far less common than the quest to acquire. We should not be put off by Tolkien's serviceable and familiar (ordinary) prose: he has the mythopoeic gift that Haggard had, for all the steps into and through the realm of the comic or the humorous.

In fact, Tolkien strikes deep into the immemorial lode of myth, and the secret of his striking deep is in his belief, not only in Christian doctrine and the Christian myth, but in the truth of myth, as we would expect of the one who (with Hugo Dyson) convinced Lewis of this. For there is a truth to myth. Even if one does not—as I do—accept the historic truth of the Incarnation of myth into history, of the Logos as Jesus Messias, there remains such a thing as mythic truth. Even if one quarrels with Carl Jung's particular selection of archetypes and anima, hypnogogic vision and dream pattern—and I do not –, there are patterns and types (and "atmosphere") true to the human psyche. I repeat, there is a truth to myth, if not always an historical truth: one need not expect to meet a broad-hatted one-eyed old man on a pony to acknowledge truth to the myth of Odin All-father. Lewis has spoken of the "double distinction of myth from fact and both from truth" as being false and a symptom of our estrangement from the natural order of the heavens, including Deep Heaven.

But if Tolkien struck deep into the immemorial lode of myth, into what lode did Lewis strike? Not—from Tolkien's reaction to Narnia— into the same lode. As we shall see more fully in the next chapter, it is not Myth but Satire (or at least small-s satire) that is at the heart of Lewis's world. Rebellion is, of course, in both (and in Dyson, by the way, also). It may be that the Narnian books reaffirm in their readers the idea of the good rebellion, as well as the pastoral idea of the child-as-judge, as well of the child-as-warrior ("Lucy the Valiant").

Lewis is sometimes called a mythopoetic (or mythopoeic) writer (a term he applied particularly to Rider Haggard). I would claim that books simply embodying a mythic pattern (or more than one)—like the Narnia books (their myth being the Christian myth)—are not mythopoetic because there is no *poeisis*, no making of myth, though myth is there. Moreover, I believe there are recognizably different atmospheres to different mythologies (as Lewis himself observed long ago, and I have observed earlier here). Myth is, indeed, pattern—pattern story, pattern dream, pattern vision—and it may be based on a logic of place, an associative logic, as much as, or more than, a logic of time.

It is perhaps the hero with a thousand faces taking yet another: but it is more than that, for the hero is a god not yet euhemerized, and what is made is a new story, a story adding to the pattern, not merely a new face for the old hero. The myth is a myth, a story-pattern, a dream and a vision, of the divine, the unusual supernatural, and it is a myth made by a believer in the myth. Must it have a figure of mythic proportions? Yes, because the figure will be the figure of a god, even if it is a great white whale or a great fish. If there is mythopoeia to *Huckleberry Finn* (and I think there is), well, I too "do not know much about gods, but I think the river is a strong brown god." And the forest is a strong green god, with trees like men walking, or at least the sanctuary of the god. It has been noted that Fenimore Cooper's forests have classical Pagan antecedents— and Ahab tries to draw out Leviathan with a fishhook, adding a new story (but it is very old) to the stories of men that go down to the sea in ships. And Mr. Pickwick's pilgrimage is also a *pèlèrinage de la vie humaine*.

Lewis has suggested that Wagner's Ring embodies the alchemical Myth of Progress (*De Descriptione Temporum*, p. 8). Edmund Wilson (in considering the remarkable mythmaker Karl Marx) suggests that the Nibelungen cycle is a music-drama on the dialectic, implied in the relations between Wotan, Brünhilde, and Siegfried (*To the Finland Station*, p. 190). Now Wilson's view, throughout this argument, seems perilously close to Max Müller's, that mythology is a disease of language, rather than Tolkien's contrary, that language is a disease of mythology. My own view is Tolkien's, but like his, rather in the sense that pearls are an irritation of oysters. Mythology is, after all, in some sense about the gods. Our contact with (and benefit from) the oyster—unless we are eating it—is the pearl. Our contact with (and benefit from) the gods—should I venture to say, unless we are eating our God—is the language. But what kind of language? Lewis suggests a characteristic of mythopoeia that the strength of the myth, by which he means the story, is independent of the language. But the atmosphere is not.

Coleridge, by a just instinct, chose the ballad form for his great mythopoetic work. Irving's "Rip Van Winkle" (except in its playing for humor in the ordinary sense) is virtually *Marchen*, and so told. In both cases, the language has a traditional form, based in the common experience of humankind. But the more uncommon the myth, or the more random the combination of myths, the more difficult it is to find language to express it. Lewis, perhaps wisely, had recourse to the objective correlatives of our literary tradition—even the bubble-trees of the Third Heaven in *Perelandra* are found in the *Book of the Secrets of Enoch*—rather than even trying to convey atmosphere or flavor *de novo*.

Every mythology, as Tolkien and Lewis have both reminded us, each has its own flavor, its own atmosphere, somehow cognate with its language. There is a hard sun shining on Grecian heights, and the myths of the North are wrapped in mist and fog: the very bridge of the Gods rises out of clouds. Naus does not "mean" ship—behind both words is a picture, similar, but not the same. But note that the flavor is the flavor of the myth-world, not of the myth. In a way, what the myth-maker makes is not the *mythos* in either sense, but a new character in the story—Treebeard or Ayesha or Scrooge or the Ancient Mariner or Bilbo or Malacandra or Sherlock Holmes or Allan Quatermain or Uncas or Curdie—or Aslan. For here, finally, is where Lewis is a mythmaker, where his "jumble" of myths (as Tolkien claimed) becomes *mythopoiesis*, or *mythopoeia*. In more ways perhaps than he knew, Aslan, when he came bounding into the story, dragged all the rest behind him.

Arguably, Lewis added nothing to the story-pattern, no new story, but he added Aslan, and arguably, Aslan created a whole new version of the Story. It remains to ask, what is the outcome of all this? We have come almost six full chapters from the beginning of this book, but where have we come to? We have read, besides reading this book, the seven books of the "Chronicles" of Narnia—at least I trust we have—and where have they brought us? And how are the watchful dragons doing?

Because Lewis was reconverted, brought back to Christian belief, through the doors of myth, it would be a reasonable thing for him to see this as a way for reconversion—or conversion. Bruce Barton was an advertising man back in the 1920s, founder of Batten, Barton, Durstine & Osborn (BBD&O)—he wrote a life of Jesus (*The Man Nobody Knows*) portraying him, in essence, as an advertising man, and it was a runaway bestseller. Dorothy L. Sayers (also with experience in advertising) wrote bestselling mysteries and then, with the aid of Val Gielgud at the BBC, the classic radio plays making up *The Man Born to Be King*: they were reprinted by Eerdmans some years ago and they had a steady sale for quite a while, I was told, but they brought both controversy and acclaim. Artistically they were successful, but it may be one of the most important things that came out of them was the next series of radio scripts on the life of Christ, *The Greatest Story Ever Told*, by magazine editor and mystery writer Fulton Oursler.

These three are all retellings of the Story, Christ, as Miss Sayers said, in his "this-ness." But we are, of course, too close to the trees to see the wood, and particularly to trace the paths through the wood. What Lewis did in Narnia was very different. He sets out the paths, using guidebooks (so to speak) and maps prepared long ago and in another country, so that when we first become part of the pattern, or first become aware of the pattern, we will recognize it. We, like the children, meet Aslan in Narnia so that, in a sense, we may better recognize Him in our world, and, to put it more fully, may better recognize the entire Pattern in our world. (I note, by the way, that the post-1994 editions of the Narnia books have a "rationalized" capitalization, rather than Lewis's quirky original, which in my view tends from time to time to obscure the full meaning—not, as Lewis once observed, that typographical reverence is of any importance, but it doesn't make sense to me, when you can make the meaning clearer by capitalization, to forego that convenience.)

Now Ronald Tolkien, in his vast mythological (and cosmological) creation (at least nineteen volumes—*The Hobbit*, three volumes of *The Lord of the Rings*, *The Silmarillion*, twelve volumes of the *History of Middle-Earth*, and two volumes of *Mr. Baggins*), gave us something that I might call the Christian reality in a pre-Christian (thus by our world's standards a Pagan) age. The atmosphere is that of the Northwest of the Old World, particularly the Celtic (and Old English) Northwest, thus a "Pagan" atmosphere, but the rules of engagement are fully in tune with Christian doctrine. What Lewis did we have seen, though we shall see more. But the last volume of the "Chronicles" was published nearly sixty years ago. What has happened since?

There have been Tolkienian books (Alan Garner, for example), retellings of Celtic mythology (Lloyd Alexander, for example) with origins possibly in Tolkien, the slightly Charles Williams-ish books of Madeleine L'Engle's *Wrinkle in Time* series (parental rather than avuncular), now four in number, but most of all, overarching the entire world and firmament of children's literature (and "young adult" literature), in fact overarching the entire publishing world, five million prepublication copies, hundreds of people in line at midnight when bookstores open on the publication date, there has been Harry Potter.

I believe it has been said that Lewis's publishers and the Lewis Estate had it in mind to publish new "Narnian" adventures, to try to—what? Combat the popularity of Harry Potter? No, I think not. Cash in on the popularity of Harry Potter? Possibly. My own view, as I noted before, is that someone with a wide knowledge and understanding of Lewis and a reasonable ability to write as his successor might possibly be able to create a subsidiary Chronicles of Archenland, but the Narnian Story is pretty much complete as given, just as The Greatest Story Ever Told cannot reasonably be added to (or not much). It is what it is (as is said far too often, these days—but it does have a meaning).

But what is Harry Potter? As everyone knows, it is now seven volumes, one to each year of Harry Potter's school-life at the Hogwarts School of Witchcraft and Wizardry (but eight films). They have made Janice Katherine Rowling the richest woman in the United Kingdom; they run to four to five thousand pages when complete—a couple of million words; and they concern one Harry Potter, son of wizards James and Lily Palmer (murdered by the Lord Voldemort), and his struggles against this Lord Voldemort, the greatest (and most evil) wizard of his—our—time. For Hogwarts exists in our time. Harry and Ron Weasley (of the redheaded Weasleys) and Hermione are very much teenagers (and for two volumes "pre-teens") in our world. Their schoolboy and schoolgirl pranks and rivalries, their language, their questions about love and dating, put them firmly in contemporary context, though at a remove created by the fact that they are all wizards (except a few Muggles who come their way). Of course, these are in part coming-of-age novels. They are certainly Arcadian novels, as schooldays are Arcadian days (Kipling shows us this in *Stalky* and Owen Johnson showed it to an American audience in his Lawrenceville stories, but of course it was Kenneth Grahame who first analyzed the connection of Arcadia and childhood).

In a way, if J.K. Rowling has not turned the dictum that "he who sees strange sights should not himself be strange" on its head, at least she has knocked it slightly askew. The whole world of wizardry (with schools of wizardry) is strange, and the Headmaster of Hogwarts, Albus Dumbledore, is more than strange—he is, as his Head Boy tells us, mad. Harry and Ron and Hermione and the others are part of that world, and J.K. Rowling makes its strangeness very clear in (for example) her descriptions of wizards trying to act and especially dress like muggles (non-wizards). But beyond that strangeness, Harry and Ron and his brothers and sister and Hermione and Neville Longbottom and the other students are recognizably real, if sometimes archetypical or idealized.

In that sense, they are not strange. But they are scarcely common-place. The books have been attacked as both escapist and as "wish-ful-fillment" fantasy (bad sense), what Lewis in a different context called "morbid castle-building." My own view is that, if they are preaching, they are preaching the same lesson that is in Tolkien—"Good and evil have not changed, nor are they one thing for men and another for elves and hobbits." Good and evil have not changed, nor are they one thing for wizards and another for us. The other attack that has been levied against the Harry Potter books is that they are un-Christian and even anti-Christian.

The truth of that attack I am not interested in here. The fact of that attack is worth our notice. I am told that one of the things Lewis's pub-lishers wanted to do with the proposed "New Narnia" books was tone down Lewis's Christianity. Again, whether that was true or not is not my concern here. But the fact that people have believed it (look at the "MereLewis" website some years past) is worth our notice. Apparently the dragons on both sides are very watchful. Yet Harry Potter's story shares a number of characteristics with Narnia as story, if not as Story. Remember our remarking on at least one of the Narnia books as being in the category—even *genre*—of Edwardian adventure story: Harry Potter's story shares characteristics with this Edwardian adventure story:

It is framed in familiarity and the familiarity is time-specific (and the more familiar for being our time). The characters—other than the chil-dren—are types. Nature is realized and even personalized, as with the Whomping Willow. Though Harry Potter starts off alone, his adventures are not solitary. (So also Lucy, of course.) Moreover, the world is essen-tially an aristocratic world, or at least a wizard's spin-off from an aristo-cratic world. Even the evil wizard Tom Marvolo Riddle rearranges his name to say "I am the Lord Voldemort." Also, the actions of the charac-ters are more in black and white and less in shades of grey than we are used to in "realistic" fiction—though that is a part of the traditional school story also, as well as of the traditional children's story, and the traditional fairy-tale, and the Marchen. Of course, being a school story, there is in Harry Potter an Arcadian impulse toward the "out-of-bounds," which is at most only tangentially part of Narnia.

But is it anti-Christian? I suspect the answer to that question depends on one's definition of what is Christian. I live in an area where the following interchange has been heard more than once: "Are you a Christian?" "Yes, I'm an Episcopalian." "No, I mean a *Christian*!" The authors collected at Wheaton include the Seven (Chesterton, Tolkien, Barfield, Sayers, Williams, Lewis, MacDonald), plus Madeleine L'Engle. I count two Roman Catholics, five Anglicans or Episcopalians (counting Madeleine L'Engle), one of them an Anthroposophist and one a believer in Magick (sometime member of the Order of the Golden Dawn), and a Universalist.

My point is that there may well be readers who make their particular Christianity the sole benchmark for children's literature (or any literature). They will approve of Narnia because it is (in their view) Christian, and disapprove of Harry Potter because (in their view) it is not. I have no quarrel with them, even if I disapprove of the bounds they set. (That, in the parlance, is "on them.") But I do not think they were the audience for whom Lewis was writing. And there is always, for our consideration, the case of nine-year-old Laurence, an American boy (in 1955) who became concerned because he loved Aslan more than he loved Jesus. Laurence's mother had written Lewis through his publishers, and in ten days there was an airmail letter from Lewis.

Laurence had been afraid that, by loving Aslan (more than Jesus), he was being an idol-worshiper (*Letters to Children*, p. 52). But Lewis told Laurence's mother that 1. even if he were it wouldn't be idol-worship, 2. he couldn't love Aslan more than he loved Jesus, because when he thought he was loving Aslan, he was loving Jesus, and if he simply meant he was loving the lion-body of Aslan more than the man-body of Jesus, well, after all, he's nine, and even if he is loving the lion-body more than the man-body, that will pass—and he goes on to talk about prayer, which was important for him and for Laurence (and Laurence's mother), but not for us here. In a later letter (mentioned in *Letters to Children*, p. 61), Laurence asked Lewis why the children in *The Last Battle* didn't know about the promise of resurrection in the Apostles' Creed, which led Lewis to reflect on which of the children knew the Creed. He decided Eustace and Jill probably did not. I daresay that is highly probable, but of course the question comes from someone who already knows the Story. And the Kilmer children were Roman Catholics. I was a confirmed Episcopalian—and not one of the children for whom the books were written—when I first came on Narnia. But though Americans in general are much more likely to be church-goers than the English (or most other nations), so that American responses to Narnia may be (in some sense) skewed, Laurence's response makes it quite clear—as we have suggested already—that Lewis's great (and mythopoeic) achievement in Narnia is the creation of Aslan.

As we know, Lewis argued that he was asking what would happen if the Savior Christ in some world took the body of a lion (*Letters to Children*, p. 52) —which is not theologically parallel to God being born as a Man, and is in fact a formulation that is theologically suspect. In the Narnian books, Aslan is not the Savior who took the body (or form) of a lion. He is a lion, and not a tame lion. And when asked who he is, he responds that he is himself. (Three times, as the seer of the negative in one of G.K. Chesterton's Father Brown stories responded three times, "I want nothing." What I tell you three times is true.) Lewis's artistry in creating (or as Tolkien would say, sub-creating) Aslan has made him a real lion, and it was his attempt to explain what he was doing to a nine-year-old that may have led him into an appearance of near-Docetism. And this should not be allowed to detract from the achievement of Aslan.

Yes, Aslan has some of his origins in the pages of *Punch*. But what is important for us here is the "lion-y-ness" of Aslan (a parallel construction to the "dogginess" of the Talking Dogs in *The Last Battle*). Just as the Great Dance in *Perelandra* shows how hard Lewis's substance can press against his form (in that case, the eighteenth-century novel)—and shows Lewis trying to "combine characteristics which the Fall has put poles apart" (quoted in Donald Glover, *C.S. Lewis: The Art of Enchantment*, p. 93)—so here, the creation of Aslan as a real lion and new mythic figure presses against the bounds of his retelling, his reproducing the myth, the story-pattern, of the Greatest Story Ever Told.

In *Perelandra*, Lewis found a way to handle the difficulty, or his genius (old sense) found a way for him. At least one contemporary reader asked me long ago if I thought Lewis had come on his description of the Great Dance through taking drugs, since in some drug-induced states sound does appear as light: the answer was, of course, no. But we might want to look briefly here at what he did in *Perelandra*, where he took pictures (the bubble-trees, for example—he said from the child's mispronunciation of laboratory as bubble-tree), and wrote a story around them, a story repeating a pattern-story (but with a new outcome, Paradise Retained).

Now *Perelandra* is a mystical book, which the Narnia stories pretty much are not. Since Lewis apparently distrusted—and rarely experienced—mystical visions, we may reasonably ask where the Great Dance came from. But this too is "realization"—the imaginative reconstruction and filling out of what someone else's experience "must have been like," which is of course the quality Lewis has particularly singled out for praise in Malory, and which has been noted as characteristic of the "Englishness of English art." What I believe Lewis did in *Perelandra* is take descriptions—stories—of mystical experience and "realize" them; whose stories I do not know, but perhaps the Great Dance is a "realization" of what things must be like if the plain and practical advice of, say, William Law, is to be followed. (It may come through Carghill.)

But in the Narnia books, Lewis was writing—at least avowedly—for children. I am reminded of an interchange in a detective story by Margery Allingham ("The Case of the Widow" in *Mr. Campion: Criminologist*, 1977, Manor ed., p. 154), in which Mr. Campion asks Inspector Oates if he has ever been to a children's party, and when Oates says "No" then asks "Well, you've been a child, I suppose?" and Oates responds, "I seem to remember something like it." That is about where we are here. Eighteenth-century (or other—particularly other) mystics can have written and left for us descriptions of their mystical experiences, but children in any century generally do not write down for future ages their childish experiences when they are happening. For those we are each of us required to remember something like being a child.

In Lewis's case, I suggest, the "something like" was less like ordinary childish experience than would have permitted the kind of "realization" he carried out in *Perelandra*. He led a largely self-contained, sometimes solitary, very bookish child's life of a kind that was more common in the days of his childhood than since—and he knew he had to go beyond that when writing for children in the mid-twentieth century. He did hate tight clothes as a child and all his life, he was manually clumsy, and he was a precocious speaker, but only the first of these comes into Narnia, because it was only the first he saw as a universal in childhood.

For, after all, if Aslan tells no child any story but that child's own, the author can tell the child no story, in the end, but the author's own. And if the author is telling a story for children, he can do one of three things. He (or she) can make his children into something else in his story, as Tolkien did with the Hobbits (most notably with Pippin = Peregrin Took and Merry = Meriadoc Brandybuck in *The Lord of the Rings*) or Kenneth Grahame did with Ratty and Moley and Toad in *The Wind in the Willows*), or (perhaps) Beatrix Potter with *Peter Rabbit*. He (or she) can take his (or her) children from observation as he (or she) is writing the story (did the fights between Cor and Corin came into *The Horse and His Boy* from David and Douglas Gresham?)—the real exemplar here is not Lewis but J. K. Rowling. Or he (or she) can, as one of my English professors once said, do the "Tomlinson routine" ("And the God that you took from a printed book / be with you, Tomlinson!")—that is to say, he (or she) can use literary models for his (or her) children, which is mostly what Lewis did.

This goes back to the avuncular or parental voice (though Lewis Carroll and Edward Lear were avuncular but with real children). It goes back to the question of the reality of the children being at cross-purposes with fantasy or pageant (though not with pilgrimage or pastoral). Let me repeat here a couple of points made above about reality. In E. Nesbit's Bastable stories (*The Treasure Seekers, The Wouldbegoods*) or *The Railway Children*, one hears the mother's voice and the children are real. And one hears the same voice in the Five Children stories, so the children are real, and by accepting the children as real, one can accept the events as real.

When we read Tolkien's stories for children, he is telling John and Michael and Christopher Tolkien bedtime (or rainy-day) stories, and then going off to write them up after telling them. G.A. Henty begins by telling Charlie and Hubert and Maud and Ethel Henty stories about Charlie and Hubert and Maud and Ethel Hardy *Out on the Pampas* and then going off to write them up after telling them. Kipling is telling stories for his children, Dan and Una, especially in *Puck of Pook's Hill*. Kenneth Grahame is telling his son stories of Ratty and Moley and Toad and Badger and the Weasels and the Stoats.

But Lewis, as we have said, except possibly for *The Lion, the Witch, and the Wardrobe*, is simply writing children's stories and then dedicating them to children he knew—though he may have done minimal rewriting with the dedicatees in mind (as perhaps with Cor and Corin in *The Horse and His Boy*—with David and Douglas Gresham in mind).

Yet, we remind ourselves (and close this chapter by reminding ourselves) of Lewis's continual reminder—"No-one is told any story but his own!"—"No-one is told any story but their own!"—"Child! Do you really need to know that?" Over and over again the children in Narnia are reminded that Aslan (or Christ or God) tells us only our own stories, and to try to learn someone else's is quite simply wrong. Are Lucy's story, and Edmund's story, and Peter's, and some of Susan's, and Eustace's, and Jill's, and Digory's and Polly's (and even a story about Cor and Aravis) ours? It seems that all the Narnian stories—the whole Narnian Story—must belong not only to the children in each but to the children in all, and to us. How successful, in the end, we find the Narnia stories—how highly we rate Lewis's achievement (after deciding what it is and what the stories are)—will depend on our conclusion as to whose stories these are meant to be, and whose, in fact, they are.

We will turn to that (and much else) now, in our Conclusion, beginning with a word we have mentioned from time to time thus far—"satire"—and a mention of Michael Ward's vision of Narnia. Here we remind ourselves of the distinctions between and among 1. the furniture of an author's mind, his sources and analogues; 2. his methods of composition and what he intended; and 3. what he produced. Dr. Ward has exhaustively discussed one set of the furniture of Lewis's mind—the "Discarded Image" or "Old Western" set (or at least a portion of it)—though he makes some assumptions about the methods of composition and what Lewis intended that I cannot agree with—and which weaken (I believe) his view of what Lewis produced.

For what Lewis produced is still a species of satire or irony—not for nothing (Northrop Frye might remind us) does *The Magician's Nephew* begin with cityscapes, both alive and dead.

[7]
A Good Swift Kick
toward Success

It is sometimes instructive to read contemporary reviews of books when they first come out—often preserved, with paperbacks, as cover-material. When *That Hideous Strength* came out, one review, in *Time* magazine, briefly described that book as "well-written, fast-paced satirical fantasy." Moreover, one of the science-fiction writers most influenced by Lewis (James Blish) repeatedly emphasized the satirical nature and purposes of science-fiction generally. And Lewis was at this point probably best known among the reading public as the author of the satirical *Screwtape Letters* and (though much less) of the satirical *Great Divorce*. He was known among his friends as a wit, a satirist, and, of course, an Irishman—not an Irishman like Nevill Coghill, still less like any of the "Irish Irish"—and not even, I think, like his father (see what I take to be his misunderstanding of his father as Irishman, in *Pudaita Pie*).

More—to go back to the eighteenth century Lewis so favored—more like Dean Swift, one of his favorite writers, whose humor (even the scatological?) he much appreciated. When, a number of years ago (nearly twenty-five), I wrote a paper on Lewis's eighteenth-century antecessors ("C.S. Lewis's Ransom Stories and Their Eighteenth-Century Ancestry" in Schakel and Huttar, *Word and Story in C.S. Lewis*), I did not miss—but perhaps did not sufficiently emphasize—the obvious links between *Gulliver* and *Out of the Silent Planet*—but Swift and Narnia? True, Swift was an Irish Anglican, like Lewis, besides being a satirist, like Lewis, but are the Narnia books satires?

Perhaps not, but they are certainly satirical, and children are perhaps natural satirists—as Lewis himself certainly was, as a child. If the Boxen stories give us a myth of (Ulster) grown-up-ness, the myth is a satirical one. But Narnia? Let us look a little at the evidence. And in looking, let us remember that Lewis's non-eighteenth-century antecedents include the satirist Thackeray, the satires of Andrew Lang (*Prigio* and *Ricardo of Pantouflia*, though they have moments of genuine faery), the (Fabian) near-satires (at least) of Edith Nesbit Bland, the satirical pages of *Punch,* and (viewing the whole with an amused irony perhaps), Lewis's mentor, the man who personally linked the ironies of *Alice* with those of Mark Twain, and brought the great *house in the country* into Lewis's life, George MacDonald. We noted back in our introductory chapter that Lewis's schoolboy attitudes may be a kind of strength in his children's books—and schoolboys (at least the ones I have known over the past six decades and more) are natural satirists.

Lewis told us that he learned Arthur through *A Connecticut Yankee in King Arthur's Court.* I daresay—and the irony, the satire, lingered. He was an Old Western Man—how could he look at the New West and bear it, except satirically. It may not have been the same kind of satire that children seek—and find—as necessary, or at least advisable, in their daily life. But like calls to like. The Professor, at the beginning, is so very ancient and so very hairy and bearded, and so much a figure of fun ("Bless me! What do they teach them in these schools?"), that he is scarcely a person at all. He is an archetype, and at this point, an ironic one. The figure of Tumnus, a very Victorian-genteel (but rather lower-middle-class?) faun, the whole tea-time *après-midi d'un faune*, is not an archetype, but it is satirical or ironic. Doubtless it may remain uncomprehended by the child brought into the story—but it is part of the ironic breaking and remaking of reality lying behind Middle-Earth (and especially The Shire) as well as behind Narnia—and the child knows it speaks to his or her spirit of resistance to a dullness in daily life.

But why would all of this be a recipe for success as a writer of children's books? Let us get it out of our minds that his success comes from an identity between the furniture of his mind and the furniture of the minds of his readers. I might myself be an exception here, but then the furniture of my mind was set in order (or possibly disorder?) by Lewis himself, before I read the Narnia books. The indefatigable and learned author of *Planet Narnia* has exhaustively examined that furniture (though under the musically-induced belief that Lewis's Narnia books are far more planned and organized than I am willing to admit), and we need not do it at length here (and of course Lewis did it himself in *The Discarded Image*, though elsewhere as well, as in *Spenser's Images of Life*).

But are our children's minds, or even ours, so furnished with the seven planets (that is, not Earth, but Moon, Sun, Mercury, Venus, Mars, Jupiter, Saturn) and their images and all they bring with them, that they will sell millions of books and make Narnia a phenomenon through two centuries (or at least half of one and part of another, so far)? It almost looks as if the answer must be *Yes*, for what is the alternative?

The children in *The Lion, the Witch, and the Wardrobe* are not much fleshed-out, not realistic portrayals of children—not as realistic, certainly, as E. Nesbit's. Given their literary antecedents, and given Lewis's pronounced bachelorhood (at least until the Narnia books were published)—and given, of course, his remarks on *Alice*—that is not a surprise. I have heard it suggested we may be dancing around the edges of an intentional fallacy here—perhaps Lewis did not create realistic children simply because he didn't have it in him, rather than because it might unbalance the books—but a look at Swift's Lemuel Gulliver, not to mention Defoe's Crusoe, warns me against that easy interpretation.

The characters of the children, in the books, have been amended for the films, presumably to permit a more "interesting" story line, more action, more adventure. And yet, the books have been unquestionably successful, and not just with those who give them to the children. In a word, why?

What we have looked at in our first six chapters should hint at a clue, or a set of clues. Let us begin with what we noted when we talked of Lewis's conscious decision to write a children's book. If we look at Lewis's reading as a child, still more immediately after, we find it (to recapitulate) perhaps a little unexpected: Conan Doyle's *Sir Nigel*; Mark Twain's *A Connecticut Yankee in King Arthur's Court;* E. Nesbit's trilogy, *Five Children and It* (1902), *The Phoenix and the Carpet* (1904), *The Story of the Amulet* (1906); *Gulliver* (illustrated and unexpurgated); an almost complete set of old *Punches*; *Tegner's Drapa* in the Longfellow version, possibly *Heroes of Asgard*. The curious thing about this childhood reading, as he recounts it, is how little of it was books that other children of his time seem to have read—but against this we may set his choice (for the "Book Club" as noted in a letter home 22nd November 1908) of *The Strand* (with Warnie getting *Pearson's* and "Field *The Captain*").

In *The Strand*, which we know he read, we find, besides Conan Doyle and E. Nesbit, H.G. Wells ("The First Men in the Moon" in 1901), W.W. Jacobs, Morley Roberts ("The Fog" in 1908), Somerville and Ross (*The Further Adventures of an Irish R.M.* in 1906), even (in 1901) Lewis Carroll. In my mind—and certainly retrospectively in Lewis's—these stories have a mythic quality. But like the mythic "grownup-ness" of Ulster in *Boxen*, these are modern much more than classic myth. In Chapter 2, "Creating Narnia," we pointed out that almost all the Narnian stories involve the children from our world, not only because the stories are being told in our world, but because it is when things happen that the children are needed—or is it that the children are needed when things are to happen or are happening (to bring resolution)?

Or is it that the mythic patterns—from our world—are in the children, who thereby make sense of Narnia—for us? This is, I believe, connected with Lewis's looking at events from the "inside"—as within the soldiers in the Trojan Horse or from the point of view of the "divine" entities who are being summoned, thus giving an internal meaning to the events. In any case, the children are there when things happen, and when they are not there, apparently, "things" do not happen. I see in this something I have become more aware of as I have studied Lewis's (and Williams's) Arthurianism—and that is the distinction drawn by Robin Collingwood (another Magdalen fellow, and Lewis's fellow Martlet) between chronicle and history. Here is a relevant passage from Collingwood's posthumously published *Idea of History* (Oxford 1946, 1st pb edition, 1956, pp. 202–03):

> This distinction serves to distinguish two very different things: history and chronicle. The names of the great Greek painters, as handed down to us by tradition, do not form a history of Greek painting: they form a chronicle of Greek painting. Chronicle, then, is the past as merely believed upon testimony but not historically known. And this belief is a mere act of will: the will to preserve certain statements which we do not understand. If we did understand them, they would be history.
>
> Every history becomes chronicle when related by a person who cannot relive the experiences of its characters: the history of philosophy, for example, as written or read by people who do not understand the thoughts of the philosophers in question. In order that there should be chronicle, there must first be history: for chronicle is the body of history from which the spirit has gone; the corpse of history.
>
> History, so far from depending on testimony, has no relation with testimony at all. Testimony is merely chronicle. So far as anyone speaks of authorities or of accepting statements or the like, he is talking of chronicle and not of history. History is based on a synthesis of two things which only exist in that synthesis: evidence and criticism. Evidence is only evidence so far as it is used as evidence, that is to say, interpreted on critical principles; and principles are only principles so far as they are put into practice in the work of interpreting evidence.

Collingwood's own field of history was Roman Britain; he is the author of the first part (*Roman Britain*) of the Oxford History of England Volume I, on *Roman Britain and the Anglo-Saxon Settlements*. His portrait of Arthur is in that book (pp. 321–25) and it lies directly behind

Dimble's discussion of Arthur in *That Hideous Strength*. (The matter of the differing visions of Arthur among the Inklings has recently become a topic of new interest since the publication of Tolkien's *Fall of Arthur*—there is no doubt in my mind that Lewis's vision is Collingwood's.) The example of the difference between chronicle and history that has been in my mind for years has to do with Abraham's declarng Sarah his sister to hide the fact she is his wife (Chronicle), whereas in fact inheritance in the polygamous societies of the Ancient Near East (including Abraham's) was determined by declaring the principal wife to be also the sister, giving her son a stronger claim to succeed to wealth and title (History)—which I learned long ago from Speiser's notes in Volume I of the *Anchor Bible*. Those notes breathed new life into the chronicle corpse of Abraham's day. But how does Narnia fit in with this?

The events of Narnia's days are simply chronicle (in Collingwood's sense) without the presence of the eight children from our world to give them meaning, and make them history. (The eight are, of course, Peter, Susan, Edmund, Lucy, Eustace, Jill, Digory, and Polly—the Earth-born children.) The meaning comes through the children (to the children, and others, who read the books), but it comes from Lewis—in the furniture, surely, and still more the contours, of his mind. That is, his school-boy-ishness, his satirical view, his sympathy with child against master or mistress, his (occasional) inspired silliness (the dogginess of the dogs in *The Last Battle* perhaps)—and perhaps most of all, in the wildness of Aslan. For children are natural rebels, after a point, and the lesson that, no more than Aslan is a tame lion, is God a tame God, is (I believe) one of the keys to the success of Narnia. One (or more) of the other keys, as we shall see shortly, may be found in the ways in which the past is alive in the present. Familiarity and ritual are involved in the reader's reaction to "straunge strondes" and "sondry londes."

It was said above (away back in Chapter 2) that we would look later at the atmosphere of Narnia (in connection with our speaking of the importance of atmosphere in myth). What is that atmosphere? In a way, Tolkien put his finger on it when he spoke of what he did not like about Narnia (at least in *The Lion, the Witch, and the Wardrobe*), what I think of as its helter-skelter Widdecombe Fair mixing of almost everything from our world. And there's the key—from *our* world—or perhaps one should say, *from* our world. Think, in the description of Merlin's memories of Mount Badon in *That Hideous Strength*, how Collingwood's real knowledge of Arthur's days (whoever Arthur was), passed on to Lewis, changes Chronicle into History, gives life to the story of a time fifteen centuries ago. The atmosphere of Narnia is the atmosphere of the

Medieval—Narnia as a country of the mind is medieval, distanced from us not so much by being another world (it is very like ours) but in a different Time.

Now time—our time—has brought a strange benefit to Narnia as popular children's fiction. One might construct a variant on Auden's lines on another Irish poet, who lies perhaps behind Merlin in *That Hideous Strength*: "Time that by a strange device / Gave us thrones and Fire and Ice / And Men and Elves to fill the hole / At the center of the soul"—from which we can go on to the lines Auden did write: "Follow poet, follow right / To the bottom of the night / And with uncomplaining voice / Teach the still heart to rejoice."

What has happened (and a little of it may be Lewis's own doing) is that the Myth that gives life at the center of the Story, the First Larger Life as it were, that enlivens the Chronicle into History, that appeals (in quite a different sense from the ordinary) to the inner child—say the inmost child—is the Myth of the Medieval. Of course the history is feigned, but the spirit of the Myth is real.

I hesitate to bring to bear the particular and improbable canon I have in mind here, but it has been helpful to me in considering the matter of Lewis's success with Narnia. On that library table in the house where I grew up, with some of Lewis's books and a couple of Charles Williams novels, was—very much the odd book out, I thought—Martin Buber's *I and Thou*. I never found out for sure why it was there, though on my first reading I found some links with Charles Williams and his mantra, "This also is Thou; neither is this Thou." But what I found later on was something to our point here.

What I did not realize when I first read Buber (who is, by the way, not especially easy to read) was that he fell into the same tradition of the Goethean Way of Knowledge into which fell Owen Barfield, Lewis's "second friend." It was, in fact, Owen himself who set me on the track, later on, in the 1970s. Let me rehearse a few of Buber's statements.

> That which will eventually play as an accustomed object around the man who is fully developed, must be wooed and won by the developing man in strenuous action . . . Like primitive man the child lives between sleep and sleep (a great part of his waking hours is also sleep) in the flash and counter-flash of meeting . . . [the] movement of the [child's] hands will win from a woolly Teddy-bear its precise form, apparent to the senses, and become lovingly and unforgettably aware of a complete body . . . [this] is the correspondence of the child—to be sure only "fanciful"—with what is alive and effective over against him . . . This fancy . . . is the instinct to make

everything into *Thou*, to give relation to the universe . . . The development of the soul in the child is inextricably bound up with the longing for the *Thou* . . . (pp. 26–28)

Through the *Thou* a man becomes *I* . . . a time comes when [the *I* of the *I-Thou* unity] bursts its bonds, and the *I* confronts itself for a moment . . . as quickly to take possession of itself and from then . . . consciousness of itself . . . now the separated *I* emerges, transformed . . . and takes possession of all It existing 'in and for itself' . . . only it can be arranged in order . . . [but] a world which is ordered is not the world-order. There are moments of silent depth in which you look at the world-order fully present. Then in its very flight the note will be heard; but the ordered world is its indistinguishable score. These moments are immortal, and most transitory of all . . . (pp. 28–31)

The world of *It* is set in the context of space and time. The world of *Thou* is not set in the context of either of these. The particular *Thou*, after the relational event, has run its course, is bound to become an *It*. The particular *It*, be entering the relational event, may become a *Thou*. . . . It is not possible to live life in the bare present. Life would be quite consumed if precautions were not taken to subdue the present speedily and thoroughly. But it is possible to live in the bare past, indeed only in it may a life be organized . . . [and] hear this: without *It* man cannot live. But he who lives with *It* alone is not a man. (pp. 31–34)

Lewis spoke from time to time of this *Thou* in its context as the numinous. As Lewis grew up, what became the furniture of his mind, which we have looked at, became part of the whole child (the *I-Thou* unity), and then of the ordered world of *It*, and then fleetingly, in moments of *Sehnsucht*, of Joy, was again if fleetingly transformed by relation into *Thou*, the numinous, the Spirit of the world, the present world, ordered by the past. I am reminded that during the 1960s, in Madison, during the interminable building of the Elvehjem Art Center, as a silent witness of revolution and rumors of revolutions, Dow demonstrations, Army Masth Research Center explosions, tear gas and all, the words "Frodo Lives" stood on the fence on Park Street, to remind us of our shared world in Tolkien's vision of the Past. Frodo lives! And Aslan—but in not quite the same way.

Those who have seen in Narnia something of Jungian archetypes may remind us that Jung also professed an allegiance to Goethe. Perhaps the Lion and the Witch are hypnogogic visual impressions of those archetypes, out of dream. Let that pass. To return to the books on our Library table at home, one of the Lewis books was *The Abolition of Man* (1946, I think, 1st American edition), and there, long ago, on p. 49, I found Lewis's comment that in studying the *It*, one must not lose what Martin Buber would call the *Thou* situation. And this sent me back to *I and Thou*. In any case, what has happened with Narnia, I believe, is that Lewis, studding his narrative with correlatives (*It*-correlatives, objective correlatives) to his perception of the numinous *Thou*, taking from the world of the *I-and-Thou* of the child (possibly from his own childhood) has given it place in the *It*-world from which the child grown boy or girl and eventually adolescent and young adult, finds in that part of the *It* a way back to the ever-fleeting and numinous *Thou*, the moment of Joy. Back into—because it is the past that organizes the present (and recall that in Bakhtin past carnival is the key to present carnival).

As with Alice it is the child-as-judge—until, at the end, it is Aslan as Judge and not, you will notice, the great Emperor-over-Sea with his Williams-ish title. Did Charles Williams talk to Lewis when he first conceived the Narnia stories, perhaps in the days of the Evacuation of children from London, or is this only from working on Williams and with his manuscripts in preparing *Arthurian Torso*? Whatever the case may be, it is Arthur who personifies the great Myth of Return, the once-ness-and-futurity of the Once and Future King.

But if the Eight Children in Narnia represent an "Arthurian" myth of return, then it is told more or less from the Arthur's point of view—and the Arthur, for all that the children are not "real" chidren, is recognizably and avowedly from our present world. If Lewis has not created individual children but only children-at-a-remove, they are still good enough for their readers to build on, and his avuncular or at least God-fatherly voice is mostly good enough for his purposes. Or so his readers have found it. (But perhaps telling it from Arthur's point of view involves irony and satire, as it did with T.H. White.)

Let us now back up for the moment and look at what we have found so far about this whole Narnian enterprise. At least one key we have found—whether in Edwardian adventure story, or *Bildungsroman* or Fairy-tale or satire—is the past alive—pleasantly alive—in the present. Not horribly alive. Ronald Tolkien long ago put his finger on a difference between child and adult, in the matter of a child asking the story-teller about dragons. When the child asks if dragons are real, he is asking a practical question, to which the answer is, there are no dragons in England *now*: you do not have to worry about one's appearing in the garden. There is another difference: when I tell the child a story, he wants it told just as before. One can tell a new story, but when telling an old story, one tells it the same old way, in as many of the same words as possible. The past and the present meet in the repetition of ritual. The Narnian Gifts are the same gifts a thousand years later.

For this purpose the story-teller must be older than the listener, and a kind of fixture, like the dog and the postman and the man-next-door. He should have—and arouse—an instinctive sympathy for and in his readers—which is why Lewis's own Swiftian characteristics may have "kick-started" the success of Narnia. But time and again, as we have read the books, and gone over them here (though only in a patchy way), we have seen variations on a few central themes or characteristics or *motifs*, over and over again. The great house in the country, the past alive in the present, the life of the imagination, the mixture of familiarity and new adventure, pageant and satire, a kind of suggested subversion, the child-as-judge, the child-as-warrior, the question (perhaps) what is really the larger life?

All this, I think, plays a role in the success of Narnia. So also do some of Lewis's failings—if that is what they are. He had, as you will recall from Chapter 2, some of the presumed makings of success—"a great stock of the makings of a poet: strong visual memory, strong recollections of childhood: desperately strong yearnings for lost Paradise and hoped[-for] Heaven ('Sweet Desire'): not least a strong primitive intuition of the diabolical (not merely the horrific). In fact his whole life was oriented and motivated by an almost uniquely-persisting child's sense of glory and of nightmare.

> The adult events were received into a medium still as pliable as wax, wide open to the glory, and equally vulnerable, with a man's strength to feel it all, and a great scholar and writer's skill s to express and to interpret. It is almost as though the adult disciplines, notably the technique of his verse, had inhibited his poetry, which is perhaps, after all, most evident in his prose. I think he wanted to be a poet more than anything . . . But if it was magic he was after, he achieved this sufficiently elsewhere.

Remember that we suggested earlier a limitation implicit in his remarks about writing a sonnet.

There were indeed, we have thought, watchful dragons—and some of them at least were in Lewis. One particular strength in his Narnian story (or stories) comes from the strength of childhood (and the things of childhood, the images of his childhood, even of Ulster and Boxen) in him and in his mind—with his adult abilities to learn and write—and it comes from the strength also of the position that the Christian story had taken in his mind. The objective correlatives are those important to him, the Romantic glimpses are his, the success of Narnia as generally understood lies (so far as we are concerned here) in his success in seeing the Christian Story in these terms. (Not a success that came easily to him, I think.) When it becomes most actual, most objective, or most allegorical, we are furthest from this part of Narnia's success. The neater the tying up of the story, the further we are from the suggestive, from the atmosphere, from the pictures, the visions, the dreams, from the allusiveness, the illustrative, the Romantic, the Romance—from any type or kind of the Larger Life.

Narnia had some of its origins in E. Nesbit; it is a kind of pastoral; it is Arcadian; and it can be traced in some ways to a huge amount of Lewis's childhood and boyhood experience, including childhood and boyhood reading—Hawthorne (*Seven Gables*) and Longfellow, Thackeray (*Henry Esmond*) and Chesterton, and most especially, Lewis's long-time longing not so much for a form as for atmosphere. And it is comic and funny and comedic and humorous, sometimes in a music-hall way, approaching Thackeray in *The Rose and the Ring*, sometimes Andrew Lang in *Prince Prigio*, sometimes E. Nesbit. It links realism and dream and "at least has the hint of a shadow of a suggestion that this is connected with dream and dream can be real" (quoting myself)—and of course not only are things not always what they seem, but places may be sometimes there and sometimes not there.

We have looked at the idea of the past alive in the present in *Prince Caspian*, at the character development of Eustace Clarence Scrubb ("And he almost deserved it") in *The Voyage of the "Dawn Treader,"* at the question "What exactly is the real world?" in *The Silver Chair*, and the cry "For Narnia and the North" in *The Horse and His Boy*, trying to do justice to the book itself, not merely as an illustration of the central point. Here let us suggest there is a point central to all the books, and it is not the one suggested by the learned Dr. Ward. It is in the subtitle to Chapter 4, "Realizing the World of Dragons"—that is, making the World of Dragons real. As we noted before, this may seem odd.

After all, it is only in *The Voyage of the "Dawn Treader"* that there is a dragon, though, to be sure, there are dragon-like beasts who have come down into the Underworld and are asleep there in *The Silver Chair*. And of course Prince Caspian is about the same world in the same age as *The Voyage of the "Dawn Treader,"* and while there are no dragons (or even dragon-like beasts) in *The Horse and His Boy* (any more than in *The Lion, the Witch, and the Wardrobe*), their absence there points something out, or at least suggests it. The dragons come in the more Medieval and more "Old Western" parts of the Chronicles of

Narnia—they are, so to speak, where (in our own history and mythology) they belong. As Boxen went from contemporary times to the medieval, so, in a way, did Narnia (complicated by the fact that the more contemporary Narnia is in A.N.—Anno Narniæ—1000–1015 and the more medieval in and after A.N. 2300). Lewis's answer to the problem of making his invented world real, dragons and all, lies in part in adopting the mode of narrative appropriate to the time and the world.

This is not what he did in *The Lion, the Witch, and the Wardrobe*, or not so much. There he went by the pictures, pretty much allowing them to form the story. But the other books (perhaps *Prince Caspian* the least) are constructs, made stories. We have seen how often we have voices (or Voices) and references to story and the right kind of books (thus far) in the "Chronicles of Narnia"—in *Voyage* and *The Silver Chair* and *The Horse and His Boy*, Lewis chose voice and story-pattern appropriate to his material.

The Voyage of the "Dawn Treader" is Edwardian adventure story; *The Silver Chair* is nineteenth-century invented fairy-tale; *The Horse and His Boy* is *Marchen*. All are humorous or even comic in nature. All use techniques appropriate to their type—which, of course, is a very different matter from whether the techniques are used well. It is unfortunate that Ronald Tolkien did not read some of the later books in the series, when the jostling pictures were no longer creating the jostling story (or stories), when it was Lewis acting as *makar* of the Chronicles. (The word *makar* is the Middle English and especially Middle Scots for poet, literary creator. It is our word maker, but given a special meaning.) Tolkien could have told us whether Lewis was successful—in Tolkien's informed view—in making the world of dragons, the world of Faerie, come alive—and if so, was it because he was conforming to time-tested techniques and time-tested types. One thing, of course, is sure: when Lewis was speaking of the very limited amount of description in fairy-tales, he was not speaking of his own Narnian books.

In the end, as we have said, these books are filled with greater wonder than the Boxen stories, but much of it comes from references to (or objective correlatives from) *The Greatest Story Ever Told*, and the corpus of "Old Western" literature. Lewis echoes his sources and analogues, has passages of brilliant—and of simply good—description, has built a structure of mostly traditional story and a world that many have admired. We looked at the beginning and the end, *The Magician's Nephew* and *The Last Battle*, the book-ends. They turned out to be book-beginning and book-end, and in the beginning is the end, and in the end is the beginning. We mentioned in particular the judgment at the end of

The Last Battle—but also and especially the judgment at Harvest-Home in the very beginning of Narnia.

The whole story of Narnia—History, not Chronicle—begins with Prologue, and goes on from there to Final Judgment—it is not the "There and Back Again" of many of Lewis's models, though it is a form both of pageant and pilgrimage (both, as I have argued elsewhere, appropriate to pastoral). And in the whole, and especially in the shift from Prologue, the author is present; the shift is part of the form; the form gives the pattern of events—one might even say gives the pattern to events, the *mythos*; judgment is part of pastoral; childhood, pastoral, and Arcady are linked (school-stories are Arcadian stories); irony and satire inhere in pastoral (school-stories are ironic and satirical); the real world is the world of the spirit ("It's all in Plato. Bless me! What do they teach them in these schools?").

Between the cosmogonic book-ends are the various kinds of story within the Narnian world. None is truly a school-story in the Harry Potter sense, though there are school-references, and Experiment House is certainly a (dubious kind of) school-setting. They are roughly, as we have suggested, children's story after the manner of E. Nesbit, Edwardian adventure story, *Bildungsroman* (with school-story edges), Arabian Night's tale, fairy-story. These are all pretty tried-and-true sub-species within the genre of children's story (larger sense). But why are they so successful in a world so out of joint with the tried and true?

Part of the answer, I have suggested, lies in Lewis's essential school-boyishness—his satire, his irony, even a tinge of sarcasm. Is Dr. Cornelius writing out "King" Peter's challenge an entirely serious vignette? It is not. Is (to quote the American edition I was long familiar with) "Rise up, Sir Peter Fenris-Bane, and whatever happens, never forget to wipe your sword" an entirely serious warning? It is not—though it is better mock-seriousness than Sir Peter Wolf's-bane. When the boys jingle off in their armor, when Lucy eavesdrops by magic, when the Duffer Monopods become the Dufflepuds—for that matter, when the *après-midi d'un faune* involves tea and sandwiches—are we traveling in the realms of gold or is it *Saturday Night Live*, Nickelodeon version?

That is an overstatement (or unfair question) of course. There is no imbalance in Lewis, any more than there was in Swift. The various Narnia volumes are not, I believe, given their contours by appeal to the seven planets of old Astrology (or Astronomy), Dr. Ward to the contrary notwithstanding. But they are given their contours by the type of story they are and the interaction of that type with Lewis's sense of humor and his school-boyishness—allowing for some overlapping of types, and possibly some overgeneralization. What types of humor are appropriate to the cosmonic bookends? What types are appropriate for the five books in between? And we should remember, in answering these questions, that these are children's books, or at least books avowedly written for children.

In the days when Mr. Sherlock Holmes lived in Baker Street (and Jacks Lewis in Dundela Villas with passages behind the walls where one could come out by mistake in the Magician's lair?), Digory and Polly met not a thousand miles from Baker Street, and the adventures began. But *The Magician's Nephew* was published late in the Narnia series, and that reminds us there are really two ways of looking at the order of the seven books for evaluating their success. My guess is that some at least of the original readers took pleasure in organizing the books in their own mind (by Narnian time?) as they came out, and certainly will have prided themselves on their knowledge of Narnia. One can look at on-line gatherings of fans of Narnia to see what strongly links them—knowledge of Narnia is one bond (and debates on Susan Pevensie in that light), and a liking for "Narnian" stories, frequently extending to writing them—but what kind of "Narnian" stories? Do they emphasize the Medieval? I rather think so. Do they emphasize the humor? I am less sure of that than of the Medieval. Is there something faintly ridiculous about Reepicheep? Doubtless there is, but there is here as willing a suspension of disbelief as with Cyrano's nose—at least for the children—for the Arcadians.

The comparison with Cyrano is not wayward. The great success of Rostand's Cyrano was in the year of Lewis's birth: the play is as much a child of 1898 as "Jacks" was. And Lewis had even read the writer Cyrano (Savinien-Hercule de Cyrano de Bergerac 1619–1655), as a reference to the Yellow Dwarf makes clear. Of course the author of the *Comical History of the States and Empires of the Sun and the Moon* may have little enough in common with Rostand's character—but what he does have in common—and it is relevant here—is the mixture of comedy and the comic and romance and pageant, and that is held in common also with Narnia. I saw Rostand's play on Broadway (with my parents) with Jose Ferrer when I was nine and quoted—even declaimed it—extensively at the age I would have been reading the Narnian books if they had been written.

Part of the point of Cyrano lies in Roxane's lament that she has never loved but one man in her life and she has lost him twice—it is the tragedy of the good-but-ugly (a character out of Comedy), lurking behind the *bouleversement* of the fairy-tale (or *Marchen*), and a whole list of "good-but" characters in Narnia, dwarfs or warrior mice, or whatever came out of the furniture of Lewis's mind. In discussing the subject of carnival in children's literature, we made use of some of Mikhail Bakhtin's work, noting that, while the comic and the fantastic are both types of carnival, in the Bakhtinian sense, fantasy and humor need not be, and humor (in the English sense) is unlikely to be—also that the distinction between carnival and order connects with Kenneth Grahame's distinction between the Arcadians (who are frequently children) and the Olympians (who are frequently adults).

We have noted that Dickens in *A Christmas Carol* has entered that realm of carnival, of *bouleversement*, of suspension of normal rules: the very name of Scrooge has the sound of carnival. And, as Bakhtin has pointed out, carnival is linked to the past—and whence comes our first ghost in the *Carol*? Now, Bakhtin's distinction between the culture of order and the culture of carnival seems to leave out any consideration of what might be called the culture of the numinous: Lewis's achievement in the Narnian stories, as we have noted, suggests that the *numen* can dwell in either order or carnival. After Caspian's resurrection, in *The Silver Chair*, we are in carnival, when Aslan and Caspian and Eustace in his Narnian armor and with his Narnian sword and Jill in her Narnian clothes, come to the wall of Experiment House. The greatest of Lewis's achievements here, we have suggested, is the blending of carnival and the numinous in the closest thing to pure fairy-tale in all the Narnian stories, though there is still a great intermixing of types and patterns. As Buchan taught us, the great Victorian novels repeat the *Märchen* patterns. *The Silver Chair* is their heir to this.

Let us here rehearse a list given above. Tolkien's "On Fairy-Stories" rules out of that category (of fairy-stories) travelers' tales (the *Voyage*?), the beast-fable (an ancestor at least of *The Last Battle*), stories with dream-frames and in the dream tradition, many of the *contes*, retellings of folklore (not absent from Narnia), indeed all stories that do not have at their heart the primal desire for the realization of imagined wonder (in *The Monsters and the Critics and Other Essays,* p. 116). And he goes on to point out, as we pointed out above, that fairy-stories contain old elements that now by their very age speak to that primal desire—and have probably retained those elements through the ages *because* [my emphasis] they speak to that primal desire (p. 129). Which does help us, a little, with understanding the appeal of Narnia—I think. But it is the *bouleversement* that is key, in children's literature "way back then" (whenever "then" is) and now. Even though the principal agent of *bouleversement* for many may now be, not the book, but the skateboard.

We know that children, teenagers, young adults (even very young) were buying and reading Harry Potter, in the hundreds of thousands, and perhaps still are. A look among teenagers at the number of claimed scholars at Hogwarts on Facebook tells us something on that. But the Narnia books are more limited than Harry Potter in their present appeal—whether limited to the scions of Christian households I cannot say, nor whether their appeal in 2014 is much like their appeal in 1954. On that I would guess it was not—unless, of course, there were simply more Christian households in 1954 than now. Let us summarize briefly where we are now on the popularity of the Narnia stories, beginning with wonder.

Tolkien spoke of the *core* as being in the realization of imagined wonder. We spoke of the realization—making real—of dragons. Michael Ward, who was not looking at the same question, nevertheless found a kind of answer in the fascination of ancient planetary schemes and identities (in *Planet Narnia*)—but it would be an answer to our question of Narnia's success only through the maintenance (if there has been maintenance) of the core symbols (Jungian archetypes?), unchanged from Lewis's childhood to the childhood (and boyhood and girlhood) of those born a century later. For I must always remember that my usefulness as a present specimen runs out as those from whom I am a specimen become fewer and fewer in number and less and less relevant to current affairs, including current criticism.

Lewis wrote these children's stories—that is certainly what they are. But one notable characteristic of children—need we even say it—is they are not frozen in time, though they may perhaps glimpse eternity—intimations (should one say "Inklings"?) of immortality in early childhood. But some observers have seen Lewis as frozen in time, past time. No, I do not think he was—at least not wholly so, because he remained a child at heart—a quality that may transcend time. But the Inklings themselves (mostly) were emphatically from Time Past, with a few exceptions— Charles Williams (who was of no time and his own world), Owen Barfield (a sort of adjunct Inkling, who studied the evolution of the human mind), Nevill Coghill (because of the plays and the translations). Even Lewis's "scientifiction" was out of the past, and his chief creative disciple in that field (James Blish) is now forty years dead.

Of course, Lewis married a modern woman, one might say—but her influence on Narnia is uncertain, though strong on *Till We Have Faces*— his least "Narnian" book, though characteristically "Lewisian" in its irony and even satire. Two thoughts occur to me as I am writing this. First, the matter of *bouleversement*, the world turned upside down, the

Märchen in the mode of "Jack the Giant-Killer," and the mythos of irony and satire, all have in common the inverted viewpoint that also characterizes the subversion of the Greenwood and the humor of Lewis Carroll and the Nonsense of Edward Lear (and Carroll's Nonsense and Lear's humor). And these, like the child-as-judge and Henty's child-as-hero (and MacDonald's Gibbie, the child-as-saint), are part of the child's ideal world. And for all the trappings of Time Past (and some of them are indeed archetypal), this may help explain Narnia's success for most of these past sixty years.

This—these things—may explain that success—it is not his storytelling, though perhaps his pictures. Walter Hooper told me Lewis was a gifted story-teller, and in some ways he was—but a gifted plotter he was not. Professor Tolkien was closest to a relevant mark when he told me Lewis was a voracious and retentive reader—who made use of what he retained. If Buchan is right—and he is (I believe)—that there are only a certain number of plots, in *Märchen* or novel, then it is no great problem that Lewis did not invent any.

Did he pick those plots (patterns, *mythoi*) that would appeal to his readers? Evidently so. Did he tell the stories in such a way as to add to the appeal? Initially, perhaps yes, particularly if the children he had in mind were really the children to whom the books are dedicated, or at least the same kind of children. But this brings us into a problematic area, through the passage of sixty years' time. The world has changed. How much have children changed? The core of wonder may not have changed. But what of the surfaces?

Possibly with the exception of Digory and Polly (and their models are literary), there are no real people in Narnia—well, perhaps Frank, the cabbie, and Helen, his wife, for a brief moment, and even there, perhaps, the effect is ironic. But Lewis's invented characters, barring Puddleglum, are notoriously not drawn from life (and that is a satiric drawing). Do children want their characters drawn from life? Readers of fairy-tales for grown-ups do—as Lewis pointed out in his preface to *That Hideous Strength*. A certain amount of identification of reader with character—the child reading with the child in the book—is arguably necessary.

Can that be carried through entirely by appeal to the past—kings in armor, queens with bow and arrow or magic potions? That is, of course possible, even in these days, perhaps more possible sixty years ago (a faint breath reaches even the late generations)—if one mixes in Father Christmas and an eponymous lion and an eponymous witch—but the magic may wear off. We recall the Coleridgean definition of humor as "bringing forward into distinct consciousness those minutiae of thought and feeling which appear [to be] trifles, have an importance only for the moment, and yet almost every man feels in one way or another." And if we substitute "child" for "man," we may be on our way to examining the success of Narnia in a new light. Well—not entirely new—we have been looking at humor (and the comic) already. What is new here is that we have reached a kind of critical dignity, perhaps, with Coleridge.

Let me ask the question this way—or in these several ways. Would it make a difference if Lucy's book (where she cannot turn back the pages and where she reads the story Aslan will someday go on telling her forever) were a computer screen (or something like it—an inexplicable magic screen perhaps)? Would it make a difference if E. Nesbit were updated so the feast in *The Story of the Amulet* resembled more closely the feasts in Harry Potter? Would it make a difference if the railway accident in *The Last Battle* (already almost an anachronism) were to have been an airplane crash or automobile crash? Does the contemporaneity of the trappings, or the quotidian world, make a difference to the magic at the core? Since these books are, if anything of the sort, rather fantasy than science-fiction, at the core, I believe the answer is—mostly—no. Let me take a brief alongside look here, at a Lewis disciple who spent some time working in and through the matter of contemporaneity.

His name is James Blish (though his name as a critic is William Atheling, Jr.). As a novelist (for want of a better word) he wrote a tetralogy/trilogy, taking place in the past (*Dr. Mirabilis*), the present (*Black Easter* and *The Day After Judgment*), and the future (*A Case of Conscience*), each with a (satiric) core of wonder. As William Atheling, Jr., he wrote the classic critical SF essay, "Cathedrals in Space," and under both names published "Probapossible Prolegomena to Ideareal History"—the oddity of whose title should not blind us to the strength of the author's perceptions. It is Blish to whom we owe the original impetus for the use of Frye's *mythoi* in the context used in this book, and the view that science-fiction writers write ironically or satirically (and Irony or Satire is the *mythos* of the winter) even as they write Romance (the *mythos* of the summer). And it is Blish who sees in science fiction generically the kind of syncretism that drove Professor Tolkien slightly wild in *The Lion, the Witch, and the Wardrobe.*

Lewis was, of course, a science-fiction writer, indeed a writer of what I have elsewhere called Arcadian science-fiction. Science-fiction I have taken as a version of pageant—especially this Arcadian science-fiction: part of its purpose is at least related to a desire to present the science-fictional world in pageant, in a certain individuality or particularity (whereas fantasy presents the generic, the archetypal, even the mythic). *Gulliver*, the *Odyssey*, the *Navigatio Sancti Brendani*, *The Voyage of the "Dawn Treader"* are all thus on the science-fictional side of the divide, and none of the Chronicles of Narnia, though they are fantasy (as I have just argued above), falls into a category of pure fantasy (if indeed, in our world or out, there is such a thing). The question is, as noted, one of contemporaneity.

Several of my cousins and I have recently been discussing (online, which seems increasingly where everything is discussed) the question whether there was such a thing as a nineteenth-century "Young Adult" novel. Louisa May Alcott, possibly? (Odd, she shared a birthday with C.S. Lewis—and with Madeleine L'Engle.) Poe's *Narrative of Arthur Gordon Pym*? Captain Marryat? What about (later in the century) G.A. Henty (1832–1902) and Horatio Alger (1832–1899)? And what about Fenimore Cooper, at least in *The Last of the Mohicans*? (That is, of course, one of the great background pieces for *The Lord of the Rings*—and by the way, is that a Young Adult Novel? Is *The Hobbit*? Is Peter Jackson's version of *The Hobbit*?) And Robert Louis Stevenson? Mark Twain? (What is a Young Adult novel?)

These questions seem to me worth asking, in some form at least, if we are to look at the "success" of the Narnia stories. They have been widely acclaimed over fifty years. They demonstrate—over and over again—the richness of Lewis's mind, and the richness and variety of the furniture of that mind. A slew of authors and critics (mostly Christians) have praised and recommended and interpreted them. They are closer to Hogwarts than Tolkien is, I think. They got something successfully past the watchful dragons (or so their author said), and they said best what was to be said (as he also said)—but what actually was and is their success? I have warned already that I am not the best reader and critic to be answering the question because I read them originally for the same reason I re-read them now—to be more in touch with the mind of C.S. Lewis and to live with the furniture of that mind. That seems to me a highly idiosyncratic reason for reading a children's (or Young Adult) book, and a highly idiosyncratic point of view on which to base any critical view or any consideration of success.

But are there signs of weaknesses in Narnia, not as world but as story? Susan is a loose end. There is a change in Eustace's character—but is there any development in the character of Peter, or of Susan, or of Edmund, or of Lucy? They have adventures—that is, things happen to them—but except for a few set pieces (one might say, battle-pieces), it seems largely a matter of things happening, not the children doing things. (Even though, as we have noted, the things happen, there is History, because the children are there.) As Prince Cor says, "Even though Education and all sorts of horrible things are going to happen to me" (*The Horse and His Boy*, p. 197). Lest we make heavy weather of this, let us remember that this is one of the simplest of all plot lines, in *Märchen* or nineteenth-century novels. And it is, *par excellence,* the plot-line of the fairy-tale.

Here, as a reminder again is what John Buchan said—and it may be that W.P. Ker had something to say on this also. From Buchan ("The Novel and the Fairy-Tale," 1931, p. 8):

> There is first of all what we may call the picaresque motive, the story based on extension in space, on the fact that the world is very wide, and that there are a great many odd things in it . . . And the thing may be done seriously or in a spirit of comedy. It may stick close to earth or adventure into the clouds. The road may be a pleasant and bustling highway . . . or a mysterious path past enchanted forests . . .

From W.P. Ker ("Romance," 1909, p. 10):

> The *Pilgrim's Progess* is one of the results of mediaeval romance; it has the sort of plan which saves even some of the dull romances from total failure, and is found in some of the best. It is the simplest thing in the world; scarcely to be called a plot—merely a journey with adventures.

If there are very few plots, and the best or at least most characteristic plot is the kind of chapter-of-adventures journey through time and space that Professor Ker fixes as the core of Romance, then the telling of the adventures, the work of fiction as *poiema* rather than *logos*, could be a principal key to the superiority of one version over another, and perhaps even (in this case) to the survival of the "Chronicles of Narnia"—unless, of course, that survival speaks to others as it originally spoke to me—a command to read, mark, learn, and inwardly digest this, because it is written by C.S. Lewis.

It is Lewis himself who has given us some clues on "successful" or "good" reading (which is essential to the survival of a work of fiction over the years) and the distinction between *poiema* and *logos*, in his *Experiment in Criticism* (1961) This distinction is certainly connected with the distinction between "art" and "life" and a tendency at certain ages and levels to be unable to distinguish between them. Tolkien's child who wants to know "Are dragons real?" and the child who mistakes film-action on screen (or the backwoodsman who mistakes action on the stage) for reality are on the borders of that world. In his *Experiment in Criticism* (p. 75), Lewis observes that "Between the ages of twelve and twenty nearly all of us acquired from novels, along with plenty of misinformation, a great deal of information about the world we live in"—and then goes on to discuss other ways of reading fiction, good and bad. But is not this "twelve-to-twenty" reading, which on the borders of some kind of unity of fiction and fact, precisely the kind of reading that would smuggle fact (or might we say truth) past watchful dragons in the guise of fiction? Is that why a children's book might say best what is to be said? (It is certainly connected with Henty and the "powder in the jam"—the historical fact carried along on the wings of fiction, sometimes with less finesse than at others).

I can recall, when I was thirteen, reading a Dorothy L. Sayers mystery—one of the Peter Wimsey stories, presumably *Murder Must Advertise*, in which Lord Peter appears also as Death Bredon. My father asked me, while I was still engrossed in the reading, whether I thought Bredon and Wimsey were the same. I thought it was the wrong question. It took me (though I did not put it in these words then) out of the creation, the *poiema*, the fiction, the *mythos* with its atmosphere, to determine a matter of fact which was going to become clear in the end anyway, when I had completed reading the book. At this point it was a distraction. This is, so to speak, the "flip side" of the fact-and-fiction discussion in the last paragraph.

Here (*Experiment*, pp. 110–11) is a passage of considerable importance in looking at the "success" of the "Chronicles of Narnia"—and as an answer to the kind of criticism Edmund Wilson aimed both at Professor Tolkien and Miss Sayers (and would doubtless have aimed at Lewis hsad he been more popular at the right time).

> [T]he very fact that people, or even any one person, can well and truly read, and love for a lifetime, a book that we had thought bad, will raise the suspicion that it cannot really be as bad as we thought . . . The prima facie probability that anything that has ever been truly read and obstinately loved by any reader has some virtue in it is overwhelming.

And Lewis would, I believe, argue that rule applies *a fortiori* to children's books. After all, he did not first read *The Wind in the Willows* until he was in his twenties. And I would argue it as strongly from my case. I still take Henty's *For Name and Fame* down off the shelves, as I have for most of the years in the last three-score—though that may be an unfair example, since its myth and atmosphere (danger and the stony land of

Afghanistan) has become fact again. For whatever reason, Henty's two Afghan books are, in my view) among his best.

Certainly the Kilmer children read the Narnia stories well and truly, and I daresay thousands of others read them as truly, if not with the advantages of frequent correspondence with CSL. Our key is "truly read and obstinately loved"—and "well and truly read [the stories] and love [them] for a lifetime." Are they still as capable of being read that way as they were by Lucy Barfield or the Kilmers or young Master Hardie or any of the other children to whom they were dedicated (or the young man who was afraid he would love Aslan more than Christ)? Perhaps not so—or not quite. But this I would claim. They are read, in the end, for their flavor, and especially for that flavor that comes from the mind of the maker—if not the Mind of the Maker. Perhaps both. The Larger Life, the Beauty of Holiness, even with Lewisian satire and irony. For the core is wonder, I suppose, but the inner joke, the satire, the irony, is shared by the reader with that curious being, the author, who is like the postman and the dog next door, an equal in childhood's land.

In the end, then, I would claim, the special "twelve-to-twenty" reading is part of what distinguishes the children's book or boys' or girls' book, perhaps even the Young Adult novel, from other works of fiction. I would claim that this is related, as for example in fantasy or science-fiction, in fairy-tale or tale of Faerie, to a shifting border between fact and fiction—and a shifting border, perhaps, between truth and fiction, the border we cross and re-cross with the question "Are dragons real?" and our attempts to "realize" the world of dragons. Whether or not we are thrown back on Jungian archetypes—whether or not, indeed, they inform the whole schematic effort of *Planet Narnia*—it is still the case that there is something at the core, something of wonder, that demands, and apparently receives, a special reading.

And so we come back to the writers whose works underlie Narnia as our keys to unlocking Lewis's achievement. There is Bunyan, who coming through Bevis of Southampton, first recounted travels toward the Delectable Mountains on the borders of Narnia. There is Swift, whose satire and irony, like those of Lewis's exemplar Dr. Johnson—and like the carnival of Thackeray and the slyness and slippertalk of Andrew Lang, and even the Fabianism of E. Nesbit—somehow was transmuted into that core of wonder. And the core in Lewis, like that in Swift (and maybe that in Thackeray), was of ironic wonder, a part of youth's kingdom of satire. (And perhaps an Irish kingdom also.)

And in the end, in speaking of the "success" of Narnia, we must ask, what are the counters of that success? Books sold? Films made? The fame of C.S. Lewis? Books written on Narnia? Conferences held on Narnia. Or, more generally, on Lewis? The fact that Narnia and CSL are indissolubly linked? The fact that the Narnia books overbalance all his other books in the public mind? When I first read Lewis, before Narnia, it was *Screwtape* and *The Great Divorce* and the Ransom stories and the *Broadcast Talks* (and their sequels), *Miracles* and *The Problem of Pain*, *The Abolition of Man*, *Arthurian Torso*, *The Weight of Glory*, and a few outliers, including his poem "Awake My Lute." Before the final Narnia book was published, I had read *English Literature in the Sixteenth Century, Excluding Drama* (his greatest work, I think), *The Allegory of Love*, *Preface to Paradise Lost*, *Surprised by Joy*, *Till We Have Faces*, and his greatest talk, *De Descriptione Temporum*.

His best work was done before he was sixty (except perhaps for tying up the ends of his old lectures on *The Discarded Image*, and for the underrated *A Grief Observed*). He was the "schoolboy Dr. Johnson" (in Claude Rawson's phrase). He never really grew up—in some ways at least—and he burned out early. He was never, I think, youthful in the sense Owen Barfield was. Or even Major Lewis. It could even be said he was of no particular age—not like the stupidest grown-ups who are most grown-up or the stupidest children who are most childish. And let us recall what he said at the end of *An Experiment in Criticism*.

> Those of us who have been true readers all our life seldom fully realize the enormous extension of our being which we owe to authors . . . My own eyes are not enough for me; I will see through the eyes of others. Reality, even seen through the eyes of many, is not enough. I will see what others have invented. Even the eyes of all humanity are not enough. I regret that the brutes cannot write books . . . Literary experience heals the wound, without undermining the privilege, of individuality . . . in reading great literature I become a thousand men, and yet remain myself. (pp. 140–41)

The night has a thousand eyes—Christmas Night, or Night in Narnia—and I see with them all. But principally, in Narnia, I see with the eyes of C. S. Lewis. That is why I read the Narnia books sixty years ago; that is why I read them now. And perhaps, after all, that is not so very different from what other readers do.

Books Mentioned

Anonymous. *The Famous and Renowned History of Sir Bevis of Southampton*. London: W. Thackeray, 1689.

Bakhtin, Mikhail. *Rabelais and His World*. Bloomington: Indiana University Press, 2009.

Chaucer, Geoffrey. *The Canterbury Tales*. London: Penguin, 2005.

Chesterton, G.K. *The Father Brown Omnibus*. New York: Dodd, Mead, 1933.

Doyle, Arthur Conan. *The Adventures of Sherlock Holmes*. London: George Newnes, 1892.

———. *The Memoirs of Sherlock Holmes*. London: George Newnes, 1894.

———. *Sir Nigel*. London: Smith Elder, 1906.

Dumas, Alexandre. *The Three Musketeers*. London: G. Vickers, 1846; William Barrow, translator.

Frye, Northrop. *Anatomy of Criticism: Four Essays*. Princeton: Princeton University Press, 1957.

Gibb, Jocelyn, ed. *Light on C.S. Lewis*. London: Bles, 1965.

Grahame, Kenneth. *Dream Days*. London: John Lane, 1898.

———. *The Golden Age*. London: John Lane, 1895.

———. *The Wind in the Willows*. London: Methuen, 1908.

Hawthorne, Nathaniel. *The House of the Seven Gables*. Boston: Ticknor, Reed, and Fields, 1851.

Henty, G.A. *At the Point of the Bayonet*. London: Blackie, 1902.

———. *For Name and Fame*. London: Blackie, 1886.

———. *In Times of Peril*. London: Griffith and Farran, 1881.

———. *On the Irrawaddy*. London: Blackie, 1897.

———. *Out on the Pampas*. London: Griffith and Farran, 1871.

———. *Rujub the Juggler*. London: Chatto and Windus, 1893.

———. *Through the Sikh War*. London: Blackie, 1894.

———. *The Tiger of Mysore*. London: Blackie, 1896.

———. *To Herat and Cabul*. London: Blackie, 1902.

————. *Through Three Campaigns*. London: Blackie, 1904.

————. *With Clive in India*. London: Blackie, 1884.

Kipling, [Joseph] Rudyard. *Puck of Pook's Hill*. London: Macmillan, 1906.

————. *Rewards and Fairies*. London: Macmillan, 1910.

————. *Stalky & Co*. London: Macmillan, 1899.

Lang, Andrew. *Prince Prigio*. Bristol: Arrowsmith, 1889.

————. *Ricardo of Pantouflia*. Bristol: Arrowsmith, 1893.

Langland, William. *Piers Plowman*. Oxford: Oxford University Press, 2009.

Lewis, C.S. *The Abolition of Man*. London: Bles, 1946.

————. *Beyond Personality*. London: Bles, 1943.

————. *Boxen*. New York: Harcourt, 1985.

————. *Broadcast Talks*. London: Bles, 1942.

————. *The Case for Christianity*. New York: Macmillan, 1943.

————. *Christian Behaviour*. London: Bles, 1943.

————. *Christian Reflections*. Grand Rapids: Eerdmans, 1968.

————. *English Literature in the Sixteenth Century, Excluding Drama*.
    Oxford: Oxford University Press, 1954.

————. *The Great Divorce*. London: Bles, 1945.

————. *Miracles*. London: Bles, 1947.

————. *On Stories*. New York: Harcourt, 1982.

————. *Out of the Silent Planet*. London: Bles, 1938.

————. *Perelandra*. London: Bles, 1943.

————. *Pilgrim's Regress*. London: Sheed and Ward, 1935.

————. *A Preface to Paradise Lost*. Oxford: Oxford University Press, 1942.

————. *The Problem of Pain*. London: Bles, 1940.

————. *The Screwtape Letters*. London: Bles, 1941.

————. *Studies in Words*. Cambridge: Cambridge University Press, 1960.

————. *Surprised by Joy*. New York: Harcourt, 1954.

————. *That Hideous Strength*. London: Bles, 1945.

————. *The Weight of Glory*. New York: Macmillan, 1949.

Lewis, C.S., and Owen Barfield. *Mark v. Tristram*. Cambridge: Lowell House
    Printers, 1967.

Lewis, C.S., and E.M.W. Tillyard. *The Personal Heresy*. Oxford: Oxford
    University Press, 1938.

Lewis, W.H. *Levantine Adventurer*. New York: Harcourt, 1963.

————, compiler. *Lewis Papers*. Vols I–XI: 1931.

Longfellow, Henry Wadsworth. *The Works of Henry Wadsworth Longfellow*.
    Ware: Wordworth, 1994.

Lydgate, John. *Pilgrimage of the Life of Man*. Toronto: Toronto Libraries,
    2011.

Macaulay, Thomas Babington. *Lays of Ancient Rome*. London: Harper, 1894.

Macdonald, George. *Alec Forbes of Howglen*. London: Hurst, 1865.

————. *At the Back of the Northwind*. London: Strahan, 1871.

————. *Donal Grant*. London: Kegan Paul, 1883.

————. *Phantastes*. London: Smith Elder, 1858.

————. *The Princess and Curdie*. London: Chatto and Windus, 1882.

————. *The Princess and the Goblins*. London: Strahan, 1872.

————. *Sir Gibbie*. London: Hurst, 1879.

Nesbit, E. *Five Children and It*. London: Treherne, 1902.

————. The *House of Arden*. London: Unwin, 1908.

————. The *Phoenix and the Carpet*. London: Newnes, 1904.

————. *The Story of the Amulet*. London: Unwin, 1906.

————. *The Treasure Seekers*. London: Fisher, 1899.

————. *The Wouldbegoods*. London: Treherne, 1901.

Ralegh, Sir Walter. *Historie of the World: In Five Bookes*. London: British Library, 2010.

Saki. *The Short Stories of Saki (H.H. Munro)*. New York: Modern Library, 1958.

Shellabarger, Samuel. *Prince of Foxes*. Boston: Little, Brown, 1947.

Sidney, Sir Philip. *The Countess of Pembroke's Arcadia*. London: Penguin, 1977.

Stephens, James. *The Crock of Gold*. London: Macmillan, 1912.

Thackeray, William Makepeace. *The History of Henry Esmond*. London: Smith Elder, 1862.

————. *The Rose and the Ring*. London: Smith Elder, 1855.

Tolkien, J.R.R. *The Father Christmas Letters*. London: Allen and Unwin, 1976; expanded edition 1999 as *Letters from Father Christmas*.

————. *The Hobbit*. London: Allen and Unwin, 1937.

————. *The Lord of the Rings*. London: Allen and Unwin, 1954–1955.

————. *The Monsters and the Critics and Other Essays*. New York: Houghton Mifflin, 1984.

Williams, Charles. *The Place of the Lion: A New Novel*. London: Gollancz, 1931.

Books about Books. A Small List

Dartt, Robert. *G.A. Henty: A Bibliography*. Cedar Grove: Dar-Web 1971.

Dowling, David. *Into the Wardrobe: C.S. Lewis and the Narnia Chronicles*. New York: Wiley, 2008.

Hooper, Walter. *Past Watchful Dragons*. Collier, 1979.

Lobdell, Jared. *The Rise of Tolkienian Fantasy*. LaSalle: Open Court, 2005.

Phillips, M.R. *George MacDonald*. Minneapolis: Bethany, 1987.

Pevsner, Nikolaus. *The Englishness of English Art*. New York: Praeger, 1954.

Potter, Stephen. *The Sense of Humour*. London: Weidenfeld, 1954.

Walsh, Chad. *C.S. Lewis: Apostle to the Skeptics*. New York: Macmillan, 1949.

Index